How Education Works

Issues in Distance Education
Series editor: George Veletsianos

Selected Titles in the Series

The Theory and Practice of Online Learning, Second Edition
Edited by Terry Anderson

Flexible Pedagogy, Flexible Practice: Notes from the Trenches of Distance Education
Edited by Elizabeth Burge, Chère Campbell Gibson, and Terry Gibson

Teaching in Blended Learning Environments: Creating and Sustaining Communities of Inquiry
Norman D. Vaughan, Martha Cleveland-Innes, and D. Randy Garrison

Online Distance Education: Towards a Research Agenda
Edited by Olaf Zawacki-Richter and Terry Anderson

Teaching Crowds: Learning and Social Media
Jon Dron and Terry Anderson

Learning in Virtual Worlds: Research and Applications
Edited by Sue Gregory, Mark J. W. Lee, Barney Dalgarno, and Belinda Tynan

Emergence and Innovation in Digital Learning: Foundations and Applications
Edited by George Veletsianos

An Online Doctorate for Researching Professionals
Swapna Kumar and Kara Dawson

Assessment Strategies for Online Learning: Engagement and Authenticity
Dianne Conrad and Jason Openo

25 Years of Ed Tech
Martin Weller

The Finest Blend: Graduate Education in Canada
Edited by Gale Parchoma, Michael Power, and Jennifer Lock

Metaphors of Ed Tech
Martin Weller

Critical Digital Pedagogy in Higher Education
Edited by Suzan Köseoğlu, George Veletsianos, and Chris Rowell

How Education Works: Teaching, Technology, and Technique
Jon Dron

How Education Works

Teaching, Technology, and Technique

Jon Dron

◊ AU PRESS

Copyright © 2023 Jon Dron
Published by AU Press, Athabasca University
1 University Drive, Athabasca, AB T9S 3A3

https://doi.org/10.15215/aupress/9781771993838.01

Cover design by Sergiy Kozakov
Printed and bound in Canada

Library and Archives Canada Cataloguing in Publication

Title: How education works : teaching, technology, and technique / Jon Dron.
Names: Dron, Jon, 1961– author.
Series: Issues in distance education series.
Description: Series statement: Issues in distance education | Includes bibliographical references.
Identifiers: Canadiana (print) 20230438857 | Canadiana (ebook) 20230438865 | ISBN 9781771993838 (softcover) | ISBN 9781771993845 (PDF) | ISBN 9781771993852 (EPUB)
Subjects: LCSH: Educational innovations. | LCSH: Educational technology.
Classification: LCC LB1027 .D76 2023 | DDC 371.33—dc23

Image sources for part openers
Preamble. Photograph by Sam Hood, 24 March 1939, Mitchell Library, State Library of New South Wales, https://archival.sl.nsw.gov.au/Details/archive/110016958.
Part 1. Clinton Folger's "Horsemobile" delivering mail, on South Beach Street, at Hayden's Bath House entrance, n.d., Nantucket Historical Association Library, https://commons.wikimedia.org/wiki/File:Horse_drawn_US_Mail_car.jpg.
Part 2. Cartoon by Jean Marc Cote, 1901, https://commons.wikimedia.org/wiki/File:France_in_XXI_Century._School.jpg.
Part 3. Photograph by Sam Hood, 24 March 1939, Mitchell Library, State Library of New South Wales, https://archival.sl.nsw.gov.au/Details/archive/110016951.
Epilogue. Photograph by Ken Thomas, 2001, https://commons.wikimedia.org/wiki/File:John_Henry-27527.jpg.

We acknowledge the financial support of the Government of Canada through the Canada Book Fund (CBF) for our publishing activities and the assistance provided by the Government of Alberta through the Alberta Media Fund.

This publication is licensed under a Creative Commons licence, Attribution-Noncommercial-No Derivative Works 4.0 International: see www.creativecommons.org. The text may be reproduced for non-commercial purposes, provided that credit is given to the original author. To obtain permission for uses beyond those outlined in the Creative Commons licence, please contact AU Press, Athabasca University, at aupress@athabascau.ca.

Tain't what you do (it's the way that you do it)
That's what gets results

—Oliver and Young (1939)

Contents

ACKNOWLEDGEMENTS ix

PROLOGUE xi

Introduction 3

PREAMBLE: ELEPHANT SPOTTING 15

1. A Handful of Anecdotes about Elephants 17
2. A Handful of Observations about Elephants 23

PART I: ALL ABOUT TECHNOLOGY 31

3. Organizing Stuff to Do Stuff 35
4. How Technologies Work 65
5. Participation and Technique 91

PART II: EDUCATION AS A TECHNOLOGICAL PHENOMENON 123

6. A Co-Participation Model of Teaching 127
7. Theories of Teaching 151
8. Technique, Expertise, and Literacy 169

PART III: APPLYING THE CO-PARTICIPATION MODEL 205

9. Revealing Elephants 207
10. How Education Works 221

EPILOGUE 263

REFERENCES 269

Acknowledgements

I would very much like to thank every student and teacher whom I have ever known but given what this book is about that would be an absurdly long list that would include my pets, my children, and the designer of the chair on which I now sit. So, instead, and in the interest of manageability, I give thanks to all the participants in talks, lectures, seminars, social media, and other events in which I have discussed and developed the ideas presented in this book, without whom it would not have happened. Special thanks are due to my friends and collaborators, particularly Terry Anderson, whose incisive critiques, feedback, and ideas reverberate throughout the book and whose inspirational guidance has been invaluable from the start, and Gerald Ardito for long conversations and opportunities to challenge my arguments. I also acknowledge gratefully the assistance of Athabasca University, especially in giving me the President's Award for Research and Scholarly Excellence, which provided me with the time needed to get this book started (back in 2013!), a fertile space in which to explore ideas, and colleagues at the top of their fields with whom to explore them. Most of all, though, this book would not have been possible without the love, support, and tolerance of my partner, Kestra, the love of my life and greatest inspiration in all that I do.

Prologue

Imagine a stick, lying on the ground, fallen from a tree in a forest. Like this one, say.

I came across this stick when walking near my house one day. There is nothing at all special about it. Is this stick a technology? It seems to be hard to think of it as such. If it is, then pretty much everything around us is a technology, and the term has no use or value. This is just a stick, lying on the ground, like billions of others to which we will never pay any attention.

Now imagine the same stick being used to

- scratch a back;
- hold up a tent;
- point to something;
- rap someone's knuckles;
- pry the lid from a can of paint;

- support someone with walking difficulties;
- scrawl an image in the sand;
- tap a tree to produce a rhythmic drumbeat;
- play Pooh Sticks;
- entertain a dog;
- support an iPad;
- measure a window; or
- fend off an attacking wild animal.

Is the stick a technology now? If so, then it seems to be an odd definition of technology since the stick remains precisely the same as when it was lying in the park near my home, minding its own business, not being a technology at all. Yet, in (I think) all cases, a technology of some kind is being described. Many of these technologies could be named: a prop, a weapon, a beater, a pointer, a scribe, a back scratcher, a toy, a ruler, a walking stick. But the technology is not the stick. The stick, though, is very much a part of each technology.

And some of these technologies might help us to learn.

How Education Works

Introduction

> *The best education consists in immunizing people against systematic attempts at education.*
>
> —(Feyerabend, 1987, p. 316)

The Educational Machine

This is a book about the technological nature of education. What follows is thus broadly concerned with processes, methods, tools, procedures, techniques, theories, principles, and models of teaching. However, the view that it presents of education is anything but mechanical. A paintbrush is as much a technology as a manufacturing plant, and teaching is far more akin to painting than it is to manufacturing, though it shares many common features with both. Teaching can be thought of as the application of tools, methods, principles, techniques, and structures to help people learn, and we all do it, whether to ourselves or others. It never happens the same way twice, and the ways in which we might respond to it are more numerous and various than the ways in which we might respond to a painting. The mantra repeated throughout this book in many different ways and in many different contexts is that what we do (the tools, methods, principles, etc. for doing it) is far less significant than the way that we do it (the technique). And, in an invented system of the complexity of an education system, there are many different ways of doing it, almost all of which we will never think of, the vast majority of which will be awful, but many of which will be wonderful.

Moreover, the number of possible ways of doing it can expand endlessly with each novel way of doing it that we discover. Learning often makes more learning possible, softening our boundaries. Sometimes, though, we can learn things that shrink our horizons as much as expand them. Invention always makes more invention possible at a global scale, though at an individual scale it can sometimes erect hard boundaries that were formerly soft and indistinct, thereby blocking paths that we might have taken. This book explores the many ways that such softening and hardening can occur and why neither freedom from boundaries nor the creation of them is a good thing in itself: it all depends on how, why, when, where, with what, by whom, and for what purpose it is done.

This is a book about understanding the technology of learning as it is lived, as a participant, not just as a user, from a deeply and inextricably human perspective. It is about how technology, from symbols to gadgets, from pencils to timetables, from poetry to textbooks, can support or inhibit creativity, capability, flexibility, passion, delight, and of course learning.

Whether you are a learner guiding your own learning journey, a student, a teacher (you are), an author, a designer of learning, a designer of software, a manager of learning systems, a philosopher, or a researcher in education, there is probably something of value in this book for you.

Education

An education is something that we can own—to be educated is to possess an education. Education is also a field of study, an occupation, and an industry. It is a process. It is something that one can be "in" and something that one can acquire. In this book, all of these shades of meaning will emerge, but to begin with we will use something a little closer to the common dictionary definition, such as this (provided by Google Search), that education is "the process of receiving or giving systematic instruction, especially at a school or university." The "systematic" part of that definition matters a lot in a book that seeks to explain education in technological terms. However, I am not going to only be talking about the formal, intentional processes and structures embodied in educational institutions such as schools, universities, and colleges. Although these are significant technologies through which a lot of education occurs, and which will figure largely in what follows, they are just one kind of educational technology among many and part of many more. An institution is an educational technology that itself is assembled from many others, most of which are anything but educational technologies, and it affords great diversity and flexibility. Of course, it might not necessarily be the best technology for the purpose of learning what ostensibly is being taught. The technologies of education, like almost all technologies, are Faustian bargains (Postman, 2011) that almost always have harmful side-effects. I intend to show that many of the dominant technologies of institutional and formal education—courses, classrooms, assessments, timetables, and more—can be inimical, in at least some respects, to their primary function of learning. To be more precise, the technologies of which they are composed have a consistent tendency to pull in mutually exclusive directions, like gears set in opposition. It can take a lot of effort and skill to overcome such problems, and a central claim of this book is that how we have developed ways of doing so has significantly shaped and defined what we have traditionally thought of as good teaching. Many of our most cherished pedagogies and structures are simply solutions to problems caused by how we have chosen to teach. At least some of those problems can be and sometimes are solved differently, and a great many solutions create new problems to be solved.

I am not being so fuzzy in my definition as to consider everything we do as education, though it is certainly true that almost everything that we see, hear, feel, and do can be educative under the right circumstances, just as the stick that introduced this book can play an educative role, if and only if it is assembled with appropriate methods, objects, structures, processes, and phenomena that make it so.

Education above all is a process of and for learning. But, of course, though learning is the most central part of education, not all learning is a result of education, education does not always lead to the learning that we might hope for, and a large portion of what goes on in and as a product of our education systems has nothing to do with learning.

It is common to be instructed in something and to come away learning nothing particularly useful apart from how we feel about being instructed. Dogs and even cockroaches learn, but we don't normally try to educate cockroaches, and we train dogs rather than educate them, as a rule. Equally, humans can learn to fear, to love, to enjoy, to hate without necessarily being educated to do so. Mountains, crowds, and dogs rarely seek to educate us, but there are many things that we can and do learn from them. Meanwhile, education always teaches things that it does not set out to teach, and it can fail to teach what it intends to teach. This book will explain how, when, and why this is true. It will explain, in the process, how education works.

To summarize, the meaning that I will ascribe to "education" in this book is that of the systematic transformation of people's skills, knowledge, and values, whether or not it occurs in a formal setting, whether or not it involves intentional instruction, whether or not it involves someone whom we would conventionally label a teacher, and whether or not the tools, methods, and approaches used are intentionally designed to work that way. The systematization can and nearly always does involve others. As well as the learner, this process also involves countless individuals, the structures and systems that they create, the technologies, tools, stories, and methods that they construct. It is a massively complex, deeply entangled system, only parts of which are deliberately designed to teach. Timetables, classrooms, doors, doorknobs, and textbooks can and do teach, and this book explains how that happens. It is about why education is fundamentally concerned with learning technologies and the parts that we can and do play in creating, using, and in most cases being a part of them. And we are seldom if ever the only parts: almost always we are co-participants with other people, all of whom play their parts.

There Are Always Many Teachers

There is probably no such thing as a pure autodidact. Even if you were raised by wolves, wolves teach. Have you ever learned anything truly by yourself, unaided? Without reading something, without watching someone, without using methods that you have learned from others, without making use of a technology made for people to use that thus teaches something in and of itself? In the language that we normally use to describe such experiences, I teach myself many things. For instance, I try to teach myself at least one new musical instrument every year. However, I have seen and heard people play most of these instruments, or ones like them, which has taught me something of value before I even start. I actively seek YouTube videos, tutorials, manuals, images, diagrams, all written by people who are nothing if not my teachers. The instruments that I play have been designed, in most cases, to be played, with fretboards, keys, mouthpieces, and so on that invite particular kinds of use. The instruments themselves teach. I listen to the sounds that I make, that provide clear feedback on whether or not I have been successful, by criteria that I have learned from my technology-mediated culture. As I get better at playing, I start to play for and with others. I talk with other players; I observe how people react to what I play. All of these things teach. In fact, there's a wealth of teachers involved in the self-teaching process, of which I am only one. It is true that I perform a lot of the orchestration; I guide the process, choose the elements, structure the activities, choose when and for how long I learn, and so on. However, much of this remains true even when I am deliberately and explicitly taught by a professional teacher. If, say, I attend a class, then the notion that all of my learning occurs during the act of being taught is patently absurd. All of us make sense of things ourselves, integrate our knowledge, make connections, choose where to give most of our attention, perform actions, whether or not someone is deliberately teaching us. It is simply a matter of degree and, to an extent, a matter of scale (the level of detail that we choose to observe), whether we choose to call this self-directed learning or not. When we teach ourselves, we are more in control of how, when, where, and whether we learn, but there are always others teaching us too. In formal learning contexts, we just delegate (or are forced to give) more of that control to someone else. We are always co-participants in the learning process, never its sole orchestrators.

We Are All Learning Technologists

Technologies lift us beyond what nature has endowed us with. The use of technology is central to what it means to be human: it might even be our defining characteristic (Taylor, 2010). Technologies do not have to be embodied in devices or physical objects. There are just as many intellectual, psychological, legal, design, and pedagogical technologies as there are blackboards, computer programs, and desks. As I will argue throughout the book, words are technologies, and so are sentences, arguments, stories, poems, theories, models, and prayers. Our technologies play a central role in making us who and what we are. We participate in them, and they participate in us. We co-participate in them with others. They help to define how we think, and they play a considerable role in determining which new technologies we can build, in a never-ending dynamic cycle of construction, both of meaning and of the social, psychological, and physical worlds that we inhabit: language, art, writing, organizational processes, procedures, metaphors, and gestures as much as wheels, cellphones, transit systems, and houses. The complex arrangements and interdependencies of technologies and how we use them combine to form further technologies, which Arthur (2009) defines as assemblies that orchestrate phenomena to achieve some purpose: we organize stuff to do stuff, and the stuff that we organize to do stuff can be anything, including other stuff that we organize to do stuff.

Given that our technologies are so much a part of every aspect of our being, it is no surprise that we use them when learning. All educative activity and most if not all learning that we accomplish could not begin to occur without technologies. To educate, including to educate oneself, is to be a user of, and a participant in, technologies.

This book weaves a common theme across a wide range of phenomena that traditionally have been treated as separate, but that reveal new subtleties and insights when viewed as interacting, mutually constitutive technologies. Pedagogies, language, imagery, art, and group processes share a surprising amount in common with computers, screwdrivers, and buildings in their basic behaviours and dynamics, in the ways that we participate in their instantiation, and in the ways that they work with and against one another to achieve our ends. If we can get a better understanding of the nature of technologies, their dynamics, their structures, their designs, their limitations, their propensities, and their patterns of change, then we can apply these insights to build and use better technologies or at least to better recognize their boundaries and potential. Whether we are learners or teachers or both (spoiler: we are both), we are designers, users of, and participants in learning technologies, so we should probably learn to design and use them as well as we can. Moreover, we should understand how they use us, how they evolve, and how they lead to emergent and unforeseen complex behaviours that we do not control but that profoundly affect us.

All educators are learning technologists. They might differ a little in the technologies that they choose to use and how they choose to assemble them, but they all create and use technologies in order to educate. And we are all, every one of us, educators, whether explaining, showing, or describing something to someone else, teaching it to ourselves, or simply modelling behaviours that others might imitate, critique, reflect on, or deride. This book can help you to become slightly more mindful of the process, but, from a newborn baby to a grand old professor, we cannot help but be educators, in all our actions and interactions, virtually all the time. Not only do we all teach, but also we are all taught: not just by individuals but also by the combinations of individuals that make up groups, networks, crowds, and collectives that surround us and often contain us, as well as by the tools, methods, structures, and processes that they create.

Although technologies are essential to almost all learning, they are never the sole cause. For instance, our motivations, or the passion and enthusiasm of others, can play a massive role in making it happen. Technologies can do no more than help to kindle and communicate such passion. More subtly, there are aspects of technologies that themselves are not technologies—that are either a consequence of their use or a nontechnological component—but that play a significant role in enabling learning: things that make them appealing or unappealing, effective or ineffective, and so on, from the narrative flow to the colours or media that they use. "Tain't what you do (it's the way that you do it)," as the song by Oliver and Young (1939) goes, "that's what gets results." Using good tools and methods is important, but it is usually more important to use them well. The idiosyncratic, ever-changing, highly personal technique that we develop, and all the passion and creativity that it embodies, to a large extent, are what give technologies meaning, value, and form. Learning is both a social and a psychological phenomenon for which the technology can be a conduit or facilitator but never the only cause.

Where I'm Coming From

It is hard to avoid one's own cultural context when writing a book of this nature, so it might be useful for you to know a bit about me before we go much further. By profession, I am currently a distance educator. I am also the associate dean, learning and assessment, for the faculty of science and technology and a full professor in computing and information systems at Athabasca University, a distance-based open university situated in Alberta, where I have worked for over 15 years. I don't just teach but also work at a distance: I live in Vancouver, over 1,000 kilometers from the workplace that I rarely visit. Prior to that, for about 10 years, I taught, partly online, at the University of Brighton, a more conventional in-person university in the United Kingdom. I spent several years before that working with, managing, and building information and communication technologies (ICTs) in an educational context. Before that, and throughout my 20s, I sang and played guitar for a living, which will be reflected in some of the examples and metaphors used in this book and which has been surprisingly helpful in making connections between ideas and theories over the years. From an academic perspective, I have postsecondary qualifications in philosophy, information systems, learning technologies, and education, and I have followed a great many academic sidetracks along the way, many of which make their way into the text, from evolution and complex adaptive systems to architectural theory.

For me, education is more about a body of learners needing or wanting to learn than it is about a body of knowledge to be learned. Education is not just about learning skills and factual knowledge. It is more concerned with developing ways of thinking and being; of passing on, challenging, and sometimes changing attitudes, values, and beliefs, including my own. In its formal incarnations, it tends to be an instrument of cultural stability, but if it works then it is at least as much an instrument of change. Knowledge is created, recreated, and transformed, not transmitted. My job as a professional educator is not to fill vessels but, as Plutarch (1927) told us long ago, to light fires. In so doing I am not just assembling combustible materials and applying a spark but also passing on the flame that has already been kindled in me. The flame will not burn the same way in others as it burns in me, because we are all made of different stuff. Teaching others is about enabling them to know things and to cultivate ways of thinking that, as often as not, I do not and sometimes cannot know myself. And it is about others lighting flames in me: as an educator, I learn for a living. But I am just one tiny part of a massively complex and only partially designed mechanism, a piece of a rich, entangled ecosystem filled with ways to support and engender learning. Classrooms and learning management systems, pencils and iPads, and countless nameless and named people, past and present, contribute to the whole, as do the countless events, structures, technologies, interactions, and things that constitute the intertwined histories of the learners whom I support. I never teach alone.

I believe that education is a deeply situated, human, social, and cultural phenomenon, and it does a great disservice to its complexity to try to extract the researcher from the research, as much as it does to extract the teacher from the teaching. This book, by design and given its central theses, is not an objective account. You will read many passionately held opinions, personal anecdotes, and biased accounts of practice in this book, for which I make no apologies. I hope that at least some of the story that it tells resonates with you and helps you to make a bit more sense of your own practices, attitudes, and beliefs regarding learning and teaching.

About the Sections and Chapters

The book is divided into three main sections and a preamble. The preamble sets the scene, Part 1 delves into the nature of technology, Part 2 focuses on educational practices and theories themselves, and Part 3 applies the model to explain, in some depth, the scene-setting stories and observations of the preamble.

Preamble: Elephant Spotting. This brief section contains two short chapters that provide some stories and observations to illustrate some of the problems that this book will address and, hopefully, solve.

Chapter 1: A Handful of Anecdotes about Elephants. This chapter begins to set the scene with a few short anecdotes that reveal various elephants in the classroom that are seldom given more than cursory glosses in educational research: that bad teaching methods—or even no apparent teaching at all—can lead to good results; that good teaching methods can lead to bad results; that what is taught is not necessarily what is learned; and that teaching is embedded in our constructed environment.

Chapter 2: A Handful of Observations about Elephants. This chapter continues setting the scene by making a number of observations about some peculiarities of education systems: that rewards and punishments are deemed necessary to drive learning, something that we naturally love to do; that learning online is often treated as undesirable while being the most popular form of learning on the planet; that media and tools appear to make little or no difference to learning outcomes; that the ways that teachers believe to be the most effective are not, on average, at all; that personal tutoring beats conventional classroom teaching by a 2 sigma advantage; that teaching to learning styles has no benefit; and that reductive research methods in education are seldom very useful.

Part I: All about Technology. This section provides the theoretical basis for the rest of the book. Although it does have a number of important and useful things to say about educational systems, tools, methods, and techniques, it is primarily about the nature of technologies themselves, which, given the fact that the key premise of this book is that education is primarily a technological phenomenon, should be useful. Some of this might not seem to be immediately relevant to the needs of educators, but I ask you to take it on trust that it is. This is a necessary foundation for understanding the next, more education-focused, section.

Chapter 3: Organizing Stuff to Do Stuff. This chapter explores a range of different meanings of the word *technology*, which turns out to be a complex and difficult word to pin down. I settle on Arthur's (2009) definition of technologies as orchestrations of phenomena to some use and his insight into the nature of technologies and their evolution as a process of assembly. Among other things, this analysis allows us to see pedagogies, along with other methods and processes used in education, as technologies in their own right.

Chapter 4: How Technologies Work. The purpose of this chapter is to delve more deeply into how technologies work, how they evolve over time, and how they exist in relation to one another. It draws extensively from a variety of complexity theorists—including Brian Arthur, Stuart Kauffman, Scott Page, and John Holland—to help frame not just the complexity of technological systems but also some of the deeper patterns that they embody.

Chapter 5: Participation and Technique. This chapter unravels the different ways that we participate in technologies, using the concepts of soft and hard technologies to distinguish between participation as an active creator and participation as part of a mechanism. I discuss some existing uses of the hard/soft technology distinction and reframe them, extending Arthur's work to include the roles that people play in technologies, not just as users but also as participants.

Part II: Education as a Technological Phenomenon. This section is where everything that comes before aims. It applies the model of technological systems developed in Part 1 directly to the process, theory, and practice of education.

Chapter 6: A Co-Participation Model of Teaching. This chapter explores the kinds of technologies that we normally label as pedagogies and the roles that pedagogies tend to play in technological assemblies. In particular, it helps to explain how and why the pedagogical process is inherently distributed, how learning is a feature not just of brains but also of the complex systems of which we are parts, and how there are always many co-participants in any deliberate act of learning.

Chapter 7: Theories of Teaching. This chapter shows how the co-participation model sheds light on existing families of pedagogical theories and models, providing a frame for understanding how, in assembly, theories of teaching, learning, and knowledge can successfully complement one another and be used to do what each does best.

Chapter 8: Technique, Expertise, and Literacy. This chapter provides insights into the technological nature of and the complex interplay between ourselves and our creations and how the co-participation model sheds light not just on the process of education but also on the nature of learning itself. It applies the co-participation model in order to understand the nature of technique (our roles in enacting technologies), expertise, and the value and nature of different kinds of literacy, revealing the notion to be highly situated and intrinsically linked to the many overlapping cultures to which we belong.

Part III: Applying the Co-Participation Model. This section uses the theory developed over the first two sections in order to explain the elephants in the room that initially made an appearance in the first two chapters. I thus hope to show how and why the co-participation model matters as a means of understanding learning and teaching.

Chapter 9: Revealing Elephants. This chapter explains the anecdotes presented in the first chapter in terms of co-participation theory, thus helping to demonstrate some of the ways that it can be used to guide and interpret learning and teaching practice.

Chapter 10: How Education Works. Through the lens of the observations initially made in Chapter 2, this chapter uses the co-participation model to explain why many of our most cherished attitudes toward and practices in education, assessment, and especially research on education are inherently flawed. It shows that much of our research—including attempts to compare the effects of different media, to examine the effects of teaching on learning styles, or more broadly to identify generally effective teaching methods—is often misdirected. It explains how attempts to solve teaching problems inevitably generate new teaching problems to solve and that often-ignored but ubiquitous technological elements of the process—from classrooms to timetables to assessment practices—work directly against our intent to educate. The chapter shows how distance and online educators have needlessly inherited pedagogical solutions to in-person teaching problems, along with most of the problems that those solutions created, even though the essential challenges of online learning in many ways are almost the opposite of their in-person counterparts, and many of the checks and balances that allow in-person education to work might not be available to online learners. Along the way, I present some tentative solutions to some of these issues.

PREAMBLE
ELEPHANT SPOTTING

1 | A Handful of Anecdotes about Elephants

> POLICEMAN: *Where are you going with that elephant?*
> DURANTE: *What elephant?*
>
> —from the film *Billy Rose's Jumbo* (Walters, 1962)

There are elephants in the classroom of education, seldom seen but towering over us, filling the space. Over the next couple of chapters, I will provide a few glimpses of where they are standing. This chapter is just a handful of anecdotes that you can interpret how you will, and the next chapter contains more direct observations of a few of the more notable anomalies with which educators live but that they largely ignore or try to explain in unconvincing ways. I will return to these anecdotes and observations in the last two chapters of the book, this time with a flashlight so that we can see the elephants clearly and know why they are there.

"You're Not Teaching Me"

In the days when I had an office and taught in a traditional campus-based university, a student once came to talk to me about one of my classes that he was taking. He was quite angry. I cannot recall the precise words that we exchanged, but the gist of our conversation was roughly as follows.

"You're not teaching us anything," he complained.

"But are you learning anything?" I asked.

"Oh yeah, tons. Actually, come to think of it, much more than I've learned on any other course till now. But you are not teaching me anything. I have to learn it all myself."

I nodded as sagely as I could, trying to repress a smile.

He paused in thought for a moment, and then his face broke into a broad grin. "Ah ha!" he said. Those were his exact words.

I love to hear those words.

When Good Teachers Do Bad Things

I was once called upon to help a colleague prepare his pedagogical statement of relevance when he was nominated for a national teaching award. He had already written a lengthy draft statement describing his methods of and approaches to teaching that I read in advance of our first meeting. In my naive arrogance, I was shocked that anyone would consider nominating him for such a prestigious award. His statement was a litany of what I understood to be some of the worst instructivist teaching practices and pedagogies that I had ever seen. As I recall, it consisted of descriptions of his full-frontal lectures, flash tests designed as threats to the unprepared, ways of punishing those who failed to keep up, and a defense of the value of objective testing. It seemed to me to be awful, authoritarian, and controlling. I would have held it up as an exemplar of everything bad in learning design.

I was so wrong.

To my great surprise, none of this prevented him from being a brilliant teacher. In fact, the more I spoke with him and those affected by him, the more I realized that he was among the best teachers I had ever known. His students were enthusiastic and competent. The best and the worst were motivated and saw great improvements in both grades and attitudes during his courses. The majority loved him, and it was clear that he loved them. They went on to do well in their field. Many sought his help in obtaining graduate degrees. His teaching spilled way beyond the deliberately taught courses and into the broader community. He was an inspiration to his colleagues. By any measure, save what I believed to be the use of good pedagogical methods, he was at the top of the field. A brilliant, passionate, and caring teacher whose results, no matter how they were defined, and certainly by the criteria that I thought should matter, were stellar.

It was a humbling experience. He got the award.

No Teacher, No Problem

When I was studying for my O-Levels (at the time, a qualification taken by many schoolchildren in the United Kingdom, normally at the age of 16, that typically came at the end of a 2-year period of study), my mathematics teacher, a charismatic and amiable man who had been quite an inspirational teacher during our first year, became ill for most of the year leading up to the final exams. The school did its best to provide substitute teachers but, for the most part, failed. If we were lucky, then we might get a student teacher for a week or two who would attempt to mark our assignments. Much of the time, they were unable to answer our questions. Some of the time, no one turned up at all. Even when they did, we were usually left entirely to our own devices and told to follow the exercises in the textbook. So, we spent somewhere between a third and a half of our math course without any (apparent) teacher. At least, there was no one playing the didactic role, hardly anyone helping us to solve problems apart from ourselves.

To the surprise of many, the class broke all records for O-Level achievement that year by a remarkably large margin. We enjoyed ourselves too.

An Earth-Moving Learning Experience

I once attended an e-learning conference during which an earthquake took out all the power for a day. Although a few people gave up presenting completely, some soldiered on. Most discarded their carefully prepared PowerPoint slides and extemporized, turning their talks into conversations. It was actually a far better learning experience for most people than would have occurred had things gone as normal. The sympathetic camaraderie of the audience meant that a great deal of interesting conversation resulted, especially since the cancellations gave more time for discussion than normally would be available. Later presenters picked up ideas and approaches from those who spoke earlier, and by the end of the day the whole conference was buzzing in a way that might not have been possible had the earthquake not disrupted the proceedings. I was rather disappointed when the power came back on later that night, in time for my own presentation the next day. The rest of the conference was interesting but not nearly as thought provoking or engaging as it was that day.

One presenter, however, took a different tack. Although his audience consisted of perhaps 20 people—a good number for this particular multi-track conference—unfortunately he was scheduled into a lecture theatre designed to hold hundreds of delegates, with no windows and only dim emergency lighting. The audience was dispersed across the lecture theatre, and using his laptop computer on battery power the presenter held it up to the audience and gave the PowerPoint presentation that he had originally prepared. He was quiet spoken, and without a microphone—a necessity in such a large room—and with English as his second language it was hard to understand what he was saying. Only those with good eyesight in the front row could see anything on his laptop screen. He repeatedly had to turn his screen toward him so that he could remind himself what he was supposed to be talking about, illuminating his face with classic horror movie lighting. Everyone applauded sympathetically at the end, despite having learned virtually nothing of what he was trying to tell us. As a postscript, I was lucky enough to chat with him a few years later. His work was actually quite fascinating, and I thoroughly enjoyed our conversation.

Although what I learned had little to do with what the presenter hoped to teach me, this was a profound learning experience.

Boats That Teach

I am writing this on my old, rickety sailboat that (more or less) floats in a marina near my home. The boat has evolved over the past 30–40 years to embody—and to transmit—much of the learning of its previous owners. From the (repositioned) mainsheets, to the ingenious feeding of lines from fore to aft, to a self-steering device (which tends to steer the boat in circles—not all technologies work as intended), this boat captures the problems and solutions of its former owners, as well as its original builders, in countless ways. I have added some tweaks of my own over the years that I have owned it. Not only have all of us made it easier and safer to operate the boat, but also we have left concrete explanations of our learning, not in words but in changes that we have made to the boat itself.

My boat sits in a marina next to other sailboats, many of a similar vintage and size, which solve similar problems in different ways. Some embody solutions to problems that I hadn't even realized were problems. I am constantly taught not just by my own boat but also by comparing it with those around me. The boats teach; the marina in which they are moored teaches.

My boat is surrounded not just by other boats but also by the people who sail in them. These people are a rich source of knowledge, drawn together by their shared interests and problems. Most of us have only a partial understanding of the art and science of sailing and boat maintenance. There is a rich and arcane vocabulary involved—gudgeons, pintles, and so on—that few of us know in its entirety, but we teach one another and, through repeated use, learn it ourselves. It is rare to spend more than a few minutes working on my boat (which I do far more often than sailing it) before someone passes by and offers some help or (sometimes welcome) advice. Whenever one of us figures out a solution to a problem, others learn from it. When I devised a makeshift contraption involving shackles taped to chimney-sweeping poles that I ran up the backstay in order to free a shackle that I had carelessly trapped at the top of my mast, there were cheers when I managed to pull it free again. Somebody came to shake my hand. We had all learned a new and useful trick.

2 | A Handful of Observations about Elephants

My roommate got a pet elephant. Then it got lost. It's in the apartment somewhere.

—Attributed to Rod Schmidt

The observations in this chapter are of diverse phenomena, each of which seems to me to raise a number of questions that need to be answered. In the final chapter of the book, I will explain these observations and answer those questions, but for now I simply present them as curious phenomena that are sufficiently widespread, either in their effects or in the research that they engender, to matter to a lot of people.

People Must Be Made to Learn

We are all born with an insatiable thirst for learning. When we want to learn something, as children or as adults, we need no special encouragement. We do it as naturally as we breathe, drink, or eat. It is intrinsically fulfilling to overcome challenges, to become more competent (Ryan & Deci, 2017), in almost anything, including many things that others (and perhaps we too on reflection) would find pointless or trivial. There is an intense joy in learning that almost everyone has felt at some point. Learning is its own reward, yet, in formal teaching and training, we usually force people to do it with rewards and punishments. In doing so, we could not send a stronger message that the activity itself is undesirable (Kohn, 1999). Even when apparently successful—usually measured by grades—a remarkable amount of what is intentionally learned under such conditions is forgotten once the rewards or threats are removed, though we might remember how we felt about it. This is perfectly natural. Just as we usually remember the number of our hotel room while we are staying there but forget it almost immediately when we no longer need to know it, so too, once the grade or credential has been achieved, or the punishment has been avoided, we tend to forget much of the information that we needed at the time. It can also teach us limited, dependent, and often ineffective ways of learning that rarely serve us well throughout our lives outside a few atypical contexts. It is also probable, worryingly, that we learned little or nothing in the first place. I am sure that neither you nor I ever cheated on a test, but we are in a minority. In some cultures, over 80% of the population admit (anonymously) to cheating on assessments (Ma et al., 2013). In the United States and Canada, over half of students admit to it (Jurdi et al., 2011; McCabe & Trevino, 1996).

At least some of our dominant teaching methods, whether or not they result in the intended learning in the short term, are counterproductive in the long term, too often resulting in learners with no desire to learn more, little recollection of whatever they were supposed to learn in the first place, and little passion for what they have learned. Given our natural love of learning, this is more than a little strange.

Online Learning Dominates in-Person Learning—Except in Formal Education

What do you do first when you need to discover some information or learn something? The odds are that your answer will be an internet search, most likely through Google or one of its close competitors. If not, or maybe as a result, depending on your field of interest and learning needs, you might visit Wikipedia, or Stack Exchange, or a bulletin board or Q&A site for your field, or YouTube, or ChatGPT. You might send a message—an email, a direct message, a tweet—to someone whom you believe can help you. You might even ask someone nearby. The chances, though, that your first port of call is a library, let alone a course of some sort, are fairly slim, even though you might use internet technologies to find one and it might help to guide a good part of your learning journey later. For those of us with access to the internet, it has fundamentally changed how we acquire knowledge and skills. We are now used to being able to discover more or less anything almost wherever and whenever we need it. Whether the knowledge that we gain in the process is reliable, sufficient for our needs, appropriate to our understanding, or relevant to our wishes might remain a hit-and-miss affair. Nonetheless, we are all learning, most of the time, anywhere, anytime, anyplace, and we are doing so online. Moreover, we do so without coercion, without the threat or reward of being graded for it. If we are talking about intentional learning, then it appears that online learning dwarfs its in-person counterpart in quantity if not necessarily in quality.

So why is it that, in formal education, online learning is often considered to be a poor second cousin to in-person learning (Protopsaltis & Baum, 2019), and, when given the choice, many people prefer to avoid it? And who is teaching us when we learn this way?

No Significant Difference in Learning Outcomes No Matter Which Media or Tools You Choose

Common sense suggests that, if people are taught in different ways, the results should be different. For instance, as alluded to in the previous section, many people believe that online learning is inferior to in-person learning. However, a large body of research over many decades has shown fairly definitively that, on average, this belief is false. The no-significant-difference phenomenon has been observed for a long time in the case of different learning media. Russell (1999) catalogued 355 explicit examples from 1928 to 1999 that illustrate the phenomenon that the mode of delivery appears to be insignificant (on average) in achieving effective learning. The same is true of online learning. In what is likely the largest metastudy to date, conducted by the US Department of Education, researchers looked at over 1,000 comparative studies and revealed no significant difference (Means et al., 2009). Indeed, metastudies of such metastudies equally reveal no significant difference between learning outcomes for online and face-to-face learning (Allen & Seaman, 2013; Pei & Wu, 2019). Similarly, large-scale individual studies tend to show little or no difference in outcomes (Cavanaugh & Jacquemin, 2015). A few metastudies reveal a slight tendency toward better outcomes for online and distance learning, and slightly better still for blended approaches, but that can usually be explained by demographics of students, competence of early adopting teachers, publication bias, or other methodological flaws (Chen et al., 2010; Tamim et al., 2011). This is not to suggest that there are no consistent and important differences in the online learner experience between in-person and online modalities. There are huge differences. But the learning results, as they are normally measured (which I will question in Chapter 10) tend, on average, to be pretty much the same for online learners as those for in-person learners.

Perhaps even more surprisingly, not even considering media or tools, it makes little difference how one teaches. In what must surely be among the most rigorous and influential metastudies of metastudies in the field of education, John Hattie (2013) synthesizes over 800 metastudies, relating to millions of learners, drawing from this vast catalogue those strategies, techniques, and methods that research shows to be most effective. Perhaps the most central message that we can draw from all this is that, as Hattie (pp. 34–35) himself puts it, "almost everything works. Ninety percent of all effect sizes in education are positive. Of the ten percent that are negative, about half are 'expected' (e.g., effects of disruptive students); thus, about 95 percent of all things we do have a positive influence on achievement."

How is this possible? Surely the ways in which we teach must make some difference. Yet, as most teachers know, not only do different methods appear to work equally well, but also we can use what appear to be the same methods repeatedly over multiple iterations of a course yet achieve utterly different results.

The Best Ways to Teach Are Not the Best Ways to Teach

Social constructivist pedagogies, typically drawing inspiration from Dewey (1916) or Vygotsky (1978), are widely taught to teachers around the world, used across the educational spectrum, and often upheld as models of best teaching practice, with good reason: theory suggests that they should be effective, and many published studies seem to indicate that the theory holds in practice. However, the empirical evidence to support such beliefs is not compelling. For example, Andrews et al. (2011) investigated the effectiveness of active learning (broadly covering a range of methods inspired by constructivist epistemologies that demand engagement with, rather than absorption of, knowledge) in a random sample of college biology courses, finding little or no benefit to learners who had been subjected to an active learning pedagogy compared with those who had been taught in a more conventional fashion. In some cases, at least by the crude measures of success employed (mainly terminal grades), things were actually worse.

The researchers surmised that previous research had involved researchers skilled in the use of active learning pedagogies who were enthusiastic about and engaged in what they were teaching. When applied by the rank and file of teachers with limited skill or engagement with the methods, there were no significant benefits to be seen. This is not an unusual finding: Klahr and Nigam (2004) found much the same thing when comparing direct instruction and the active approach of discovery learning, and Mayer (2004) has long made similar claims. De Bruyckere et al.(2015) make the more nuanced assertion that problem-based approaches can be useful to extend existing knowledge, but not to acquire it in the first place, and that discovery learning can sometimes be effective, but only with the right guidance and support. Hattie (2013, p. 331) draws from many metastudies to conclude that minimally guided, facilitative approaches such as problem-based, inquiry-based, and project-based learning tend, on average, to be relatively ineffective.

For most teachers who have undergone any kind of teacher training in the past 50 years or so, this tends to come as a surprise.

No One Has Solved the 2 Sigma Problem

Bloom's (1984) paper on the 2 sigma problem shows, among other things, that one-to-one tutoring leads, on average, to a 2 sigma improvement in performance compared with "conventional" didactic teaching (again according to the measures used). This has since become the gold standard for educational interventions, especially in online learning. No methods identified so far have consistently achieved that gold standard. Given the tens of thousands of papers written every year since Bloom set his challenge, which represents only a small fraction of millions of teaching interventions, this might seem to be a little surprising. Why is one-to-one tutoring so much better than any other method of teaching?

Matching Teaching Style to Learning Style Offers No Significant Benefit

People are different, and (self-evidently) different people learn better in different ways. Common sense suggests that we should therefore teach them differently. Following this intuition, numerous learning style theories postulate that individuals have one among a fixed range of persistent learning styles or preferences and that they will learn better when teaching is designed to fit with their identified style or preference. The boldest theories claim that learning styles are unalterable traits and field independent, whereas others make the weaker assertion that they are potentially changeable states and/or field dependent (Curry, 1983). The meekest theories claim only to identify learner preferences, rather than fixed styles, though this is a much less useful claim that might have little impact on teaching practice because the most preferred ways of learning might not coincide with the most effective ways of learning. In fact, the odds are against it (Clark, 1982). A vast majority of professional teachers believe that learning style theories—often as expressed in their strongest, trait-like, field-independent form—are valid (e.g., Boser, 2019; Dekker et al., 2012). There are many reasons to challenge this belief, such as that these theories cannot all be true, that misapplication can disadvantage those inaccurately diagnosed, that people seem to learn any which way when they have to, and so on. But perhaps the most obvious reason for doubt is that there is virtually no reliable evidence to support any of them, despite countless studies and thousands of papers published on the subject every year for several decades (Coffield et al., 2004; De Bruyckere et al., 2015; Derribo & Howard, 2007; Hattie, 2013; Husmann & O'Loughlin, 2019; Pashler et al., 2008; Riener & Willingham, 2010). If different individuals do learn better in different ways from one another (and this is undoubtedly true), then why is it that, when we adapt our teaching methods to ways that should suit them better, such adaptation does nothing to improve the desired learning outcomes? Is it just that we do not yet have a good theory, or is there some other reason?

Experimental Educational Research Methods Appear Not to Work Very Well

There have been hundreds of thousands of randomized controlled tests (RCTs) and null-hypothesis significance tests (NHSTs) performed in educational settings over many decades that seek to discover or confirm what causes learning. Yet, apart from in some very limited and rigidly proscribed contexts, we have little proof that any generalizable method is much better than any other (Hattie, 2013), and there is little evidence that education has improved significantly in quality over the past several decades. Makel and Plucker (2014) observe that, in top educational journals, only 0.13% of experimental studies replicated earlier studies and that, of those few that successfully replicated the originals, the vast majority involved some overlap in authorship and thus might be subject to similar errors and biases. Why is it so difficult to find proof of things that work? Given the massive investment in research time spent on education, has there been so little obvious improvement in outcomes? Why is it so hard to replicate success?

Explaining the Elephants

The apparently diverse phenomena described in these two chapters are closely related to one another, in fact, and they all stem from similar, closely entwined causes. Much like the parable of the "Blind Men and an Elephant," each allows a glimpse of one part of a single phenomenon.[1]

In the chapters that follow, I will offer some unifying explanations of these phenomena and plenty more. These explanations emerge naturally from the nature of technology and especially the nature of the technologies through which we commonly learn. They are among the consequences of how technologies are designed, how they work with (or sometimes against) one another, and above all how we and our technologies are intimately and irreversibly entwined, as essential parts of one another. Before offering my explanations, though, it is necessary to understand the whole elephant. The starting point for this must be the nature of technologies in general and, later, how they can contribute (positively or negatively) to learning. This is the purpose of the next few chapters.

---

[1] For the parable, see https://en.wikipedia.org/wiki/Blind_men_and_an_elephant.

PART I
ALL ABOUT TECHNOLOGY

A Summary of What You Are about to Read in This Section

If we wish to understand education as a technological system, then we should first have a clear idea of the character and form of technological systems. In this section, I will therefore explore the nature of technology, examining many of its complex meanings as well as uncovering some of its universal regularities. Along the way, I will reveal some interesting and occasionally surprising implications for learning, teaching, and educational research, but my main purpose is to provide the necessary foundations for the next section of the book, in which those implications turn out to be considerable and profoundly important.

Chapter 3 delves deep into the complex and diverse meanings of the word *technology*, what it includes, and what it excludes. Drawing heavily from Brian Arthur's insights into its nature and evolution, I present a case that technology is best understood as both the process and the product of organizing stuff to do stuff. Importantly, again drawing from Arthur's work, the stuff that is organized nearly always includes other stuff that has been organized. Thus, technologies are seen to be assemblies of technologies and other phenomena, forming a hugely complex, recursively intertwined technological web.

Chapter 4 discusses some of the most significant structural dynamics of technologies, viewed as complex entangled assemblies. Among other things, recognizing this complexity, it draws attention to the importance of the boundaries that we choose to consider when discussing technologies, observing that it is too easy to focus on one part of this entangled assembly—a computer, say, or a pedagogical method—and to treat it as a synecdoche for the whole, leading us to many unwarranted and counterproductive conclusions and actions. The technology of greatest interest is usually the complete assembly as it is enacted, not the parts of the assembly. The chapter goes on to discuss how technologies develop, and how they can guide but (beyond limited local contexts) almost never determine behaviour, and it explains some of the evolutionary dynamics and structural patterns that affect their development, use, and enactment, including ways that they can narrow and ways that they can expand our horizons as we explore the adjacent possible empty niches that they create.

Chapter 5 builds upon the understanding of technology that emerges from the two previous chapters to describe how we participate in rather than simply use technologies. We are not just users but also parts of our technologies, and some of them (e.g., language, arithmetical procedures, theories, and principles) are parts of us. Sometimes the parts that we play in their enactment are predetermined and fixed, such as when we flick a switch, follow a prescribed procedure, or spell a word correctly. I label such technologies "hard," by which I mean that our roles as parts of them are inflexible: if they work, then what we must do to make them work is entirely determined in advance. Sometimes our roles are far less precisely determined, such as when we draw with a pencil or write with a word processor. I label such technologies "soft." Hardness or softness is a characteristic of our roles in assembling and orchestrating the technology, not of the parts that it contains. Nearly every technology is an assembly of soft and hard technologies. Softness to hardness is a fuzzy continuum, not a binary distinction. Softness or hardness is a measure of the extent to which we must or may add our own orchestrations to the mix. The larger the gaps that may or must be filled, the softer the technology.

There is already a common English word for this human role in technologies: *technique*. A technique is the way that we become parts of our technologies, and for any technique there will be at least some hardness in how it is done, some pattern, perhaps some archetype or ideal that it aims for, and usually some softness, something idiosyncratic, something personal, something creative.

Combined with the observations and principles from the preceding chapters, the soft/hard distinction provides the basis for the theory of learning and teaching that I will develop in the subsequent section of the book, in which teaching is seen to be a vastly complex, distributed technology assembled from countless technologies, engaging and enacted by countless co-participants (especially learners); where method plays second fiddle to technique (and it is the technique of many, not of one); where every situation and every learning event is unique and unrepeatable; and where learning is never just an individual behaviour but also a collective act in which we are, ultimately, all complicit.

3 | Organizing Stuff to Do Stuff

How does one speak about something that is both fish and water, means as well as end?

—Ursula Franklin (1999, p. 6)

Before we can begin to understand education as a technological phenomenon, it is necessary to understand the nature of technologies. Unfortunately, "technology" is a slippery term used in many formal and informal contexts, with meanings that vary vastly in precision and application, some of which are contradictory. As Schatzburg (2018, p. 10) puts it, "the definition of technology is a mess." In this chapter, I hope to unpack much of that mess or at least to explain it. As a result, we will slide down a few rabbit holes together here and there because there is a great deal of complexity, ambiguity, and multiple layers of meaning to unravel, and (if you are anything like I was a few years ago) no doubt you have plenty of preconceptions about the subject that can cause confusion down the line. It might therefore be helpful to know that the end point that we are heading toward is that eventually I will define "technology" as "the organization of stuff to do stuff," derived directly from Arthur's definition of it as "an orchestration of phenomena to our use" (2009, loc. 783–786). Both "stuffs" in my definition can be literally any stuff: real, imaginary, physical, conceptual, virtual, supernatural, or whatever. Most notably, the "stuff" includes other stuff organized to do stuff: technologies are made of technologies, they make up further technologies, and they participate in a vast technological web. The "organization" can refer to either a process or a product of a process (sometimes both at once).

Etymology and History

Although we should be extremely wary of using etymology to help define current usage, it might be helpful to seek the origin and history of the word *technology* to understand at least some of its shades of meaning and its nuances of application. For the ancient Greeks (at least through the closely related word *techne*), technology covered "everything from farming techniques and ancient medical practices to political techniques, gymnastics and arts" (Zhouying, 2004, p. 135), a meaning that certainly included educational practices. This was the central meaning that the word retained until not much more than 100 years ago, and strong shades of it remain today. The word *technology* itself first occurred in the early 17th century to represent the study of *techne*. This was a logical use of the word, reflecting most other "ologies" such as psychology, anthropology, and neurology. It started to acquire its less intuitive current meaning during the early part of the 19th century (Kelly, 2010), but it retained various parallel meanings for a long time. Nye (2006) notes that it was still more common up to the late 19th century to find the word referring to a book about a practical art or craft than describing the products of such skills.

The term continues to evolve and encompasses a complex set of attitudes, beliefs, and assumptions, leading Nye (2006, p. 15) to describe its current usage as an "annoyingly vague abstraction." This vagueness, at least in English and some other languages, has led some to use a different term, such as "technics" (Mumford, 1934; Stiegler, 1998), in an attempt to capture the shades of meaning that we intuit naturally when thinking about the example of the stick with which this book began. A similar meaning, translated directly from the French, is found in the use of the term "technique" by Ellul (1970). Unfortunately, the use of these terms is as confused and diverse as that of "technology" itself—Webster's dictionary from 1828, for instance, defined the word *technics* as "the doctrine of arts in general; such branches of learning as respect the arts" (Schatzburg, 2018, p. 235), closely reflecting the original meaning of *techne*. None of these alternatives has entered common usage, and modern meanings of the word *technology* range from "the stuff that we buy at technology stores" to a catch-all encompassing pretty much all human activities and artifacts. If we are to understand what we mean by the word, then we need more clarity.

Technology and Tech

Alan Kay once described technology as "anything invented after you were born" (cited in Brand, 2000, loc. 189). Many take this definition to heart. For example, Oppenheimer (2003) argues improbably against expenditure on technology in schools because it means that less is available to be spent on Bunsen burners, pencils, and textbooks. The word *technology* has gained a usage much like that of *chemicals* in foods that proudly and implausibly proclaim themselves to be *chemical-free*. We kind of know what they mean even though the words themselves make no sense.

It is becoming increasingly common to make our meaning clearer by talking of "tech," a more precise term that usually refers to the subset of technologies that includes devices, gadgets, gizmos, and software as well as some other science-informed technologies such as gene editing or advanced materials engineering. This term helps to distinguish older, arts and crafts–based *techne* and the products of the modern, science-infused technological age (Borgmann, 1987). However, education (like this book) is about technology, not just tech. If we are to understand education as a technological phenomenon, then we need a clearer and more inclusive definition.

Not Just Physical Objects
It is common to think of technologies as physical objects. For instance, (Akerson et al., 2018, p. 3) describe technology as "organized around a concept or principle and . . . expressed in a physical component form." This, too, is wrong. Plenty of things that are not physical objects are commonly recognized as technologies, from university regulations to mental arithmetic to operating procedures for factories, and what made the stick

that introduced this book a technology was not the stick itself but what was done with it.

In fact, every practical invention (at least) is a technology. Things that we take for granted—such as houses, plumbing, farms, canals, and road systems—are only the most obvious, but technologies run far deeper. Time itself, as we experience it, is an invention that has evolved over millennia (Frank, 2011), as is language (Changizi, 2013; Kelly, 2010; Rheingold, 2012; Ridley, 2010; Wilson, 2012), which shapes at least to some extent our very perception of the world (Lakoff & Johnson, 1980) and may be thought of, by some persuasive accounts, as an inextricable part of our cognition itself (Clark, 2008; Heyes, 2018). Reflecting this object/process duality, Schwartz (1997, p. 21) defines technology as "the use of human intelligence to create objects or processes that change the conditions of daily life." This would not be a bad definition of education. However, the same might be said of things done by many animals, from nest building to herding, and its focus on effects tells us little about the particular nature of those objects and processes. We need to delve a bit deeper.

Not Just Tools

It seems to be natural to talk of technologies and tools in the same breath, but the two are not the same. Not all technologies can be described easily as tools. For instance, it seems to be natural to describe a pen as a tool, but not the paper on which we write with it, though both are clearly technologies, as are the things that we do when we bring the two together, such as writing and drawing, neither of which is normally described as a tool. Nuts and bolts are not, on the whole, thought of as tools, though they are clearly technologies. Tools do not have to be physically instantiated: we may use, for example, conceptual, mathematical, or theoretical tools to help us unravel a complex problem. Although many tools are technologies in their own right, some are not: sticks and stones can be tools too. What appears to be common to all tools is their relationship with an individual tool user (or sometimes a specific group of tool users) and their use to accomplish some further purpose. Whether or not they can be seen as technologies in their own right, what is done with them is almost invariably seen that way.

Technologies and Techniques

Although the term "technique" has a number of fuzzy conventional meanings and has sometimes been enlisted to refer to something different, such as Ellul's (1970) use of the term as a means to an end, I will use it here in a familiar and straightforward way to describe how a human being does something technological. Technique is how a person does a technology. For instance, we can use different techniques for playing the violin, for driving, for cooking, or for teaching. Perhaps we use more than one technique, for instance, to strum or finger-pick a guitar. The fact that we can point to examples of different techniques or talk of "perfecting" our techniques implies, correctly, that techniques are kinds of technology—essentially those in which people play a part—but techniques are more than just repeatable methods and procedures enacted by people. Techniques are often highly idiosyncratic. It is often possible to identify, say, artists, authors, or musicians (or teachers) from their techniques.

As the notion of "perfecting" techniques implies, they can evolve over time, not (usually) from one thing to another but as variations of something that approaches some kind of ideal. However, what that ideal means is often personal. There seems to be a prerequisite complexity to an activity for it to be described as a technique. It is unusual to talk of technique when there is only one way to do something: that seems to be described better as a "method" that we implement. It would make little sense, for instance, to describe the method by which we interpret the hands on a clock as a technique for telling the time because, in the context of a clock with hands, there is no alternative that works. It is not possible to tell the time from a clock badly: it is simply wrong or right. That said, we can develop techniques for telling the time quickly, at a glance, and shortcuts for approximation that might differ from one person to the next. Technique, then, seems to embody something distinctively human, vague in its boundaries, potentially idiosyncratic, and usually capable of refinement. Understanding the nature of technique is central to the arguments that I will develop in this book about the nature of education. We will return to the concept in Chapter 5 and, more fully, in Chapter 8.

Technologies as Other, Technologies as Us

Technologies are often seen as innately separate from nature or experience. As Max Frisch (1994, p. 178) puts it, technologies are "the knack of so arranging the world that we don't have to experience it." Black-boxing of technologies that hides their physical and virtual inner workings from us is a largely modern phenomenon that puts this into sharp relief; though, that otherness has always been innate in our conception of all technologies. Mitcham (2009, p. 329) describes how Aristotle places the archetypal technology of writing, for instance, at two removes from experience, separated via speech. This is often seen as a bad thing. Socrates complains that writing provides only a semblance of knowing (Plato, 360 BCE), taking away a skill fundamental to being human, much as some complain of uses of the internet today. However, it is an inevitable consequence of embedding something of ourselves in our technologies and precisely what makes it worthwhile to do so. The technology does the work so that we do not have to do it. Often it does things that we could not do unaided, such as go to the Moon or lift heavy objects. It is also the scaffolding on which we build all thought and an inherent feature of thought itself. As Heyes (2018) puts it, much of our thinking relies on "cognitive gadgets" invented by others, including not just the grist of what we think about but also the mill that lets us think in the first place. Cohen and Stewart (2001) describe this complicity of thought and technologies as "extelligence."

Technologies allow us to build upon one another's ingenuity and invention, and they are the sources of our collective intelligence, forming, being formed by, enabling, and being enabled by the cultural, physical, and social artifacts that we share (Bloom, 2000; Henrich, 2017). As Saloman and Perkins (1998, p. 11) observe, "tools characteristically play a double role: as means to act upon the world and as cognitive scaffolds that facilitate such action." It is difficult (perhaps impossible) to understand ourselves without taking into account the technologies that are not just tools that we use but also parts and implementers of the organization of our lives (Noë, 2016). McLuhan's (1994) description of technologies as extensions of our central nervous systems foreshadows a modern perspective that sees technologies as inextricable parts of our minds rather than something used by them.

Clark (2008) argues persuasively that our habit of treating the mind as a process that exists solely inside our heads is unrealistic and inconsistent with our lived experiences. From "knowing" the time (because we have a watch) to expanding our cognitive capacity with a notebook, he observes, the processes of thinking are extended beyond the mental processes that occur in brains. This matters greatly to educators because of what it implies for learning and the nature of the knowledge that they seek to impart. If personal knowledge extends beyond our brains through the use of technologies, then learning itself must also be intertwingled with the knowledge of other people, mediated through those same technologies. In a real sense, we are part technology, technology is part us, and, through technology, we are part of one another.

Humans and machines are mutually affective, but the lines between them are fuzzy and shifting (Haraway, 2013). As I will explore in more detail in Chapter 6, we are co-participants in knowing and doing. Given that technologies are self-evidently developing faster and growing in number at ever-increasing rates (Arthur, 2009; Kelly, 2010), the implications for what it means to have knowledge seem to be profound. Our minds inevitably change as the world changes. It is grossly oversimplistic to react to this phenomenon by trying to teach students better ways of learning and adapting to this exponential growth, still less to try to push against it, especially since teachers are as much a part of it (and as much out of their depth) as anyone else. If we are to cope with it, then we might need to change our conceptions of what it means to know at all. We will return to this topic, too, in Chapter 6.

Things with a Purpose

Danny Hillis, only partly tongue-in-cheek, once described technology as anything that "doesn't really work yet" (cited in Brand, 2000, loc. 189). Like Kay's "anything invented before you were born," it implies a view of technologies as tech, especially those combined with software, as opposed to a broader and more generic class of things in the world. However, as anyone who has ever experienced government bureaucracy or a university committee knows, the same inherent unreliability is true of process-driven technologies as much as it is of those with flashing lights or lines of code. What is most interesting about this definition, though, is the word *work*, which implies that technologies should do something in a particular way that achieves a particular end. However, a technology that does not work is still a technology. Intention seems to matter as well as execution.

Having a purpose (and being better or worse at fulfilling it) seems to be a critical part of any definition of technology, though sometimes—and this is often true of educational technologies—the purposes can be vague. It can be hard to provide a clear definition of the purpose, say, of a garden or painting: at the least, it might have many purposes. Part of the reason for this is that only rarely is the purpose innate to an object or process, even when the intention of its designer is clear. A chimpanzee sitting on a discarded computer is not using the same technology as its former owner because the chimpanzee not only fails to understand its intended purpose but also has no intention of using it as a computing machine: it is just a seat. Papert (1987) makes a related point that it is not possible to think of technologies other than in the context of their applications: it is not just who is using it but also why, and for which purpose. The dictionary definition of *technology* as the "practical application of knowledge"[2] similarly implies that someone somewhere is performing that application with a purpose.

There are a couple of interesting things to note at this point. The designer of a screwdriver might intend that it should be used for driving screws, but the owner of the tool might use it for many other purposes that cannot—in principle—be known in their entirety in advance (Kauffman, 2008). There is still intent by the user, though it is not the intent of the tool's creator. The owner effectively becomes the designer (or, if copying an existing use, user) of a different technology when using it to pry the lid from a can of paint or as a makeshift murder weapon. There is a broader issue of context and perception at work here: the creator of a technology and its user may experience it entirely differently even when apparently it works the same way for both. Indeed, "a dog may hear a symphony,

---

2 See http://www.merriam-webster.com/dictionary/technology.

but it will not hear what its master hears" (Feenberg & Callon, 2010, p. 204).

Many technologies can have uses other than those intended by their designers. It would be perfectly reasonable, for example, to think of education systems as technologies for filtering people for the benefit of companies seeking employees, or even for feeding the education system itself with more professors, though that might not have been the intentions of their original designers. At least some of the creators of educational institutions might have thought of them as systems for learning, and some of us still do. Even those who designed the original systems of accreditation that feed industry and academia might have thought of certification as primarily a means to judge the success of teaching or a way to signify that it had been accomplished. In this case, employers use a feature of an output of the education system—the accreditation of learning—as part of a different technology (a process for recruitment). Technologies meant for one purpose can become parts of the designs of other technologies and can be transformed through different uses into countless different technologies. Bijker (1989, p. 155) refers to this as "interpretive flexibility." We will return to this concept because it is a major feature of all technologies and central to the nature of the technologies of learning.

There is a further aspect of this repurposing that demands our attention: the fact that educational qualifications are used for filtering people has fed back into the designs of education systems themselves. Demands from employers and professional bodies have long played a significant role in determining what is taught and, in many cases, how it is taught. Feedback loops abound. We shape our dwellings, which in turn shape our lives (Churchill, 1943). Just as significantly, the development of virtually all technologies is a collective endeavour, filled with connections and feedback loops that drive complex and explicable but inherently unpredictable behaviours.

Faustian Bargains

There is another significant facet of Hillis's definition that speaks to the fact that, even when technologies do work, virtually every one ever devised has unwanted and often harmful side effects. This is inevitable because, as Olson (2013, p. 233) observes, "negative entropy in one part of the system creates entropy elsewhere." Each time we create order, we also create disorder. Technological change, according to Postman (2011, p. 192), is "a Faustian bargain. For every advantage a new technology offers, there is always a corresponding disadvantage." More mature technologies have been around long enough that counter-technologies have been developed to overcome many of their side effects. However, as well as providing short-term fixes for things that don't quite work yet, in turn they cause new problems, in an ever-escalating, endless, self-reinforcing cascade. This might not be a great idea. As Dubos puts it, "developing counter technologies to correct the new kinds of damage constantly being created by technological innovations is a policy of despair" (1969, p. 8).

It is possible that highly evolved and ancient technologies, such as our education systems, are almost nothing but counter-technologies, as will become apparent in Chapter 10. We can see the effects in microcosm in what some describe as the "technological debt" incurred by those charged with maintaining digital hardware and software, whereby the constant interplay of systems components that affect one another causes an ever-increasing burden of maintenance. In reality, it is not so much a debt as a price, the inevitable consequence of escalating complexity, and this is a feature of all technological systems. Similar dynamics can be found in legal systems, bureaucracies, and city streets that have at least as much complexity as the most sprawling and gargantuan computer software and often include elements that might go back hundreds or even thousands of years. They work (most of the time) in part because they have flexibility thanks to human roles within them and in part because we have had time to find solutions to the problems that they cause, solutions to those solutions, and so on. However, the problems that they cause often still exist, and they tend to resurface when we replace parts of them. This is nowhere truer than in education, in which modern inventions such as online learning have disrupted some of those chains of solutions in ways that we are only beginning to understand.

Rarely the Application of Scientific Knowledge

Some, including many writers of dictionaries, see *technology* as the application of scientific knowledge for practical purposes. Although it might be partly true of some branches of engineering, this is profoundly misleading. The invention of the vast majority of technologies has no more to do with science than it does with pulleys, which is to say a lot sometimes but little or nothing on the whole. Even creators and users of advanced technologies rarely have any more knowledge of the science behind their inventions than a New Caledonian crow bending a piece of wire to get at a bit of food uses the knowledge of metallurgy, ore extraction, and manufacturing processes that went into the production of that piece of wire. Relatively few inventions explicitly or directly employ science, though a fair number, especially those labelled as "tech," and much of what is described as "engineering," often do incorporate products of scientific discoveries. Most of the technologies around us, in an educational setting as much as anywhere else, are the results of different processes. Even archetypal examples of supposedly science-driven engineering such as early steam engines or the Spinning Jenny were barely if at all driven by science (Mumford, 1934, p. 215), at least as we know it today. True, there were complex webs of inspiration connecting scientific ideas and technical practices in at least the later development of the steam engine, and some relatively early examples were informed at least by advances in pneumatics and materials science (Kerker, 1961), though it is noteworthy that Newcomen, whose engine dominated the early years of steam technology, was an ironmonger, not a scientist.

In fact, the relationship between science and technology is the precise opposite of what some dictionaries tell us it is: science is the branch of technology that deals with the discovery or creation of a particular kind of systematic knowledge, itself a species of technology. As Arthur (2009, loc. 943–946) explains, "science builds itself from the instruments, methods, experiments, and conceptual constructions it uses. This should not be surprising. Science, after all, is a method: a method for understanding, for probing, for explaining. A method composed of many submethods. Stripped to its core structure, science is a form of technology."

Science, viewed as a practice, is unequivocally an archetypal technology. In fact, it is a huge set of technologies with a huge range of applications. Naturally, they are different from other technologies, just as wheels are different from classrooms. But, equally, they share some central and significant features with all other technologies, including their usefulness when combined with other technologies. Also, most incorporate technologies in widespread use in other technologies, such as nuts, bolts, language, glassware, and arithmetic. The practice of science is fundamentally technological. As Ridley (2015, loc. 2207) puts it, "once you examine the history of innovation, you find scientific breakthroughs as the effect, not the cause, of technological change."

If, as I suggest, education is fundamentally technological, then this raises some interesting issues, not the least of which is that it might not be (and indeed, I hope to show, cannot be, in most important respects) the application of science.

It is not just scientific practice that is technological. Much of the body of knowledge resulting from scientific practice, structured and connected, itself can be described accurately as technology. It is perfectly natural to talk of theories, equations, models, and so on as tools because that is exactly what they are: technologies for creating, discovering, manipulating, making sense of, and evaluating knowledge. Science's many forms are unusually successful technologies insofar as they reveal a great many phenomena that can be used in other technologies, sometimes to enable something new, sometimes to improve what is already there. Much of the knowledge uncovered by science—its discoveries rather than the theories behind them—is not particularly technological in character, though it would be hard to express that knowledge without at least some technologies. At least, its discoveries require language, or mathematics, or visual technologies to describe them. Scientifically discovered knowledge can be useful in many ways, expanding the range of phenomena that we can utilize as well as act upon with other technologies. But that is not science, or the application of science, any more than the works of Shakespeare are the application of dictionaries.

Ferguson (1977) argues persuasively that technological development is at least as dependent on art as it is on science. Although scientific discoveries can contribute to the assembly, the process of technological invention and innovation is always creative and artful. Education systems are rife with technologies, from timetables to teaching methods to paintbrushes, that have (and arguably should have) little or nothing to do with the application of scientific knowledge. They are tools, of course, but many other creatures use tools in ways that closely resemble what we would recognize as technologies. It would be hard to ascribe a scientific method to the behaviour of crows. The technological church is also broad. As Franklin (1999) observes, there are as much technologies of prayer as there are technologies of transportation. If, like Hitchens (2007), we assume that all religions are inventions (or, if you are religious, all but your own religion), then religions themselves have a strongly technological character, with processes, tools, organizational features, and methods designed to achieve some end or ends, from prayer wheels to censers to mantras to litanies.

To suggest that this has anything to do with science would be to do science a disservice. To add another nail to the coffin of the "application of scientific knowledge" conception of technology, Derex et al. (2019, p. 446) found that an accurate causal understanding of scientific principles is unnecessary in the development of complex technologies that use them: "Complex technologies need not result from enhanced causal reasoning but, instead, can emerge from the accumulation of improvements made across generations." Indeed, the complex technologies that we create collectively more often inspire science than they are inspired by it. As Henrich (2017, p. 181) tells us, "an enormous amount of scientific causal understanding ... has developed in trying to explain existing technologies, like the steam engine, hot air balloon, or airplane."

For Latour (1987, p. 131), "the problem of the builder of 'facts' is the same as the problem of the builder of 'objects.'" At least, in constructing tools, experiments, theories, and models, and in mobilizing resources to achieve their ends, there is a strong technological aspect to every scientific endeavour. In fact, one of the most fundamental tenets of scientific thinking is that all scientific theory itself is provisional. Science itself thus effectively describes its practices and discoveries as at least in part invented, a way of understanding the world that might (and probably will) be superseded by later inventions. A classic case in point is the "replacement" of Newton's physics by Einstein's relativity. In fact, Newton's theory was not replaced, for it remains a lot easier to use, more useful, and sufficiently accurate in many more contexts. Bridge builders use Newton's equations rather than Einstein's because, for their purposes, they are much easier and just as accurate. Both sets of theories are tools that can perform useful work as part of a technological assembly, whether the work is to explain what we observe, predict the path of a planet, or plan the trajectory of a spacecraft. It is highly probable that both theories will be replaced one day, or at least radically refined, when a theory is invented and sufficiently verified that fits better with what we know of quantum physics, but it is unlikely that we will completely stop using either, as long as they are good tools for the jobs that we ask of them.

Not Just Problem Solving

The fact that science tends to be seen as a method of problem solving is common to most technologies. Postman (2000, p. 42), for instance, challenges us to ask, "what is the problem to which this technology is a solution?" Arthur (2009, loc. 1370) claims that "a new [design] project always poses a new problem," reflecting a commonly held perspective of technologies as means to overcome challenges. This perspective can usually be bent, at least post hoc, to fit almost every technology. However, though certainly true in many cases, the relationship can be tenuous. We might see Christmas decorations as a solution to the "problem" of bare trees, or the "problem" of how to celebrate Christmas, or, for their manufacturers or sellers, the problem of not having enough money, and so on, but that stretches the definition a bit further than most of us would be comfortable espousing. In reality, not all technologies are designed to solve problems even if, in retrospect, we can find problems that they solve, and it is indeed common for new uses to be found for those that do.

The art of bricolage—a common technology design approach—is often less about solving problems than about seeking possibilities in the objects around us (an issue to which we will return in Chapter 6). Many are the results of what Gould and Lewontin (1979) describe as exaptations, incidental features of the design that turn out to be useful. Gould and Lewontin use the example of spandrels (the spaces left when you perch domes on walls), never designed to solve the problem of where to place statues but nonetheless serving that purpose well. Having a purpose within a broader system, or being useful, is not the same thing as solving a problem. It is also important to be aware that, when we look for problems, we usually find them. Often, we might achieve more by looking for things that work and then trying to do them even better (Cooperrider & Whitney, 2011). Rather than treating education as a problem to be solved, for instance, there are benefits in seeing it as an opportunity to build upon, a mystery to be embraced (Cooperrider & Srivastava, 1987). Many technologies create opportunities more than they solve problems, and quite a few are designed with that in mind, from content management systems to Photoshop filters. The notion that necessity is the mother of invention, with its implied premise that invention is therefore problem solving, ignores the fact that invention also has a father, an opportunistic sprite that we might call serendipity or happenstance.

Ways of Doing Things

For Ursula Franklin (1999, p. 62), technology is best seen as formalized practice, a perspective that leads her to define technology as "the way things are done around here." Although this sounds a little trite and overgeneralized and is equally true of culture (which she rightly sees as intrinsically and inseparably linked), it contains some deep and important insights, carrying with it implications of cultural and temporal specificity but, more significantly if we are seeking a definition, the notion that technology is about repeatable processes and methods—the ways that things are done. Bessant and Francis (2005, p. 97) are a little more specific, describing technologies as the "ways that people get complicated things done." Again, there is the implication of replication and method, though I would take issue with the notion that complexity needs to be involved. It often emerges from the fact that technologies allow us to go beyond what we could do easily without aid. But, equally, they can be used to do simple things better, faster, more accurately, or more consistently. Borgmann (1987, p. 28) describes technology as "the systematic effort to get everything under control," which focuses usefully on both the replicable, ordered nature of technology and the human purposes that lie behind it.

Useful though they are, definitions that include just tools (physical and/or conceptual) and purposes tell only part of the story: to be useful for a given purpose, there must be something about the tool that fits it to that purpose, or Franklin's "the way things are done around here," is as specific as it gets. With such a broad definition, it is hard to think of any human activity that could not be described as a technology, including eating (applying knowledge of what is food and the effects of biting and swallowing to alleviate hunger) or scratching an itch (applying knowledge of what has alleviated itching in the past to alleviate itching in the present). Of course, there are technological elements of all such activities, including cultural norms and shared practices. Even something as apparently "natural" as a sneeze shows huge cultural variation that has little to do with physical biology. But there is something more to a technology than applying knowledge to some purpose, or we would have to include the entire animal kingdom—including slugs—in our list of users of technology as well as (perhaps) the organs in our own bodies or the growth of plants. Dosi and Grazzi (2010, p. 173) bypass this problem to describe technology as "a human-constructed means for achieving a particular end, such as the movement of goods and people, the transmission of information or the cure of a disease."

Although they do go further than that in distinguishing the complex roles of inputs, outputs, processes, procedures, and knowledge as different though complementary aspects of the definition, this is still a little vague, inasmuch as it tells us little about the nature of that construction. It also appears to imply that humans are the only possible creators of technologies, which seems to be unnecessarily restrictive. We know, for instance, that crows make inventive uses of found objects in ways that appear to resemble closely our uses of technologies, including the pleasure that we take in using them to solve problems (Reuell, 2019). Even if we allow that some further amount of planning and shaping is needed to describe an activity as "construction," New Caledonian crows are adept at shaping different hooks for different purposes, apparently being able to plan ahead using causal reasoning, going far beyond simple trial and error or mindless imitation (Taylor et al., 2008). Although human uses of technology are part of the definition of what it means to be human, it would be arrogant and overly anthropocentric to suggest that no other organisms use it.

Things that We Do and Things that Have Been Done

Part of the reason that it is so difficult to pin down the nature of technology is that it describes both the process of doing and what has been done. Kelly (2010) describes technology as "not a thing but a verb," but clearly it is (at least) both. Writing is a technology—in fact an abstract technology that is neither a thing nor a verb—but so is a poem or book. I am using the technology of writing right now to write (a technology) a piece of writing (a technology) that you are most likely reading as a book (a technology created and instantiated by technologies). When we look at almost any physical technology as it exists when instantiated in the world, we can see that it embodies the processes and, most of the time, the other technologies used in its construction: it is a frozen act of doing as much as it is something that was done, and, to be describable as a technology at all, it must (at least latently) do something: it must have a reason for existence. Technologies instantiated by people—dance, say, or oration—are almost nothing but things that we do, yet we can also talk of them as concrete entities that exist as independent objects for our consideration: a dance performance, say, or speech. Both, by any definition, are unnatural activities, both are inventions, both are designed to achieve purposes, and both seem to be describable as technologies. Any definition somehow needs to take this dual nature into account.

Orchestration, Phenomena, and Purpose

In his book *Technology: What It Is and How It Evolves*, Brian Arthur provides some more compelling definitions that I will use as a springboard for understanding technologies in greater depth. His fundamental insight is that technologies are "the orchestration of phenomena to some purpose" (2009, p. 51). Elsewhere in the book, Arthur describes technology as the "programming" of phenomena, but this suggests an algorithmic perspective that is less descriptively rich than "orchestration" since it focuses too much on process, and it appears to downplay the equal importance of structure. By "phenomenon," Arthur simply means something that happens or something that is: a thing, an effect, an idea, a feeling, a concept, or whatever. Phenomena exist in the world, regardless of what we do with them or to what purposes we put them, though many can occur or exist because of things that we do. Some can be mythical, others simply false. Surprisingly, in many cases, we might not even be aware that we are using them, proceeding by trial and error to achieve our goals without understanding the phenomena that our technologies orchestrate: kites and sails, for example, have flown for millennia without their makers understanding the pressure differentials that give them lift or forward motion.

More precisely than what is implied in Franklin's use of "the way," Arthur's use of the term "orchestration" neatly encapsulates not just a way but also a constructed and repeatable method of organizing diverse phenomena to achieve a purpose. Phenomena can be as varied as the physical characteristics of objects to the believed nature of divine beings, from the effects of gravitation to the assembly of ideas, from the ways that wheels reduce friction to our perceptions of how people learn. Orchestrations can be diverse, from connections between transistors to methods of teaching, from assemblies of cogs to assemblies of the rules of the road, from designs of buildings to the writing of poetry. Given the growing recognition of the many actors and complex interactions involved in almost every educational process, for this reason the term "orchestration" has seen increasing use in educational literature, especially in the field of learning technologies, in recent years (e.g., Prieto et al., 2015). Arthur's use of the term extends far beyond an educational context, and is more general in its application, but it speaks to the same need to understand the interplay of imposed order and emergent complexity in a diverse universe. When we orchestrate, we do not just aggregate a collection of phenomena. We make them work together in order to achieve some end. Ridley (2015, loc. 2120), inspired by Arthur, similarly describes technologies as ordered pieces of information, "an imposition of informational order on a random world."

To put it more colloquially, we organize stuff (real or imagined, mental or physical, designed or not) to do other stuff. I prefer this view to Arthur's more precise formulation of the same basic idea because it works better to highlight the deeply recursive nature of how technologies are made, to which we turn next.

Technologies Are Assemblies

Crucial to understanding Arthur's insight and the argument of this book is that the phenomena orchestrated can be (and nearly always are) provided or exhibited by other technologies.

The phenomenon that a wheel can reduce friction, for example, means that it can be utilized in a drawer to make it easier to slide the drawer in and out. The phenomenon that a personal computer can display images means that it can be utilized to present visual information to learners, which in turn uses phenomena such as our understanding of how people learn, to bring about more effective learning. When we make intentional use of such phenomena to achieve some end, we create technologies that might be (and, as we shall see, nearly always are) composed in part or in whole of other technologies. Virtually all technologies are assemblies, often mutually constituted. Figure 1 illustrates the general dynamic of this, though in real life the implied hierarchical layers usually run much deeper, can be recursive, can loop, and the phenomena and orchestrations tend to be much more diverse than this simple diagram suggests. As Arthur (2009, loc. 567–570) puts it, "a technology consists of building blocks that are technologies, which consist of further building blocks that are technologies, which consist of yet further building blocks that are technologies, with the pattern repeating all the way down to the fundamental level of elemental components. Technologies, in other words, have a recursive structure. They consist of technologies within technologies all the way down to the elemental parts."

The assembly can involve a great many people as well as the technologies that they use. As Read (1958) wrote over 60 years ago, no one person even knows how to make that humblest of technologies, the pencil. It is made from, and is the result of, innumerable technological processes that stretch indefinitely far and wide, involving literally millions of people, undirected by any centralized governing process, the result of a massively interconnected distributed intelligence that diffuses through time and space. This is not just a feature of manufactured items: many human-enacted systems, such as pension schemes or the internal operations of a university, are only partially understood (at best) by most of us.

Arthur's definition neatly sidesteps the assumption that technologies must involve physical objects while avoiding the over-embracing fuzziness that makes everything into a technology. A stick fallen from a tree, by any definition, is not a technology at all. It is just a stick. However, if someone picks it up and uses it to reach for an apple on that tree, it has become a tool assembled with a method (the orchestration) using a technique (manual dexterity and pattern of movement) to achieve a purpose (getting an apple). The user of the stick utilizes the phenomena of length, rigidity, ease of handling, sharpness, and so on of the stick, along with the propensity of apples to fall when prodded, in tandem with some processes and methods to bring the two into conjunction, in

Figure 1. The Assembled Nature of Technologies

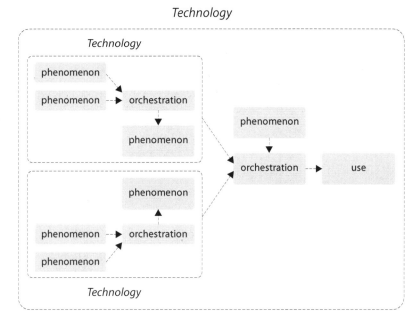

order to achieve a goal that might not be possible without this or some other assembly of technologies: to get an apple. Conversely, if the stick is then rubbed against another stick to light a fire or used to point to a picture on a whiteboard, then it is not part of the same technology at all, because different phenomena of the stick are orchestrated to different purposes, assembled with different methods and techniques.

The technology of interest in any given context is rarely the one that we would say, in conversation, that we are using. It is the technology that occurs when we use it. Nothing has changed about the stick whether we use it as a pointing device, a back scratcher, or a dog's toy: what makes it a distinct technology is the precise combination of the phenomena that we are able to orchestrate to a particular use or uses. That orchestration itself is the technology that matters most.

The same is true all the way up the technology stack. It applies at least as much to computers, classrooms, and learning management systems as it does to sticks and screwdrivers. They are parts of other technologies and not necessarily (or even often) the main technologies of interest when thinking about education as a technological phenomenon.

Arthur's definition also encompasses cases in which physical objects are not a necessary part of a technology: business processes, rules of acquisition, examination processes, and timetabling are technologies orchestrating phenomena for a purpose as much as cars and computers, as many others have observed (Arthur, 2009; Bessant & Francis, 2005; Franklin, 1999a; Orlikowski, 1992; Zhouying, 2004).

Arthur's definition embraces theories and models: they orchestrate phenomena to some use and in turn may be used for many other purposes in many orchestrations. It explains why technology is not the application of scientific knowledge but can (and often does) make use of phenomena discovered using scientific methods. Finally, the definition succeeds where others fail because it applies equally to both process and product. Franklin's (1999, p. 6) dilemma of how to describe something that is "both fish and water"—both process and product—is thus neatly resolved. Technology is both something that we do and something that has been done. A computer or a nail is a technology, but so is the process of creating that computer or hammering that nail into wood. In the process of doing, we create something that has been done, and both are equally well described as the orchestration of phenomena to achieve a purpose. This is a vastly complex state of becoming, not one entity or action in isolation but a dynamic network of many, each playing its part in an overall assembly.

Arthur's definition also embraces much, but not all, of how we communicate with others, how we express ourselves, and how we think. Although some have speculated that humans might have an innate ability for language (e.g., Hauser et al., 2002; Pinker, 1994), even if that were so, language itself is indisputably an invented and constantly reinvented toolset orchestrated to a multitude of uses such as thinking, arguing, reasoning, and communicating (Wittgenstein, 2001); naming ships and creating marriages (Austin, 1962); and, of course, teaching. It is the archetype of technologies, perhaps the most powerful of them all (Deutscher, 2006), the primary form and example of what Cohen and Stewart (2001) call "extelligence." As McLuhan puts it, "language as the technology of human extension whose powers of division and separation we know so well, may have been the Tower of Babel by which men sought to scale the highest heavens" (1994, p. 80). Some support for this view is found in the fact that there appear to be close similarities in the use of brain regions when engaged in physical tool use and in language tasks (Higuchi et al., 2009; Uomini & Meyer, 2013) and that broader networks in both physical tool and language use are very similar (Stout & Chaminade, 2012). It appears that we use words in much the same ways that we use other technologies, though which came first remains an unanswered question. McLuhan, with delightful self-referentiality, does not even bother to draw the distinction, so closely are they intertwined: "Each of man's artefacts is in fact a kind of word, a metaphor that translates experience from one form into another" (McLuhan & McLuhan, 1992, p. 3).

Not only spoken language but also other means of communication such as painting, drawing, dance, and music are not just technologies but also, like language, occupy a special place among our technologies inasmuch as they are also among the most important means through which the ability to create and use technologies can be passed on to others. Without them, we would be like apes, imitating one another's use of tools, but not extending them, signalling but not signifying. Kelly (2010, loc. 209) puts it well: "Even if we acknowledge that technology can exist in disembodied form, such as software, we tend not to include in this category paintings, literature, music, dance, poetry, and the arts in general. But we should. If a thousand lines of letters in UNIX qualifies as a technology (the computer code for a web page), then a thousand lines of letters in English (Hamlet) must qualify as well."

More poetically, William Carlos Williams (1969) describes a poem as "a small (or large) machine made out of words." A painting, poem, or piece of music is not just the product of technologies but also a technology in and of itself, orchestrating phenomena not just of the media that it uses but also beliefs (not necessarily true or complete beliefs) about the effects that it might have on others. This affective aspect is more obvious in highly purpose-driven communication such as street signs and propaganda, but even our most abstract non-purposive signals are innately infused with communicative intent. Indeed, whether or not the intent of artists or creators is to convey anything at all, the uses to which we put their work (e.g., to decorate our homes, to listen to while working, to simply enjoy) give them a technological character: we—the viewers, listeners, readers, and so on—actively orchestrate phenomena ourselves as co-participants in their enactment. In fact, an original creator might not be required at all. My home is decorated with a fair number of found objects such as rocks and pieces of driftwood. The fact that they have been chosen, and that their placement has been chosen for aesthetic, sentimental, or practical purposes, makes them as much technologies as the human-formed sculptures and paintings with which they share the space. The same is true of many of the things that we do with nothing but our own bodies—singing, dancing, and acting, for example, as well as engaging in athletic sports and competitive games, in which phenomena provided by our own minds and bodies are orchestrated for some purpose. The fact that we tend to talk of such behaviours as "expressing" something does suggest, however, that there is something to express that might be non-technological.

There are some fuzzy boundaries between technological and non-technological forms of communication. For instance, body language can communicate someone's state of mind or intention without being in the least bit technological. If I spontaneously twitch, or laugh, or cry, or cross my arms, then there is little or no deliberate orchestration and certainly no conscious purpose, albeit that these forms of expression can be learned and influenced by the culture to which I belong. Yet it would be a technology if I were consciously to adopt a pose or, as an actor, mimic a particular kind of body language. I would be orchestrating phenomena (my beliefs about how people will interpret what I am trying to convey, my ability to manipulate my own body, and so on) to some use (to convey to others that I am feeling, revealing a plot line, or pretending to feel a certain way to avoid hurting someone).

There are also some personal technologies that can involve no direct communication with others, such as yoga, meditation, and self-hypnotism. Most approaches to meditation and hypnotism follow a prescribed set of procedures to bring about a particular kind of mental state manufactured by an individual, making use of the phenomena of the effects of such procedures on consciousness to achieve calm, serenity, focus, or the lack of it. Equally, when we construct mental models, use words to generate ideas in our minds, memorize multiplication tables, or perform long division in our heads, the fact that they are not visible or corporeal does not make them any less technologies. This extends into many aspects of life, not all of which are even slightly technological in and of themselves but can be technologized through processes, methods, and tools designed to affect them. We are partly made, in effect, of technologies. In fact, increasingly, we tend to see ourselves as technologies. As Feenberg (2006, p. 5) puts it, "not only are we constantly obeying the dictates of the many technical systems in which we are enrolled, we tend to see ourselves more and more as devices regulated by medical, psychological, athletic, and other functional disciplines. Our bookstores are full of 'operating manuals' for every aspect of life: love, sex, divorce, friendship, raising children, eating, exercise, making money, having fun, and so on and so forth. We are our own machines."

Things That Are Not Technologies

For all the technologies that we enact in thought and social behaviour, there are many things that we, as humans, do that can be engendered or transformed by technologies but are not technologies at all. Here is a list of a few arbitrarily chosen things that are phenomena that can be used or engendered by technologies but, on the whole, are not technologies:

- Values
- Beauty
- Length (though its measurement is a technology)
- Dreaming
- Love
- Entertainment (though it is almost always enabled by technologies)
- Fire (though there are technologies of fire)
- Blue
- Brittleness
- Noisiness
- Camaraderie
- Belief
- Excess
- Friendship
- Laughter (usually)
- Motivation
- Excitement
- Travel (though it is nearly always mediated by technologies)
- Sadness
- Expectation
- Desire
- Knowing something (sometimes)
- Crying (usually)
- Floating
- A tree (usually)
- Humour
- Mountains
- Balance

- Water (though there are technologies of water)
- Fish (mostly)
- Women
- Danger
- Relative positions
- Learning (though there are technologies of learning, and it is nearly always mediated by, and often embedded in, technologies)

Some of this arbitrary list is equivocal. Could crying be a technology? Some people can cry on demand and do so to achieve some purpose. It is a skill demanding a method and, usually, a significant amount of practice. They utilize phenomena, such as their own ability to elicit tears on demand, and the expected effects of tears on those who observe them, to achieve some end, such as to elicit sympathy or persuade someone to buy them a new car. The technology is not the tears but how they are used in an orchestrated assembly to achieve an end. Again, it is the orchestrated whole that should be seen as the technology of interest in any given situation, which can include non-technological phenomena as well as (in most cases) other technologies.

Taking a slightly different perspective, a tree might be the result of a technological process (from simply watering it to cultivating a bonsai), plus there is a whole technological field of arboriculture, not to mention the application of genetic engineering, and a tree can certainly be used in many technologies (e.g., as a windbreak, as decoration, or to delimit the edges of a garden path), but viewed in isolation the tree is not normally a technology in and of itself: it becomes one only when used as part of an orchestrated assembly. And, of course, the taming of fire is the beginning of some of our most important technologies and a vital component of many, but fire itself is no more a technology than the stick on the ground. It is a phenomenon that occurs with or without humans or any other conscious agency. Beyond poetic or metaphoric uses, and notwithstanding its roles in natural systems that may be described teleologically (e.g., fire as a means of achieving ecological balance), fire (in itself) does not have a purpose. Sometimes the lines are fuzzy. Walking, for instance, is not a technology in itself, but ways of walking—from an intentionally controlled walk in a dance or march to the exaggerated walking in Monty Python's Ministry of Silly Walks—certainly can be.

A great deal of what makes us human and allows us to identify other humans as beings like us has no direct relationship with technology. Although almost always we use technologies to achieve non-technological ends, from Facebook to sustain friendships, to plays for entertainment or edification, to language for pursuit or support of our loves and loathings, these ends are no more technologies than cats or dogs. But it is complicated. There are plentiful technologies of cats and dogs, and some ways that dogs (at least) can be seen as technologies, for example in sheep herding, hunting, or guarding our homes, not to mention that many are the results of technological and intentional breeding processes. Even cats can loosely speaking be trained as support animals. Indeed, virtually all domesticated animals are the results of technologies (from selective breeding to husbandry to genetic engineering) and often serve technological purposes, from companionship to decoration to entertainment to pulling carts.

Among the many non-technological things that can be described, explained, employed, or engendered using technologies, learning is of most interest in the context of this book. We will return to this topic in earnest in Part 2, in which I will try to unravel how pedagogies (by which I mean pedagogical methods, models, and principles) work, but it is worthwhile to spend a moment now to reflect, in broad and incomplete terms, on the relationship between learning and technology.

Learning for humans is usually (in part) the direct result of using technologies, from words and pedagogical methods to books and YouTube. When we talk of "learning technologies," we are talking of those that engender, or are meant to engender learning, that make it easier, more effective, faster, more satisfying, more amusing, more interesting, or simply possible where otherwise it would not be. Learning can also be embedded in technologies, from notebooks to computer software to door handles (Clark, 2008; Norman, 1993). But learning itself—whether we think of it as something that occurs in our brains or as something more distributed or ill defined—tends not to be a technology so much as a purpose or result of technology. Babies learn, crows learn, and even evolution can be thought of as a learning process (Cohen & Stewart, 1997 p. 96). Technology does not need to come into it.

There is likewise a great deal that can contribute positively to the learning process that has nothing to do with technology: seeing passion in others, imitating the behaviours of those whom we admire, the thrill of overcoming challenges, the delight of working with other people, the need for autonomy, aesthetic pleasure, some foodstuffs, feeling empathy, having enough sleep, and many more non-technological phenomena are typically among significant contributors to an effective learning process, without at least some of which it is unlikely to happen. Equally, negative phenomena such as distractions, physical impediments, illness, pain, or coercion (Kohn, 1999) can play large roles in making learning ineffective (or sometimes, such as when we learn from putting our hand in a flame, more effective) and have little or nothing to do with technologies. These are phenomena that can be exploited in a technological process, enhanced by technologies, and become important parts of educational technological assemblies, but they would exist, and many kinds of learning would consequently occur, whether or not technologies played any role.

Learning can also be affected deeply by serendipitous events, from general feelings of wellness to thunderstorms, from being surprised by novelty to being conditioned by familiarity, none of which needs to have anything to do with technologies of any kind.

Equally, many important aspects of a teaching role, whether in a formal setting or not, have little if anything to do with technologies. Knowing when a student needs a hug, or a break, or a challenge, for example, largely emerges from being human and knowing how humans feel. A great deal of the effectiveness of teaching can come from personal characteristics such as kindness, compassion, passion for a subject, hard-to-define charisma, even a twinkle in the eye or a certain hairstyle. Education is a process of learning to be a human in a human society, and much of what is important about it derives from the fact that we are a profoundly social species that has evolved in ways that lend survival value to our abilities to mimic, to admire, to cherish, to depend on, and to support others. Although all can be affected by and orchestrated in technologies, none is essentially technological in character.

Technologies provide the means to go further (often much further), faster, better, or more reliably than what could be achieved without them. All of the many non-technological things that contribute positively or negatively to what, how, and how effectively we learn are parts of the stuff that we organize to do stuff or the reasons that we organize it: passion and compassion, especially in teaching, provide much of the energy that drives us to do what we do. Emotions are among the phenomena that we can orchestrate to bring about learning. For instance, if people learn better when they are aware of the enthusiasm of others, then there are technological methods (mindfulness, method acting, and so on) that can cultivate enthusiasm. We know that technologies (with appropriate skill and technique) can be used to help kindle almost any kind of emotion, and that emotions can be part of their orchestration, because technologies are what make painting, music, poetry, dance, acting, and every other art possible. Technologies can both provide and reduce distraction. Teaching methods and organizational structures can be designed to bring people together with shared learning purposes or to afford greater autonomy. Pedagogical designs can be created to support achievable challenges that learners can overcome and feel joy in having done so. Words help us to move one another, as much as levers help us to move heavy objects.

To describe education as a technological system is anything but an attempt to reduce it to a set of mechanical rules. In fact, my intention is the opposite: to reveal education as a deeply entangled, complex web of passionate, meaning-imbued people and their creations, in which we all play unique, creative, mutually affective roles. It is to show that technology is not a thing that is done to us but a thing that we do together in endlessly recursive and ever-unfolding ways. It is to shed light on what it means to be human, to be part of the many entwined collectives that make us part of one humanity, to share our passion with others, and to kindle our passions with the passions of others.

4 | How Technologies Work

> *[Techne] is a way of making [or] . . . of bringing something into being whose origin is in the maker and not in the thing.*
> —Aristotle (cited in Illich, 1971, p. 84)

Given that technologies are always situated, capable of being used in different ways, differ from one use to the next, and constantly evolve, if we are to understand education as a technological process, then it is useful to have some idea of how technologies change and how they adapt. This chapter explains some of the central dynamics of technologies and technology development, drawing mainly from complex systems theories, to lay foundations that will explain much of the nature of educational systems in the chapters to come.

We Shape Our Dwellings . . .

The development of technologies follows a complex recursive dynamic that is partly extrinsic, shaped by social, environmental, political, conceptual, and creative forces, and partly intrinsic and self-reinforcing. Changes that we make to our world in turn affect us, in an endless cycle of affect and effect. As Dewey et al. (1995, p. 154) put it, "the organism acts in accordance with its own structure, simple or complex, upon its surroundings. As a consequence, the changes produced in the environment react upon the organism and its activities. The living creature undergoes, suffers, the consequences of its own behavior." McLuhan (1994, p. xxi) puts it more simply: "We become what we behold.... We shape our tools and afterwards our tools shape us."³

However we express it, there is a constant interplay between the technologies and structures that we create and their effects on us, in turn changing how we build them and what we do within and with them. This does not just make them complicated. It makes them complex; technologies can and do result in behaviours and forms that are difficult or impossible to predict in advance. Looking at their components is seldom very useful, because the whole is different from the sum of its parts, just as a body is more than a collection of cells, a poem is more than just a collection of words, and a community is more than just a collection of people. A complex whole emerges through the multiple, many-layered interactions of its elements.

Even tiny differences can matter. For example, the sentence "the man bit the dog" contains the same words, grammatical structure, and general form of the sentence "the dog bit the man." In almost every respect, it is an instance of the same combination of technologies, and both sentences work equally well to convey meaning, but their meanings are utterly different. The same dependence on small details of arrangement is true of virtually every technology, from guitars to teaching methods. And, like the sentence "the man bit the dog," a great deal depends on the surrounding context: what other stuff exists and how it relates to the technology of interest.

The Importance of Boundaries

It is of little use to think about technologies unless they are the ones that matter in the context that we are researching. Because technologies are assemblies (and often assemblies of assemblies of assemblies . . .), we can choose different boundaries around different parts of the assembly and thus see different technologies. Boundaries are how we give and discover

---

3 In fact, though attributed to McLuhan and no doubt used by him as cited, this phrase is attributable to his friend, John Culkin (Culkin, 1967).

form in the world. They are the impermeable, semi-permeable, or entirely permeable lines that we draw to distinguish one thing from another—a heart from a lung, a property from a street, a married couple from an unmarried couple, and so on. They do not (necessarily) separate objects; instead, they define what they contain (Cilliers, 2001). Different problems and different behaviours emerge at different boundaries (Holland, 2012). They pass and make use of different signals internally, not all of which will matter in other parts of the assembly. For instance, if we place our boundary around a computer-based tutorial and a learner, then what matters is the extent to which the learner learns from the lesson, how it fits with existing knowledge, and so on. Because we have chosen this particular boundary, the computer, the operating system, the application's code, and other important constituents of or containers for the application are not our immediate concern, though they can play a causal role in how it achieves its purpose. The things that matter are the behaviours of what lies within the boundary that we have chosen, notably including the learner's own orchestration, the primary process that leads to the technology about which we care. If we place our boundary around the lesson and the teacher, then what matters is how easy it is to write that tutorial, which authoring supports it offers, how it fits with future plans, the teacher's skills, and so on. This means that knowledge relevant at one boundary can be completely irrelevant or at best partial or tangential at another. The signals that pass from a brake pedal to a brake assembly (whether electrical, pneumatic, or whatever) matter greatly to the engineer designing a car, but it is the effect of foot pressure on the pedal, and how that affects the overall slowing of the vehicle, that matter more to the driver. Where we choose to place our boundaries depends on our interests and current needs.

The importance of boundaries is shown in particularly sharp relief when we examine computers and their uses in learning. The computer is a universal tool, medium, and environment, which means that it can become pretty much any other technology—that is the overarching phenomenon about the computer that makes it useful. The computer is a technology in itself only from a few perspectives, of interest mainly to computer scientists, purchasers, marketers, and creators of the product.

Mostly it is the means by which we create other technologies, a part of (and a container for) an indefinite number of much more interesting and complex assemblies. For a computer used to run, say, a quiz program in a school, it is a different technology for the student, for the teacher, for the programmer, and for the technician supporting the machine. Each different user utilizes some of the same phenomena, some that are different, and some that are differently orchestrated, for different uses. Although the computer might be a necessary constituent part, it seldom makes sense to think of the technology that matters the most as a "computer," and even then context matters too: when buying a computer, we usually have at least a sample range of uses in mind. If we do choose to use the term, then "computer" is usually a synecdoche for a host of other technologies: it is a part that signifies a whole.

Unfortunately, it is common and entirely natural to pick the wrong boundaries, to blur the computer technology and the vast number of technologies that result from its use into one, leading people to ask (and often proceed to answer) misleading questions such as "do computers improve learning?" (Bouygues, 2019) or "is Google changing our brains?" (Brabazon, 2007) or even "do CRT monitors interfere with learning?" (Garland & Noyes, 2004). When posed as general questions related to all possible uses of the technology, they make no sense at all, but they are not much better even when applied to specific instances, unless seen as part of an assembly of the technology that we are in fact investigating. The problem with such questions is that they mistakenly conflate an arbitrary range of different technologies that happen to use the same element as part of their assembly into a single part that happens to be common to all of them. We could choose different boundaries just as validly.

We might, for instance, ask "do transistors improve learning?" or "are cooling fans changing our brains?" The answer is undoubtedly "yes" in both cases, but this tells us little of any value because we are looking at the wrong assembly: we are choosing the wrong boundaries. It is reasonable to ask if such things can affect learning, in positive or negative ways, as part of a design process in which we consider the strengths and limitations of particular components in order to think how we might use them. It is also reasonable to ask questions about some specific uses of them, or about specific uses in a common context, or to compare different uses to find out how they differ. However, it is not reasonable to pinpoint one generic part of the assembly that could make any number of positive or negative contributions, depending on its relationship with the rest of the assembly and the orchestration that brings them together. It is the wrong boundary. We might equally (and perhaps with greater reason) pick a broader boundary and ask whether the institutions in which they are used are changing our brains (yes, definitely) or improving learning (sometimes yes, sometimes no).

Choosing the Right Boundaries

Misattribution of boundaries occurs all the way down the line to detailed cases. Even when two technologies appear to be the same, and are used in similar ways, other processes are often—and, in an educational context, usually are—more significant. Indeed, as any experienced teacher will tell you, there can be a world of difference between two instances of the same lesson plan using more or less identical pedagogical methods and tools on two different occasions. Again there are different boundaries (encompassing a different group of learners, all of whom introduce their own processes and pedagogies) in each case. For much the same reason, it makes no sense to talk of Google Search (and especially not, as some have suggested seriously, Google) as changing our brains in any particular way. Some of the ways that Google Search can be assembled with other technologies (including processes and methods for using it and the purposes to which we put it) almost certainly will have some effect because we will learn something, and learning always changes our brains—that might even be a fair working definition of the word *learning*, albeit incomplete for reasons that will become clear. We can even find regularities—for example, biases introduced by Google's algorithms that cause replicable effects—but each different assembly can have different effects, each of which will affect us in different ways. A critical attitude toward any technology, be it a part or a whole, is vital, but we have to be very clear about the boundaries as well as about which phenomena, orchestrations, and uses are contributing to the effect. If there are statistically significant things to be said about the effects of computers, say, as a whole on learning, then this is useful information, and it should cause us to question the reasons behind it, to look more closely at the actual technologies, and the contexts in which they are used, that are having this effect and why. However, to blame one piece of a technology assembly, especially when we know that those effects are not seen in every case, is lazy and intellectually incoherent.

The effects that we see are the results of many technologies, many forces, and many co-dependent and independent factors, of which a given technology is only a visible feature that we have chosen as our boundary. Although there might be a statistical correlation between computer use and (say) an inability to concentrate, surface thinking, and a host of other ills (as well as a host of benefits), it is almost never the computer or a given piece of software itself that is the cause but the assemblies of which it might form a host or a part, its contexts of use, and the consequent purposes to which it is put. We know that there are ways of using computers that do not cause these problems, so it is not the computer that is the issue. Studies suggesting that computers have potentially limited value in classrooms such as OECD (2015) and Bouygues (2019)—the latter with far greater care and discernment—describe not the value of computers in specific instances of learning per se but the value that they have (on average) as part of a particular kind of technological assembly that includes (on average) a certain kind of test, set of pedagogies, structural power relationships, and organizational methods common to most schools. Enthusiasts—and I am one of them—might justly counter-claim that the problem is not with the use of computers but with the processes and other technologies in schools with which they are assembled. Such studies often highlight inadequacies in the technologies with which we attempt to assemble them, or in weaknesses in the ways that we use them, not in computers (at least without a great deal of further argument). If the parts of the assembly are not working together, then of course, regardless of whether they work separately, the whole technology will not work. It is as foolish to put computers in classrooms without changing the rest of the assembly (or adjusting computer use to fit it) as it is to put a V8 engine on a pushbike or to use a fork for eating soup. These parts of the assembly might make more sense if we were to strengthen the bicycle or make the soup chunkier. But perhaps such issues should encourage us to rethink our strategy altogether.

It is always possible to use technologies differently, to assemble them with others, to apply orchestration to different phenomena, to orchestrate them in other ways. It is important to analyze these assemblies but futile to demonize or extol one part without considering the rest and without thinking about ways that it might be used differently with different effects.

Although some rigid, prescriptive, and dominative technologies—laws, production lines, exam regulations, and so on—can and do strongly determine behaviour (part of the stuff that they are organized to do or how they are organized to do it), for the most part, especially when we are considering types of technology rather than specific instances within specific assemblies, in themselves they do not. All technologies, of course, do have affordances (often the reason that we use them) and limitations that affect their use, but they do not entail so much as enable consequences (Longo et al. 2012). The consequences that we observe are only some among (sometimes) many that could have been with a slightly different assembly. We might see consistent patterns and assume that they are causal, but in fact they are normally the results of what is enabled (or disabled) by technologies rather than direct results of using them. For example, asynchronous online learning (a massive class of diverse technologies) typically enables people to learn at any hour of the day, and it is constrained in ways that slow down the pace of communication, both of which undoubtedly lead to more common uses of certain patterns of pedagogical design, distinctively skewed demographics, physiological commonalities (e.g., learners can be tired after a long day working), and so on. Similarly, until recently, computers did require that we sit down to use them, often in limited physical contexts, and many still do. That matters: it is among the phenomena that result from using them, and it can be among the phenomena that we orchestrate to achieve our goals or that stand in the way of effective learning. But, again, it is not a relationship of entailment: computers do not cause any particular kind of learning. What causes it, or inhibits it, is how they are organized with other stuff.

Rarely, we might conclude that there is indeed inevitable harm from a specific technology, though even that depends on the context of use. A gun, for instance, though deliberately designed to cause great harm, can make a serviceable paperweight, doorstop, or decorative item. Some people believe (with a little justification) that the ubiquitous glow of our device screens or (with no justification) the broadcast of wifi signals can have bad effects on our brains. If some incontrovertible evidence emerged that screens cause harm, or that wifi signals do adversely affect some people, unequivocally contradicting copious and overwhelming evidence to the contrary, it still would not tell us that computers as a technology are bad. It would tell us only that we need to fix those screens (e-paper screens, perhaps, or filters) and figure out a better way to send signals around (light, for instance, or shielded wires). Perhaps we would have to put them (or affected users) inside a Faraday cage. It is always possible to imagine different assemblies, each with its own weaknesses, strengths, and things that it enables or prohibits.

Equally, there can be default behaviours or particular kinds of orchestration that have consistent or regular effects (harmful or otherwise) that are phenomena that need to be considered when we use them. For example, the delays that computers typically impose (time to start up, load data, access a network, and so on) can be sufficiently harmful in some assemblies (e.g., web page load time, leading us to abandon an otherwise useful search) to render potentially useful technologies worse than useless. Again this is a signal that something about the technologies needs to be fixed, not that the types that they represent are inherently bad. And the fix might not be to make them faster: it might be that different uses could be made of the time spent waiting. Sometimes new technologies can result from exaptation rather than design.

Statements about particular technologies—be they computers, teaching methods, cars, or poems—are always, and must always be, provisional because technologies can always be changed, improved, assembled with others (including other methods), and used differently. We need to look critically at the past, choosing the right boundaries and observing the salient characteristics, because we should always aim to improve our technologies, and they can always be improved. However, we should not assume that our analysis of what happens now necessarily predicts the future. Technologies are not natural, invariant phenomena; they are inventions. Analysis of current behaviour can be little more than a good story: it can, say, warn us of potential failures, provide hints of what leads to success, enrich our design vocabulary, or inspire us, but it cannot provide us with an invariant law.

The Adjacent Possible

Every new thing in the world opens up possibilities that were not there before. This is what powers the ratchet of evolution. Eyes could not have evolved had light-sensitive cells not already evolved, for instance. A fallen rock can provide a step up to reach fruit from a tree that was previously unreachable. Space travel as we know it would not get off the ground without metallurgy, bolts, or radio. Ideas depend on other ideas to form, most famously recognized in Newton's unoriginal assertion, perhaps made in a barbed reference to his (very short) bitter rival, Robert Hooke: "If I have seen further, it is by standing on the shoulders of giants."

New things in the world, especially when (as in the case of technologies) evolution is involved, increase what Kauffman (2000) frames as a formal concept of the "adjacent possible." The adjacent possible, or more precisely the "adjacent possible empty niche" (Longo et al., 2012), describes the potential next steps that any development might take, and it alters as the world around it and the things being developed in the surrounding system change (species, chemicals, technologies, etc.). For things that reproduce with variation, such as species, or for things that are reproduced with variation, such as technologies, such possibilities are additive. Succeeding generations do not immediately, if ever, replace their forebears but can, and normally do, coexist with them, interact with them, and sometimes help to constitute them or incorporate them into their own constitutions. Sometimes they compete with them. This concept of additive expansion of the adjacent possible applies in many areas and in many ways. In the context of culture, Wilson (2012, loc. 1403) describes the process as autocatalytic: each advance makes new advances more likely. Of knowledge, Ridley (2010, p. 248) tells us that, "the more knowledge you generate, the more you can generate." Of technology, Nye (2006, loc. 65) explains that, "when humans possess a tool, they excel at finding new uses for it. The tool often exists before the problem to be solved. Latent in every tool are unforeseen transformations." Of language, Melville (1850, p. 1162) put it more poetically: "The trillionth part has not yet been said; and all that has been said, but multiplies the avenues to what remains to be said."

The creation of a new kind of thing, based upon something that came before it, rarely immediately negates the possibilities available to its forebear, at least when viewed at a global level—what Arthur (2009, loc. 78) refers to as the collective of technology. Locally, we may replace one type of technology with another (a blackboard with a whiteboard, say) and thus block some former channels of possibility for those affected, but globally the technology that we replaced typically continues to exist somewhere, and often it remains a latent possibility locally. Over time, the new technology might come largely or eventually to replace its predecessor completely. However, at the point of its creation, it seldom prevents its ancestors from doing what they always did, notwithstanding occasional issues of forced dependency (e.g., the availability of ink cartridges for discontinued printers).

New technologies are sometimes created to do something that could not be done before, sometimes to do the same thing better, more cheaply, more accurately, or simply differently. As a result, though one technology can completely replace another in a local context, the sum of technological possibilities in the world grows with every novel change or new assembly. As Kelly (2010, p. 309) says, "more complexity expands the number of possible choices." And, thanks to a combination of the power of assembly and the relentless expansion of the adjacent possible, the technological world is becoming more complex at an ever-faster rate. We look back on the past to what we perceive as a simpler age not just through nostalgia but also because it actually was a lot simpler. It had fewer possibilities, fewer choices that could be made, and considerably less variety. Whether we choose to see this as progress or not depends a lot on our context and point of view, but the inexorable dynamic of the adjacent possible means that there has been without doubt an ever-accelerating rate of technological change.

There are mainly cognitive and pragmatic rather than intrinsic limits to this acceleration, a fact all too evident for a long time. Melville's positive assertion cited a couple of paragraphs ago, for example, is followed immediately with a phrase that echoes a very modern complaint: "It is not so much paucity, as superabundance of material that seems to incapacitate modern authors" (1984, p. 1162). The rate of technological change has been on an upward curve for many generations and likely for many millennia. For each generation, the curve becomes steeper, and the discontinuities become greater, because the adjacent possible expands exponentially. This makes it harder to know everything that might be known and easier to know that we do not know it.

The greater diversity that results from effervescent change more often than not also provides possibilities for combination. The ability to create lightbulbs, for example, relies on a wide range of foundational technologies, each of which provides new opportunities, but together they make a lightbulb not just possible but also likely to be invented. Indeed, it was invented independently at least 23 times prior to Edison's "invention" of it (Kelly, 2010), each within a few years of one another. The combination of glass-blowing, knowledge of inert gasses or vacuums, electrical generators and batteries, wires, metallurgy, manufacturing methods for filaments, and a host of other technologies enabled an adjacent possible of the lightbulb when they were assembled together. It was not inevitable by any means (technological determinism is extremely rare, if it exists at all), but the combination made it far more likely that it would be developed, particularly given the overwhelming need for cheap, bright, clean lighting at the time. This need itself was driven by other changes, such as more widely available literature, industrialists' desires for longer productive hours, and overcrowding that affected safety on streets.

The electric light developed not because a proto-lightbulb existed prior to it but because the pieces were ready to be assembled and because there was a need for better lighting. Once it was available, it was used and adapted for a great variety of other purposes, from heaters to signs to electronic valves (and hence radios, TVs, and computers). This is the foundation of the basic evolutionary dynamic noted by Arthur (2009), that technologies evolve through assembly and recombination. As we have seen in many different ways, human intelligence resides only partially in the heads of individuals. It is a collective and emergent phenomenon. We never learn alone, we never think alone, and we never invent alone. This is as true of educational technologies as it is of lightbulbs.

The Adjacent Impossible

Whenever we create, we become able to create more. New possibilities, new potentials, new assemblies become possible and change what we do and how we progress. However, technologies can also be subtractive as well as additive. If we replace old technologies with new ones, then new constraints typically emerge, and avenues untaken remain closed, sometimes (at least at a local scale) more than ever before. We create boundaries and barriers, whether through rules, regulations, and processes or through physical restrictions or the propensities of our tools and systems. From digital rights management (DRM) to immigration restrictions, we find new ways (at least locally) to restrict what we can do by inventing new technologies that take away from what we could do before. When we replace multiple learning management systems (LMSs) in a university with one centralized technology, for instance, we lose the adjacent possibles of those that we replaced. Although the adjacent possible expands globally with each new invention, for those forced or cajoled into using prescriptive, dominative technologies, the former possibles become impossibles. For some technologies, notably those that Schwartz (1997) describes as "ideologies"—technologies of ideas—the effects on us can be profound. Echoing Churchill, McLuhan, and Dewey, Schwartz (2015, p. 10) claims that "we 'design' human nature, by designing the institutions within which people live." By way of example he describes how behaviourist models of work and learning inherited from Adam Smith, B. F. Skinner, Frederick Winslow Taylor, and others have become self-fulfilling prophecies. Smith's jaundiced (though, as Schwartz is careful to observe, misunderstood and unsubtly interpreted) view that people do not want to work and must therefore be incentivized to do so was very influential, particularly because it happened to fit neatly with industrial revolution technologies of mass production demanding that individuals behave in cog-like ways. This way of thinking, originally a misleadingly partial observation of human nature, has been inherited and embedded in our schools, businesses, hospitals, and other institutions to the extent that it has become self-fulfilling: many people do not want to work because they have been trained to believe that they do so only because of incentives. They are working for pay rather than being paid for work; pay is a (or sometimes the) reward rather than being an award. You do not normally need to give incentives unless you believe that the activity is unpleasant. By removing challenge, meaning, and autonomy, rewards and punishments have become a viable means of sustaining some level of compliance, albeit less effectively than would be the case were individuals allowed to find intrinsic motivation. As Schwartz explains, what was an invention can now be, for social scientists and psychologists, a discovery, a phenomenon to be studied and used. In the conditions that were invented, based upon the erroneous belief that people are inherently reluctant to work, rewards and punishments have some effectiveness, in large part precisely because they make people reluctant to work.

The same is true of the use of grades and credentials to shape behaviour in our education systems. An invention based upon a mistaken premise (or, as I will argue later, a side effect of how the system was constructed)—that people must be made to learn—now plays a critical role in the educational machine and directly causes people not to want to learn. This phenomenon can then become an object of further "scientific" research that, unsurprisingly, proves it to be true because the system has been designed to make it true. I use the scare quotes around "scientific" because, though the methods used can be similar superficially to reductive methods used in natural sciences, what is investigated is a contingent invention that exists in a web of other contingent inventions, all of which are in a constant state of flux, changes to any one of which will likely change the phenomena being investigated. Unlike scientific investigation of the natural world, it is therefore extremely unlikely that generalizable knowledge will result from such practices. They can still be useful, at least for those building or using such a system for the moments that they remain stable, but (as we saw in the case of the demonization of computers) it is extremely unwise to extrapolate the results beyond the bounds of a specific design intervention. Such use of the trappings of a reductive scientific method in an inappropriate context is what Feynman (1997) scathingly refers to as "cargo-cult science."

Technologies can profoundly constrain learning. If we create a room with no light, then we will be unlikely to have much success with a drawing appreciation class, though it is an interesting exercise in learning design to come up with ways to do so. I have faced a similar problem in adapting a course on computer game design for blind students: it can certainly be done, and the result is often better for everyone because it forces us to think of more diverse needs. But some constraints are truly deterministic. If we do not have technologies of communication, for instance, then we will have little success with social pedagogies that demand interaction at a distance, regardless of the potential value of guided didactic conversation (Holmberg et al., 2005) in partially simulating dialogue.

Technology Evolves by Assembly Rather Than Mutation

Technologies evolve through reproduction, variation, and competition for survival. They virtually never spring from an inventor's mind fully formed, without predecessors, but make use of, assemble, and repurpose existing technologies. However, though they do evolve and it is possible to draw an evolutionary tree for all technologies, the evolution of technologies is significantly different from the evolution of natural species. Technologies evolve by assembly, not through mutations of genes (Arthur, 2009). Technologies evolve within a social and technological context, and they embed many beliefs and assumptions that spring not from the technologies themselves but from the world that they inhabit (Bijker et al., 1989). They are not neutral. Page (2011) observes that some of the significant ways that creative and evolutionary systems differ include the following.

- In evolutionary systems, every variation has to be viable, or the mutation will die. Creative systems do not, at first, have to work at all. We can create prototypes, glorious failures, and not-quite-working technologies.

- In evolutionary systems, everything must follow from its immediate ancestors: unlike a technology, a creature that evolves today cannot arbitrarily incorporate features of one that existed millions of years ago or thousands of kilometres away.
- Creative systems can make large leaps, sometimes without intervening steps.
- Creative systems can define their own selection operators: success or failure can be measured in many different ways, not simply in terms of survival.
- Creative systems can be created in anticipation of the future: we might knowingly create, for example, an app for a device not yet on the market.

For all those differences between natural and technological evolution, the essential dynamics are similar and Darwinian in nature. It is possible to observe species and lineages for technologies that in many ways are similar to those that we might draw for natural species, albeit perhaps more like bacteria inasmuch as there is a huge amount of reuse of parts across "species" (e.g., nuts and bolts appear in many manufactured items). New technologies are invented as the adjacent possible expands around them. Each new invention opens up possibilities for further inventions and often creates new problems for new inventions to solve (Rosen, 2010), but it is firmly grounded in the assembly of technologies of which it is constituted and tied to what came before. For instance, the traditional university relies on buildings, books, cataloguing systems, pedagogies, lecture theatres, timetables, doors, enrolment systems, regulations, statutes, and countless other technical inventions that were necessary before it could achieve its present form.

Technological development and change are far from deterministic. Longo et al. (2012) describe the dynamic as one of enablement rather than entailment: technologies open up adjacent possibles and thus provide a normally large but constrained range of possible futures that might or might not come to pass.

Technological determinism is largely false for the simple reason that there can be no prestatable entailment in any complex emergent system

(Longo et al., 2012). Although we can trace back, at least in principle, from any technology to identify its antecedent causes, at any point we cannot predict what will happen in the future because, not only are there vast numbers of adjacent possible empty niches for most technologies (especially those that we will recognize later as soft), but also those niches are mutually constituted and affected by all the other complex parts that surround and co-evolve with them, stretching indefinitely far in every direction.

The direction of technological evolution is far from arbitrary, however, as the near-simultaneous invention of so many technologies, from the lightbulb to the telephone, reveals. There is a momentum, as Nye (2006) explains, to the change that gives it direction. Technological momentum exists not just because of the dynamics of entailment but also because we often create boundaries that, without further invention, are difficult to cross. Once we have settled on, say, a particular standard for electrical voltage, anything that does not comply simply will not work. The case is similar in education systems. Radical reinvention is extremely rare, if it exists at all. For instance, distance education institutions, though fundamentally different in many ways that we will explore later, were built upon foundations laid by in-person forebears and inherited many structures and processes of their ancestors, from curriculums to convocations. Furthermore, they exist within a broader educational context—including funding bodies, credentialing norms, and hiring pools—that greatly limits the possible ways in which they might develop. Constraints can greatly influence behaviour, and there are strong patterns to this influence, to which we turn next.

The Large and Slow

The large and slow in any complex system influence the small and fast more than vice versa, a phenomenon that Brand (2018) describes as pace layering. This is a universal law of complex systems whether natural or artificial. A mountain will have greater influence on the trees that grow on it than vice versa. Beneath the trees, shrubs and animals will have their lives constrained by the shapes, shadows, and chemistry of the trees.

Within the gut of a mouse that makes its home under the root of a tree can be thousands of species of bacteria unknown to science (Jones, 1999), whose entire world is shaped and constrained by the ecosystem provided by the mouse's gut.

Pace layering is a strong feature of educational systems, in which buildings, classrooms, LMSs, legislation, regulations, curriculums, and a host of other relatively slow-moving elements influence pedagogies and student learning far more than vice versa. Although it makes no sense, for reasons that will become clearer as this book progresses, to put pedagogy first in any educational intervention, the reasons that many educators loudly claim that we should are understandable, inasmuch as pedagogy is unlikely to have natural precedence. Similarly, the centralization of resources, especially when organized hierarchically, tends to result in disproportionate levels of control at the top, which is why such systems have been popular in the past, but (without great care in construction) they can greatly reduce agility for those inhabiting the levels below. In an education system, which relies heavily on creative individuals free to experiment and try new ways of thinking, this can be harmful.

Unlike natural systems, human systems can be and sometimes are redesigned. It is not that the small and fast can make no big change to the large and slow, especially when they work together. It is merely that changes of the large by the small are much less likely to occur and will occur less often because they are more costly in almost every way, at least in the short term, than adapting to the large and slow. Without the stable foundation of the large and slow-moving, the small and fast cannot (individually) thrive.

Crowds and mobs obey a different dynamic but often can be treated as a single large individual, what Kauffman (2016) describes as a "Kantian whole" or what I and others have described as a "collective" (Dron, 2002; Dron & Anderson, 2009; Segaran, 2007). This is most obvious in eusocial animals, such as termites and ants, that exhibit collective intelligence through the phenomenon of stigmergy (work done by signs left in the environment, such as pheromones) as well as in mobbing or herding species, such as locusts and wildebeests (Bonabeau et al., 1999), but it is also a factor in human systems, including those involving learning technologies (Dron, 2004).

In general terms, the larger and slower parts of a system act as a brake on progress. However, a certain amount of stability is essential to maintaining system metastability and evolutionary growth, avoiding the traps of a Red Queen Regime, in which co-adaptation is continuous and unchecked, so that the system is always running to stay in the same place, and the Stalinist Regime, in which nothing ever changes (Kauffman, 1995). Neither extreme of system dynamics allows for development, evolution, and adaptation to occur.

However, pace layering is a symptom, not a cause, of a further underlying structuring pattern. The dynamic that drives this effect is that things within a system that are less flexible and more unchanging (which I will describe later as harder) have a greater effect than things that can adapt and change faster (which I will describe later as softer) than vice versa. This is a matter not just of empirical observation but also of logical necessity. If fast-moving things affected slow-moving things more rapidly than vice versa, then slow-moving things would not be slow moving anymore. Things are slow or fast in relation to something, and they are slow because something else has changed at a more rapid or less rapid speed than their own. Similarly, the larger parts of a system exist either in a relationship of containment (e.g., a house contains its rooms, a mountain contains the trees that live on it) or, more generally, in a relationship of confinement (e.g., a rock that stands in the path of a herd of wildebeests or a hill that diverts a stream). If something contains another, then it cannot change more rapidly than its contents, and it must be larger. Similarly, if something confines another, then, relatively speaking and by definition, it is a greater influence on what it confines than the thing that it confines and again must be of sufficient size to have such an effect: if that relationship changes, then it no longer confines the smaller, faster-moving thing and thus is no longer the larger, slower-moving thing. The bounded are subordinate to the boundary.

Path Dependencies

The pattern of the inflexible disproportionately affecting the flexible can be seen as part of a still larger family of path dependencies. When we make changes to our environment, further changes are built on top of them, solidifying and embedding them in ever more solid strata, thus making those that came first less easy to change because of the disruptions that such changes will bring to things created in their context. This is the nature of assembly: what comes after builds upon what came before. In many cases, it results in a complex network of interdependent relationships that can lock us in to an arbitrary pattern that, if we were to start again, might be designed completely differently.

There are many classic examples of this in the development of technologies—the standardization of the QWERTY keyboard, the dominance of VHS tapes over Betamax, the widespread use of Microsoft Word, or the persistent use of lectures in education, for instance. These are not inherently large and slower-moving parts of the system—originally, they competed with similar technologies (most of which were only slightly less fit, some of which were objectively superior by some but seldom all measures) and were agile, but they became fixed parts of the landscape as investments of time, money, space, and expertise cemented their positions, and the costs of change began to exceed the benefits. It is much the same as the dynamic that drives natural evolution. Often what survives does so by chance, affected by sometimes random events that change the fitness landscape, from meteors to sea level changes to accidental isolation. But, once it has survived, it crowds out alternatives: it both adapts to and changes its environment so that, in a sense, its environment adapts to it. However, lucky breaks do happen.

The spread of invasive species shows that, at least sometimes, things can change. The same is true of technologies, including education, as Christensen et al. (2008) argue, in which disruptive innovation may occasionally supplant older, more established species. However, it is important to note that disruptive innovations seldom if ever compete head on with their forebears at first: they tend to sneak into niches that give them time and space to develop before spreading out to challenge the entrenched.

The same thing drives speciation in natural evolution: boundaries, often geographic, lead to different selection pressures in different places, and speciation always occurs most rapidly in isolated domains (Calvin, 1997). It is not coincidental that much of Darwin's evolutionary thinking evolved while visiting the Galapagos Islands, where different species of finch had evolved in the different ecological niches of the different islands. If radical disruption ever occurs in education systems, then it is unlikely to come from within the existing tightly interwoven system itself. If it happens at all, then most likely it will come from an area not currently connected in any meaningful way to the greater whole.

An archetypal example of the path-dependency lock-in effect is that the size of the rockets used on the space shuttle, arguably among the most advanced transportation technologies ever created, was predetermined by the width of Roman warhorses (Kelly, 2010, p. 180). The chain of events started in Roman times with chariots built to accommodate the width of two large warhorses, which meant that carts were built with wheels set to the same width so that they could follow the ruts left by the chariots, which led to roads built in Britain to accommodate Roman carts, which led to tramways designed to accommodate horse-drawn carriages built for those roads, thence to railway tracks in England, thus to railway tracks in the United States (because workers imported from the United Kingdom used familiar tools and jigs), onward to the space shuttle engines built in Utah that had to be transported by rail to Florida, going through tunnels that could not accommodate more than, as Kelly quotes an anonymous wag as saying, the width of two horses' arses. In this, as in any evolving system, there were countless possible ways in which things might have evolved differently. Each decision made is a branch in a track, leaving other branches untaken. Once decisions are made, they tend to be baked in and accrete further props as they continue to persist. People make investments of time, money, legislation, and passion that would be lost if things were to change. Even when change would be easy in a physical sense, attachment to things with which we are familiar and into which we have invested time and emotional energy makes us inclined to keep them the way they are, notwithstanding a counterbalancing love of novelty that helps to drive change. Many of our educational institutions have a history stretching back at least a millennium, and in some cases millennia, so they have inherited many such dependencies.

Path Dependencies in Education Systems

The effects of path dependencies on educational technologies are immense. To give a simple example, once an educational institution decides on an LMS, it usually results in a great deal of content being created, a great deal of training and on-the-job learning of its quirks and capabilities, and a large set of expectations in a student body of how learning content and process will be delivered. This investment is almost always orders of magnitude greater than the cost of the LMS in the first place. The costs of change are even greater, which is one of the key reasons that what many have argued is a substandard system such as Blackboard (which entered the market early on with what appears to have been in retrospect a half-formed product that, till at least not long ago, was a patchwork of code bases that barely fit together) could retain both its high price and its market share for many years, despite widespread dislike of the product. Customers are forced to follow upgrade paths if they wish for secure, competitive systems that meet needs created by the adjacent possible that earlier versions opened up, an effect exacerbated by the low motivation of the company to make its data portable. Moving to a different system altogether takes both great bravery and great resources, and few are willing to take that step lightly. A substandard system that is a known devil is usually better than none at all.

Blackboard's lock-in is not complete, as evidenced by its steady loss of customers over the past decade. One major reason for its demise is what Cory Doctorow (2019) describes as "adversarial interoperability." It refers to situations in which competitors (against the wishes of market leaders) attempt to take advantage of a thriving marketplace by making their own, independent tools compatible with those of their competitors, classic examples being support for proprietary and unpublished Microsoft Word formats in multiple alternative word processors and the exponential growth of IBM PC-compatible microcomputers in the 1980s using BIOSs (basic input/output systems that provide interfaces between an operating system and hardware) that replicated the functionality of IBM's own without using any of IBM's code. Although its own database structure is famously opaque, Blackboard, under pressure for many years from the market as well as internal needs, has supported a certain amount of data export, albeit with the loss of some of the structure and data that might matter. Competitors have taken advantage of this and made migration a great deal easier than it might otherwise be by using the limited export tools that Blackboard provides and reverse-engineering how it stores its data. The path dependency remains, but it can now be built upon by further toolsets that increase the adjacent possible.

The development of the LMS as a class of technologies in the first place follows a similar dynamic of path dependency. Those building online learning technologies in the 1990s originally (and I speak from direct experience) based their designs on the functions that they observed in existing educational institutions. To be effective tools for learning, they did not have to embody courses, classes, teaching roles, presentations, discussion forums, and assessment tools, but they did, because that was how the environment of education systems into which they needed to slot had evolved. They did not have a blank slate: they had to be assembled to fit the larger, slower-moving systems of which they were to become parts, or no one (least of all their creators) would have a use for them.

The same pattern of path dependencies can be seen all the way down the line in education systems: infrastructure such as libraries and classrooms defines limits on how teaching might occur, and their use is strongly encouraged by those who have made the investment. Accreditation systems standardized and embedded across society are difficult to change, leading to great disruption and resistance from many sides when even minor changes occur. Chains of dependencies run through these deeply embedded systems, each dependency embedding it further.

The decision to use a new technology in a novel situation is a relatively easy one, but the decision to replace an entrenched one is far harder to make and can have far greater repercussions across a system that depends on it. The larger the boundaries that the technology embraces, the more profound its resilience to change: smaller pieces are more easily replaced. This is unfortunate in the case of large, centralized toolsets widely used by many people—Facebook, Blackboard, or Microsoft Word, for instance—because the costs of replacement can be much higher than the costs of suffering their multiple dire consequences. The greater the number of people who use a technology, the more embedded it tends to become and the more assemblies it becomes a part of. To make things worse, without great care in construction, large centralized toolsets can be extremely constraining and, to add further constraint, need to be constructed to suit average or majority needs, which can stifle diversity. As a result, monolithic technologies play a strong (and seldom carefully considered) role in establishing norms and practices and in setting boundaries where none needs to exist.

The survival of a substandard system is not entirely regardless of its utility. A truly useless or dangerous technology eventually and typically will fail to survive, though it might persist for a long time, and inevitably it will be propped up by counter-technologies that embed it further. However, constructed differently, were we to sit down and start afresh, we would often do things differently and much better. Unfortunately, what exists in national and sometimes international education systems is so deeply embedded with other stuff that substantial change is virtually impossible from within. The massive network of embedded connections, themselves often linking large and slow-moving networks such as education systems and legislatures, emergently becomes the most determinant large and slow-moving feature. We will return to this theme in Chapter 10.

It was a rational choice for the makers of early LMSs to situate their technologies within traditional education systems: had they gone back to basics and reconsidered how learning might be enabled using online technologies, it is highly unlikely that there would have been a market for them. That particular possible was far too far away. However, just because education systems are deeply embedded does not mean that change cannot occur. As Christensen (2008) observes, disruptive innovations nearly always come from outside the field, where they can develop without the hindrances and interdependencies of large, established systems, exactly as finches in each of the Galapagos Islands developed independently of one another.

Path dependencies, as the example of the space shuttle shows, can stretch back a long way. Existing higher education systems derive directly from the exigencies emerging from the decisions by cities such as Paris and Bologna in medieval Europe to attract rich students by forming centralized places of learning where scholars, books, and students could come together (Norton, 1909). As much as the width of two horses' arses need not have led to the dimensions of rocket motors in space shuttles, things could have been different in higher education. Indeed, had we followed the Bolognese model of universities, in which students determined who taught, and what and how it was taught, rather than the Parisian model, in which such decisions were made by faculty, things would be very different today. Better? Not in every way and certainly worse in some. But change is possible, it appears to be happening, and it is the change that matters more than what results from it. This is because what it is likely to lead to is not the replacement of what we already have (unless it really is significantly better in every way, in which case so much the better) but the coexistence and co-evolution of different ways of doing things. Old technologies seldom if ever die, so the demise of institutional education probably will never happen, or at least not in the space of a few generations, so whatever comes next will add to, rather than fully replace, what currently exists. This means an increase in the adjacent possible, which, like all technological change, builds new adjacent possibles as each avenue is explored, thus moving us forward into a richer future filled with new as well as old ways of learning. On balance, this is a good thing.

It is worth noting finally that large, scale-free networks of the sort that link education and other core social systems, though highly tolerant of perturbation, sometimes (depending on their form) can fail catastrophically (Watts, 2003) and, when faced with compelling competing networks that can emerge outside the education system, can be depleted of so many nodes that they cannot thrive and must transform. This change might be in progress right now as networked technologies combine and mutate in a breathtaking crescendo driven by the exponentially emerging adjacent possibles of new technologies and ways of thinking. From MOOCs (Massive Open Online Courses) to Wikipedia, from the Kahn Academy to Sugata Mitra's Hole in the Wall experiments, from fast-track bootcamps to open mentoring systems, different models and conceptions of teaching are emerging as a direct consequence of new technologies outside or on the fringes of academia. Similarly, free universities, in person and otherwise, have started to emerge both online (e.g., the University of the People) and in person (e.g., the Free University of Brighton) and are separate from their institutional peers.

Meanwhile, alternative forms of credentialing are creeping in, from OpenBadges to LinkedIn endorsements. Tools and standards to record and manage the process independently of institutions are beginning to hit the mainstream, notably TinCan (also known as the Experience API or xAPI) and e-portfolios. Apart from MOOCs, these are not yet seen as competitors to traditional education. Indeed, in many cases, they are being incorporated so as to bolster the old ways. But they are beginning to fill in some of the gaps that might lead to a new adjacent possible. Other technology standards, from newsfeeds to LTI (learning tools interoperability), allow different online systems to interoperate—for one technology to become part of the operation of another—and thus to extend the adjacent possibles of both. Again this opens up the potential for change, though these interdependencies create yet more path dependencies and hardness (inflexibility and resistance to change) in the overall system. Technologies are not determinate and not predictable in advance, so it is hard to know whether these or any other initiatives will tip the balance, but the ever-burgeoning adjacent possible is leading inevitably to combinations and assemblies that likely will provide, at some point, serious competition for the incumbent institutions that comprise most of what we recognize as education systems today. If or when they do, however, they will incorporate into their assembly much of what came before, and likely they will create adjacent possibles that will feed back into the technologies of the institutional systems that they (partially) replace. The world will change, but much of it will remain familiar because of the nature of technologies as assemblies.

5 | Participation and Technique

> *A man provided with paper, pencil, and rubber, and subject to strict discipline, is in effect a universal machine.*
>
> —Alan Turing (1948, p. 113)

Virtually all technologies demand some kind of action or activity from us, from turning a dial to painting a masterpiece. We are not just using technologies when we do this: the use itself is a form of technology, a process that we enact so that the technology of which it is a part can perform the purpose that we wish for it. Thus, we do not just use technologies but also—as they are instantiated in specific contexts—participate in them. We are part of them, as either elements of a predetermined mechanism or as assemblers and orchestrators of something novel (and, typically, both). This participation can usually be described as "technique." As I use the term, "technique" is the human-enacted part of any technology. An important feature of many technologies, and especially educational technologies, is that we are co-participants, directly or indirectly, with other people.

Sometimes our participation in a technology is predetermined, from actions as simple as pressing a button or operating a microwave oven to activities as complicated as correctly singing a piece of music or solving a differential equation. The techniques that we use must be enacted with precision, or the technology will fail to work. I will describe these as hard technologies.

Often, however, we have to (or choose to) perform some of our own organization in order for the technology to do what we ask of it. Technologies, from pencil and paper to learning management systems, leave a great deal unorchestrated, yet to unfold. They leave gaps that must or may be filled idiosyncratically and, often, creatively by their participants. The techniques that we use can vary considerably, potentially differing each time we use them. I will describe these as soft technologies. It is important to take note, though, of where the boundaries of such technologies lie because the softness is not inherent in the parts but unfolds only in the whole. What makes it softer or harder, in its enacted unfolding, is the role of humans in the overall assembly—their techniques—not the other parts of which the assembly consists. I will describe this definition of softness and hardness as participatory, reflecting the fact that the softness or hardness describes the kind of participation required of or enabled for the human (or other intelligent) participants. Before explaining this and its consequences further, I should distinguish my own from other common uses of these terms because, otherwise, preconceptions of earlier definitions of hard and soft technologies might make the rest of the book difficult to follow. In the process, I hope to demonstrate that the participatory definition is more useful than its predecessors.

Soft Technologies and Hard Technologies

Many authors have found it useful to divide the world of technologies into those that are hard and those that are soft. Most definitions fall into one of three main camps, which I label here as binary, socio-technical, and holistic, with respective foci on phenomena, use, and orchestration. Table 1 provides an overview of each definition, as well as my own, that characterizes the major differences and similarities.

The Binary Definition

The binary hard/soft distinction is a simple and everyday way of separating those technologies concerned primarily with human-mediated human processes from those that use physical (including digital) tools

Table 1. Patterns, Examples, and Foci of Competing Definitions of Soft and Hard Technologies

Definition	Pattern	Primary technology focus	Soft example	Hard example
Binary	Physical tools versus business processes	Phenomena	Exam regulations	Pencils
Socio-technical	Liberative versus dominative technologies	Uses	Pencils	Exam regulations
Holistic	Technologies and humans as part of one assembly	Orchestration	Drawing	Exam boards
Participatory	Flexible human roles in technologies versus inflexible roles	Phenomena, uses, orchestration, and users	Drawing	Multiple-choice quizzes

(e.g., Bessant & Francis, 2005; Burgess & Gules, 1998; Hlupic et al., 2002; McDonough & Khan, 1996). This, roughly, is the definition employed by the Association for Educational and Communication Technologies (AECT) in making its own soft/hard distinction with regard to learning technologies (Lakhana, 2014), so it is frequently used in educational literature. It is also implicit in the common use of the terms "software" and "hardware." From this perspective, rules, theories, methods, managerial systems, and exam procedures are soft, whereas anything embodied in hardware or software (oddly enough)—including classrooms, whiteboards, and LMSs—is hard. The distinction might have some value in (and, for the most part, only in) management accounting, because essentially it has to do with whether technologies can be bought or sold. However, it fails abysmally to acknowledge that most technologies are mixes of the two (like the stick on the ground), and it leads to some nonsensical categorizations: for instance, a verbal quiz would be soft by this definition, but the same quiz online or on paper would be hard. That is not a useful distinction unless you are charged with accounting for your use of paper. It also seems to be unintuitive that a paintbrush is a hard technology whereas a rigid rule that cannot be broken is a soft technology. This is a confused and confusing definition if the intention is to describe a technology, and it is not the one that I will use.

The Socio-Technical Definition

Another common use of the soft/hard distinction for technology is concerned with how technologies affect us rather than their constitution. I call this the socio-technical definition. From the socio-technical point of view, softer technologies, however they are instantiated, are empowering, whereas harder technologies are disempowering, demanding that we must behave in particular ways to service their needs. As Don Norman (1993, p. 232) puts it, "hard technology makes us subservient, soft technology puts us in charge." Terms other than "hard" and "soft" are used by some writers to describe similar concepts, such as Franklin's (1999) distinction between "holistic" and "prescriptive" technologies or Boyd's (1996) distinction between "liberative" and "dominative" technologies. Baldwin and Brand (1978, p. 5) are thinking along similar but not identical lines when they say that "'soft' signifies something that is alive, resilient, adaptive, maybe even lovable." Although not explicitly defined, hard technologies, presumably, are none of those things. For them, softness relates to technologies that exist at a human scale, fitting local needs rather than organizational needs and acting for the benefit of all—including the environment—rather than the benefit of a few. For them, a bicycle or public transit system might be soft, whereas cars (and all their unequally distributed, environmentally destructive infrastructure) might be hard.

The socio-technical perspective recognizes the complexities that occur when we shape technologies and are shaped by them, the dialogue that occurs between designer and user, and the role that technologies play in shaping our working lives, our education, and our ways of being. All technologies are value laden; most behave in hard-to-predict ways when assembled, they normally cause harmful side effects, and all are deeply intertwingled with many facets of our individual and collective lives.

However, for one person, what is a hard, opaque, and ugly technology that restricts patterns of behaviour can often be, for another person, a liberating technology that opens up vistas of creative possibility. Many educational technologies are liberative for some but dominative for others. For some, the LMS is a liberating technology that extends reach and pedagogical vocabulary, whereas for others it is a repressive instrument of domination and uniformity. For most, it is somewhere between the two, frustrating when it prevents some intention, liberating when it reveals hitherto unnoticed ways of teaching. I have frequently used pedagogies that deeply inspire some students but leave others quaking in fear because of the agency that they are forced to embrace. Most probably find these pedagogies to be somewhere between the two definitions, and few would agree on the balance.

The socio-technical definition tells us little about the constitution of such technologies because it is much more concerned with their use than with their orchestration. This does have some value in understanding technology roles in socio-technical systems. It is also a useful perspective when designing systems and tools that people will actually use and that will not cause harm. This is important in an educational context, in which students are often required to follow a rigid process toward accreditation and often subjected to highly dominative and prescriptive methods of teaching both in the classroom and online. However, when we look closely at most technologies, a certain amount of hardness—in the sense of dominative and prescriptive effects—is inevitable and far from harmful, and there are technologies, from water and sewage management to protective legislation, that appear to be hard (from a socio-technical perspective) yet mainly are beneficial. It is a useful distinction, but the terms tell us little about the technology in question, and it is not how I will use them.

The Holistic Definition

For some writers, the distinction between softness and hardness, like the binary distinction, is concerned with the constitution of the technologies themselves, but in this definition humans and their intentions are what make them soft, whereas the lack of them makes them hard. It is thus a way of looking at both the technologies themselves and our intimate relationships with them. Like the socio-technical perspective, it is concerned with a continuum of softness to hardness—representing different levels of human engagement in them—but its focus is more on their orchestration and the roles that humans play in making them work. I will describe this as a holistic view because of its treatment of the entirety of the technology assembly, including the people using the technologies and the construction of the technologies themselves. For example, to Zhouying (2004), soft technologies are concerned with the human factors that are a necessary adjunct to harder processes and tools, relating to psychology, ways of thinking, and ways of using those tools. Laszlo (2003) describes hard technologies as physical embodiments of technologies and/or technological processes and methods, whereas soft technologies represent the support for individual and collective self-determination—design methodologies, decision-making processes, and so on—that they enable. Like the binary definition, the holistic definition allows that technologies can be almost anything created but recognizes that some processes are distinctly human, whether or not the technologies are physically embodied, and, like the socio-technical view, it considers the affective nature of technologies for both people and their organizations.

A more holistic perspective takes us beyond the affective definition of socio-technical perspectives, and it offers a more realistic and nuanced way of understanding the complex assemblies that form our technologies than the binary view. It is the closest of all families of definition to my own. However, it runs the risk of providing a definition of soft technologies that few would recognize as technologies at all. Although (following Arthur, 2009) psychological factors can indeed be phenomena in an assembly that are necessary for a technology to perform its job, they are no more technologies in themselves than the passion of an artist or the sensitivity of a musician; instead, they are features that describe users of those technologies and the impacts of those users on their use. Soft, yes, and significant phenomena in many technology assemblies, but not technologies, because they exist whether we incorporate them into a technological assembly or not. So, though the general principles behind the holistic definition are laudable and rich in their application, and this definition allows us to examine both phenomena and their orchestration as parts of a single whole, it goes a little too far in including the non-technological, and thus its value as a differentiator is undermined, especially if we take on board the complex nature of technologies as usually being assemblies of multiple technologies.

The Participatory Definition

My participatory definition takes into account Arthur's (2009) insights into how technologies are formed and evolve through orchestrated assemblies. My definition of softness or hardness is essentially a measure of the degree to which humans participate in the orchestration of the final assembly: it is a description of the parts that we play in making the technology happen. Humans play predetermined roles in the orchestration when they are parts of hard technologies, whereas in soft technologies humans are the orchestrators. Hard technologies operate in fixed, invariable ways, whether or not they are physically instantiated, whereas soft technologies are pliable, relying on humans to engage in ever new ways of enacting them. This is more in keeping with common uses of the English terms "soft" and "hard" because softer technologies (demanding that orchestration be performed by their participants) are consequently more pliable, malleable, and giving, whereas harder technologies (in which humans play fixed and invariant roles) are consequently more rigid, more resistant to change, and more brittle. The participatory definition embraces phenomena, orchestration, and use as indivisible contributors to the same assembly. The softest technologies by this definition—those involving pencils, say—can be performed in almost infinite ways, whereas the hardest technologies—production lines or standardized tests, say—must be performed in the same way each time to achieve their intended purpose, as long as they work.

There is a continuum between softness and hardness. This is because almost all technologies are assemblies that consist of soft and hard technologies, and the human role in enacting any of those parts can range from completely proscribed to almost unconstrained and usually is a rich combination of the two. For example, when we write, we must obey more or less hard rules of spelling, citation practice, punctuation, and so on and we must use the physical tools with which we write in fairly proscribed ways. However, there are limitless possibilities for creative expression and invention, and most things that we write will not have been written before. Hardness and (especially) softness are not characteristics of the parts of the assembly: they are characteristics of the whole, as it is enacted by one or more humans, in a real-life setting.

The vast majority of technologies are blends of this nature, often in complex ways, once they are brought together for some use. Typically there are many more parts to an assembly and many ways that the assembly itself is part of other assemblies, often involving iterative and recursive loops. For instance, teachers may use a hard lecture format, but students (performing their own sense-making orchestrations) may ask questions or look excited, then teachers may use those phenomena to soften what they do, which might incorporate, say, showing a hard video demonstration, and so on. As Fawns (2022) puts it, the phenomena, orchestrations, and uses are deeply entangled: they are mutually affective and ever shifting over time.

Figure 2 shows a few technologies that might be found in academic environments, listed in rough order from soft to hard. However, the order of this list can change considerably for different people, different orchestrations, different uses, and different assemblies that incorporate or might be part of these technologies. The pliability of a technology, for the most part, is a highly situated phenomenon that depends on the phenomena, the assembly, the orchestration, the use, and (above all) the way that the person uses it at the point that it is enacted. Only rarely is it a fixed aspect of a named technology in itself. Even a pencil can be hard if we are forced to use it in a particular way (e.g., to draw a straight line between two points), and, to its creator, regardless of its inflexibility to its operators, a production line can be soft. A great deal depends on where we choose to place the boundaries around the technology of interest. The boundaries of a soft technology always extend beyond the components (including methods, tools, natural phenomena, structures, etc.) of which it is composed, and extend fuzzily toward infinity, limited only by the imaginations of the participants. The description of a hard technology perfectly encompasses it and people's roles within it. This does not mean that it cannot, through assembly, become part of another, softer (or harder) technology, of course, because technologies are assemblies that can become parts of other assemblies. Again, in labelling a technology as softer or harder, we are describing human roles in enacting that technology, not its parts.

The distinction is similar to that between hard and soft disciplines in academia: put simplistically, hard disciplines can be seen as those with right answers, whereas soft disciplines can be seen as those with many possible good answers. Hard technologies, as I am defining them, are invariant, always behaving in the same way no matter how they are instantiated, whereas soft technologies can be enacted in many ways. The more room left for humans to play their roles differently, the softer the technology.

This use of hard and soft is akin to that used by Checkland (2000) in his soft systems methodology (SSM), which treats hard systems as relating to well-defined problems and soft systems as those applying to fuzzy and ill-defined situations demanding dynamic adaptation and creativity. The participatory definition differs inasmuch as its application is to the nature of technologies rather than to the analysis and design of them (by my definition, SSM itself is a soft technology). SSM is concerned with understanding complex systems, leading to ways that we might go about

Figure 2. A Notional List of Technologies Approximately Ordered by Their Plasticity

softer ↑
computer,
pencils,
email,
whiteboards,
teaching methods,
textbooks,
learning management systems,
curricula,
timetables,
expense claim forms,
examination boards,
legislation,
multiple choice quizzes,
harder ↓
citation styles

changing them. Like the holistic definition, Checkland's soft systems can include attitudes and values. The participatory definition is about the results of doing so: the technologies themselves. In my use of the term, the "fuzziness" of a soft technology is a temporary state that resolves into a concrete system when it is instantiated. By my definition, a soft systems design process can lead to a hard technology, while a hard systems methodology may lead to the design of a soft technology. The biggest difference between a soft technology and a hard technology is that part of the former is unknown and, typically, unknowable in advance, not that it is inherently blurry once it is instantiated.

Turkle and Papert (1992) make a similar distinction between a hard engineering approach to design, involving planning and a rigorous design model, and soft bricolage (or tinkering), engagement with the concrete in which a dialogue is enacted between the creator and the technology created. Like me, Turkle and Papert are concerned with the relative degrees of human engagement in the process and, more than Checkland (2000), interested in the product as much as the process. However, their interest in the product lies in how it differs (internally) as a result of a soft or hard design process. This might be of no consequence to end instantiators (users) of the resulting technologies. By my definition, the hardness or softness of those resulting technologies has little to do with whether they were built by engineering or bricolage. It is just as easy to enact a technology that is restrictive, inflexible, and resistant to change using bricolage as it is through engineering, and some of the softest, most pliable technologies in the world (e.g., most of those involving computers or pens) are more likely to be made by engineers than bricoleurs.

Finally, there is a connection between this definition and what Bijker (1987) describes as "interpretive flexibility": that is, the ways that different technologies can be adapted or appropriated for different contexts. However, Bijker is concerned with the environmental, economic, cultural, and social conditions under which technologies can be adapted and appropriated, and particularly with how classes of technology can be adopted within a society, whereas my distinction concerns the nature of the technologies—as concretely enacted in particular situations—themselves. My understanding of technology is more closely related to actor network theory (Latour, 2005; Law, 1992) and activity theory (Engeström, 1999), inasmuch as it conceives of technologies as inextricable parts of human action and knowledge, but there the similarities mostly end.

The Enactment of Technologies

The softness of a soft technology comes from the phenomena being orchestrated anew each time it is enacted by a human or humans, whereas in a hard technology that orchestration has already been determined, whether or not it is actually enacted by humans. I use the word *enacted* to emphasize that technologies often are as much performed as they perform, whether by people or machines. When people perform them, they are participants in the technology, not just users of it: the techniques that they use are parts of the technology's complete assembly. Another way of thinking about it is that technologies can be "realized," in the sense of being made real, by humans as well as machines. We might say equally that they are instantiated, in the sense that they do not fully come into being until they are used within a specific context for a specific purpose. Technologies such as mental arithmetic, thinking in words, or just singing in our heads can be enacted (or realized or instantiated) entirely by people, whether they are hard or soft, though in many cases the enacted assembly typically includes something more tangible, be it software, bricks, pencils, fingers, or ink.

The participants' role in soft technologies is variable and often creative, whereas their role in hard technologies is predetermined, predefined, and (if successful) invariant. This is not always related obviously to the component parts. For instance, unconstrained classroom teachers may use words in many unique ways (as a soft technology), but teachers following a script to say the same words would have no choice about their part in what appears to be the same assembly, assuming that they stick to the script. Greater softness can emerge in many other ways, such as tone of voice, expression, pacing, accent, and so on: there is still plenty of room for soft technique. Inevitably, because they reify human decision making in something non-human (be it a bearing system or a set of explicit rules that may not be broken), harder technologies tend to be more constraining and authoritarian, whereas softer technologies tend toward creativity and flexibility. Soft technologies are thus often more "alive, resilient, adaptive, maybe even lovable," as Brand (1978, p. 5) suggests, whereas hard technologies tend to be prescriptive, making us subservient to their needs. However, hard technologies often do good (and, indeed, are essential since almost invariably they form parts of the assemblies of soft technologies), while soft technologies can cause harm as easily as good. There are many soft technologies of war and slavery that are far from lovable.

An archetypal hard technology such as an old-fashioned, mechanical, spring-driven wristwatch mostly performs its role independently of any intercession but demands that a human, from time to time, must wind it. Creative watch winding, if the watch is meant as a timepiece, is not recommended by the manufacturer. For the mechanical watch, at least when used as a time-telling machine, the human is a part of the orchestration, a necessary component of its assembly without which it simply will not work and in which the human has no choice but to act in a particular manner if it is to fulfill its function. There might be some small element of personal technique involved: twiddling back and forth faster or slower, for instance, or slowing down as it approaches being fully wound, or variations in ways of gripping the crown that make it easier or harder to wind, but all are just parts of the orchestration, implementations of a predefined method. The human role in the hard technology of a watch also includes reading the positions of the hands and using them to calculate the time. Creative interpretation of hand positions is rarely a good idea if the intention is to tell the time accurately. If it is to work as an accurate time-telling technology, then the person who uses it is a necessary part of a complete description of its assembly, and a complete description of the technology of telling time (including its human parts) is possible. It is also possible for the watch simultaneously to be part of many other technologies that can be equally hard (e.g., when used as part of a technology to identify location or direction) or softer (e.g., when used to indicate social status, or as a decoration, or as a metaphor in a play). The softness is inherent not in the watch, but in the way (with a human or humans) that it becomes part of the enactment of the technology that matters—the technology as it unfolds, as it is instantiated, as it is realized—be it timekeeping or status signalling. And, of course, it can be both at once but, when it is, there are two different technologies of interest, not one.

Like the mechanical wristwatch, the pencil and paper are useless without a human, but unlike the watch the human must orchestrate the phenomena that they provide, assembling those phenomena with other phenomena if they are to do anything at all. Many of those other phenomena are technologies themselves, such as methods of handling the pencil, rules of perspective, spelling, rules of grammar, and so on, as well as non-technological phenomena, such as suppositions about how signs made on the paper can influence or affect other people. There can also be some soft skills involved, such as imagery and metaphor. Without those extra parts of the assembly the pencil and paper are not just non-functioning but also functionally incomplete. They do not lack just one or two parts but are inherently open to becoming many different technologies—portraits, shopping lists, calculations, architectural plans, games, and so on—not to mention a host of entirely orthogonal technologies (e.g., a toy windmill can be made from nothing but folded and torn paper and a pencil). Separately, their adjacent possibles are at least as great. A pencil can be used equally as a stabbing implement, a coffee stir stick, a measuring device, part of an artwork, a table prop, a filler of a hole in a wall, a maker of a hole in a wall, and so on. A piece of paper can become an airplane, a dustpan, a fan, a means to wipe up a small spill, a sunshade, a coaster, a fire lighter, a hat, a filler of a hole in a wall, and so on. A complete list of all the possible ways in which these technologies can be used would be impossible to compile, both in principle and in practice.

Although pencil and paper are simple technologies, simplicity is not a prerequisite for softness. A school building, for example, is complicated but, though built mainly for the purpose of teaching, can be used for an indefinitely large number of purposes in any number of technology assemblies, from a voting booth to a bomb shelter, from emergency housing to a place of worship. At least to their programmers, computers are perhaps even softer technologies than pencils or schools, with even more possible uses, and more possible ways that they can be orchestrated or assembled, though they are among the most complex objects ever manufactured. No matter the complexity of a technology, if it allows or requires humans to use it in their own orchestrations, then it can be described as soft.

Many technologies can be soft or hard depending on use, phenomena, and orchestration. A screwdriver, for instance, can be used with precision as a hard technology to correctly drive a screw. However, as Kauffman (2008) shows, there are no limits to its other possible uses, including murder, paint stirring, and back scratching.

Perspectives and Points of View

A screwdriver can be soft or hard because humans are a necessary part of any technology in which it plays a part. This is true of almost any tool because, by definition, a tool is used by someone. Different users of the same tool may put it to different uses and organize different stuff to do so, and they may thus use an entirely different technology from one another, even though significant (and often the most visible) parts might appear to be the same. The classroom, for example, is a different technology (with varying degrees of hardness) for a teacher, a student, an administrator, and a principal because they are users of very different (though overlapping) phenomena and put them to very different uses. Similarly, to the creator of an online form, it is usually soft, but for someone required to fill it in it can be hard, and the use of the form will be different for each of them. Each will orchestrate different phenomena for different purposes.

Skill matters too. For example, the fact that I might be able to modify the code of the software that produces the online form makes it a much softer technology for me than for someone without such skill. However, this is also subject to a range of other technological constraints, such as permission to access the system where it is installed, its licence, and access to suitable software to upload the code, not to mention the time that it would take to write the code, any or all of which can be more significant in determining its softness or hardness than the software itself. What we conventionally label a single technology—Moodle, say, or Blackboard—is (when used) often far from it, depending on the boundaries that we choose and the perspective from which we approach it. Indeed, for a system of such complexity, full of softness as well as hardness in its assembly, it can be part of a different technology for every person who enacts or participates in the enactment of it.

Softness and hardness can occur in different parts of an assembly as well as in different uses of that assembly. For instance, an LMS can be hard in the sense that every person who uses it does so in the context of an architectural unit of a "course" but can be soft in its toolset (at least for a teacher). It can incorporate a rigid tool for assessment but a flexible tool for content creation. Furthermore, it is important to remember that we are dealing not just with pieces of an LMS but also with a bigger assembly, of which the LMS is only a part. Some people (especially students but often also teachers) will be required to use some of what might otherwise be softer parts because of externally applied rules, for instance, or because of its role in a course. There is a world of difference between a lecture that a student is forced to attend and the same lecture that an observer attends voluntarily: they are different assemblies, and different technologies, when we extend the boundaries to include all that are relevant (in this case, course regulations). There can also be less obvious boundaries to consider. For instance, if an online teacher wishes to engage students in debate, there might be only a single discussion forum available in the LMS provided. This is not particularly hard because (assuming that regulations allow it) the teacher might use a different system instead. However, that can demand plentiful counter-technologies (e.g., manual registration, protection from privacy violation, learning a new interface, etc.) and therefore effectively be no choice at all. Its hardness lies not in the LMS itself but in the teacher's rigid adherence to the pedagogical method and perhaps the norms and expectations of the teaching role. They contribute to setting the boundaries that we must consider when identifying the technology of interest.

Soft Is Hard, Hard Is Easy

When a hard technology is used to replace something that a soft technology could do, one of its fundamental benefits is that it demands fewer decisions to be made by those who use it: in this sense (and only this sense), it makes things easier. Whether enacted in hardware or by humans, it requires less decision making because at least some of the thinking has already been done for us. In the process, we usually gain reliability, consistency, and replicability. It can still be difficult—mental arithmetic or correct interpretation of legislation, for example, is hard in every sense of the word—but there is only one correct way to do it. Although we will encounter exceptions and provisos as the chapter progresses, hard technologies are therefore highly amenable to automation, which can increase reliability and consistency and usually save time.

Softer technologies make things harder (more difficult) in the sense that they demand decision making and invention. The softest technology would be none at all, leaving its enactor to invent everything about it. This would be extremely difficult, and virtually impossible to label, because there would be nothing fixed about it. In real life, no such technology exists. To be able to call it a technology implies that there must be at least one or two hard phenomena (usually but not always or only other technologies) to orchestrate. Soft technologies fill gaps, not unlimited empty spaces. For example, it does take a lot of time and effort to develop the hard techniques for handwriting (holding a pen, forming letters, mastering spelling and punctuation, etc.), but once they have been learned we rarely need to think much about them in the future. It is not that it is trouble free—this is why it makes sense to harden that technology further, through technologies such as word processors, spell checkers, speech-recognition tools, and typewriters—but that we seldom have to think about it: we have created a machine in our minds that does the work. If, though, we are writing an essay, a poem, a book on learning and technology, or even a shopping list, then a different kind of difficulty emerges, because we need to orchestrate those hard skills, tools, and much else besides to create something that has never existed in the world.

Technologies do not necessarily simply replace things already done by people. Often they orchestrate things that would be difficult or impossible for humans to accomplish alone, such as providing the thrust needed to lift a rocket out of the Earth's atmosphere, or calculating pi to a billion decimal places, or just moving a heavy rock with a lever. Making things easier, and/or making new things possible, are normally the reasons that we invent technologies. However, once they have been created, the same principles apply, regardless of whether a technology extends or improves what we can do unaided: a hard technology can increase the adjacent possible because it enables us to create and instantiate further soft technologies that incorporate the hard technology. It extends our boundaries, but within its own boundaries our roles (if any is left to play) can be fixed.

A soft technology can be enacted well, but it cannot be enacted correctly, because there is no single correct way of doing it. For the softest of technologies—for example, for painting or architecture—there can be no upper limit to what "well" means, no gold standard of measurement that can be applied consistently. We might recognize excellence but it will be impossible to say that it is as excellent as it could be.

Because they are closer to functional completeness, harder technologies are less flexible and less adaptable than softer technologies. They are also less open to change, less capable of evolving, less resilient to perturbation, more brittle. This is an inevitable and invariant trade-off built into the definition itself. If we make things too hard, then we take away the power of creativity, take away control, remove flexibility. But the solution is not therefore to make all technologies softer, because in doing so we introduce more potential for error, limit adjacent possibles to do more, and reduce efficiency.

Softening and Hardening through Assembly

Almost any hard technology can become part of a softer technology when assembled in the right way with appropriate methods and other phenomena (including other technologies). Even an archetypal hard technology such as an automated manufacturing machine can (say) provide warmth to dry clothes, or be used as steps to reach a light on the ceiling, and it might even make a serviceable bottle opener. It also takes little more than the application of a rule or rigidly proscribed method to turn even the softest of technologies into something much harder. Even natural movements such as walking can become a hard march or a dance that must be enacted precisely.

Of course, equally, we can replace one technology with another, softening or hardening the whole in the process, and we can make changes to parts of the assembly that will make it softer or harder, though it is important to note that simply softening or hardening one part does not necessarily affect the whole in the same way: the orchestration and the rest of the assembly usually play significant roles in this. For instance, the submission of coursework by email can be a soft technology for both the teacher and the students, allowing the teacher to accommodate individual circumstances, to cater to difficulties producing appropriate file types or sizes, or to forgive late submissions. Conversely, a hard equivalent—typical of many default LMS implementations of coursework submission systems—might prevent all those actions. However, the softness of email submission might well be overridden by hard institutional regulations or even something as simple as local restrictions on email.

Sometimes even disassembly can soften or harden a technology. Bricoleurs often take parts or even whole assemblies from one machine in order to build another, for instance, and many kinds of makeshift repair rely on disabling or removing non-working parts so that at least some functionality remains. Although this can be more restrictive and therefore harder, it can also be softer, as when a broken automatic controller is bypassed with a manual operation.

As soft systems grow softer by assembly then, as long as the additions do not restrict what was already possible, they can actually become less complete the more we add to them, each new addition increasing the adjacent possible, so they become more dependent on our creative input. A little like fractal figures that, as we zoom in to look at them in greater detail, turn out to be infinitely empty as well as infinitely full, the more we add to a soft system assembly, the greater the range of new and different options in addition to those already available and thus the further the technology moves from completeness. To a large extent, it is this dynamic that Kelly (2010) observes when he talks about "what technology wants"—the ever-expanding range of adjacent possibles drives technological evolution inexorably forward and to ever-greater complexity. Soft technologies are inherently dynamic and forward looking, always capable of change, always evolving, because with each actual comes new possibles. Think, for example, of the ways that we can build a model out of clay, in which each lump of clay opens new opportunities to place the next. This can be a curse if the need is for efficiency and focus on a problem. Sometimes, for instance, it is far better to use a restricted painting program than a full-blown installation of Photoshop because, unless we have a lot of the hard skills needed to make Photoshop do more complex things, there are too many possibilities with which to deal. However, for open problems that demand creative solutions, and in a world that constantly emerges and transforms in complex ways that are anything but designed, soft technologies can be very useful indeed. Although they often take second place in our imaginations to the flashier hard technologies that allow us to do things that we could not do before, soft technologies are at least as much engines of progress as their harder kin.

Softening through Automation

There are some possibly counterintuitive features of assembly. One particularly interesting example is that of automation. Although it is often demonized as a dehumanizing and hard technological pattern, and often plays that role when it replaces a formerly soft human process, there are many occasions when automation can actually soften a technology.

Twitter, for example, is soft because it is and can be many different things. One big reason for this is that one of its primary uses is as a connector to other resources, so it can become a critical part of a much larger assembly, adding social sharing to almost any web-connected technology. The restriction, for most of Twitter's early history, that limited posts to 132 characters might be seen by some as a deliberate hardening, but that is to misunderstand the role of Twitter as part of the assembly of a larger technology. As Rose (2012, p. 206) explains, "it has enabled Twitter to achieve a significant paradox: maximum freedom through ultimate constraint."

A big part of what makes it so flexible is that it does one small trick, like a stick or screwdriver or wheel, and like those technologies it needs other technologies, soft and/or hard, to make it complete, such as websites to display linked pages and images or user-defined mechanisms such as hashtags, abbreviations, and other processes to increase the meaning of the transmission. Its deliberate limitations are what make it so useful, because it embodies (or at least, when it was created, it embodied) one tiny, precisely delineated, but easily connectable tool that could be assembled with and into many other technologies. Unlike other technologies of the time that served similar essential purposes—for instance, social bookmarking systems—Twitter was soft enough to be aggregated in many ways with many different technologies and ways of working. Its lack of an obvious, well-defined purpose was its greatest strength.

Twitter's subsequent evolution illustrates how automation can soften. For instance, the use of hashtags (e.g., #softtech) to classify subject matter into sets, the use of @ symbols (e.g., @jondron) to refer to people in networks, and even integrated hyperlinks were not part of Twitter's original design. They started as conventions adopted by users of Twitter to turn it into a more useful technology for their particular needs, adding new functionality by inventing processes and methods aggregated by them with the tool itself (Johnson, 2010). These were both hard and human-enacted technologies: they were techniques that had to be performed with precision, or they would do nothing at all. They were prone to error, they were not understood by all who read them, and using them was a manual and not altogether trivial process, involving generic search tools to seek hashtags or @ references and scanning manually for results. Observing these patterns, the makers of Twitter subsequently automated these technologies, bringing efficiency and freedom from error—classic hallmarks of a hard technology. However, far from making Twitter more brittle or harder, this automation softened it further, because Twitter was aggregating them with the assembly, not replacing or subtracting any part of it. These additions opened new and interesting adjacent possibles (e.g., mining social nets or recommending and exploring tags). Crucially, the hardened parts took nothing away from what Twitter could do previously: users of it could ignore the new functionality if they so wished, without suffering anything worse than a few underlined links. Other features added to the Twitter ecosystem, such as photo and video sharing, have taken none of the system's original flexibility away, despite automation, but added to the adjacent possibles of the system as well as made complex tasks simpler to perform. While Twitter has undergone many changes and its future is uncertain (as I write in 2023), these lessons have been applied in many other systems, most notably in functionally similar but federated applications like Mastodon and Bluesky.

There are many similar examples, from the automation of email attachments through embedded MIME (Multipart Internet Mail Extensions) enclosures replacing the manual use of uuencode and uudecode tools, to automated parking systems for cars, to the addition of electric motors to pedal bikes (assuming that pedaling remains an option). Notwithstanding a host of undesirable consequences—greater difficulties in maintenance, increased complexities in construction, greater ecological impacts, more expensive assemblies, and so on—automation, when it takes nothing of note away from the softer technology, often can result in increased softness rather than greater hardness. Those additional consequences are often significant, however, and typically demand the creation of counter-technologies to deal with them. Technologies remain, as Postman (2011) said, a Faustian bargain.

Hardening through Automation

Automation can often lead to more dehumanizing patterns, of the kind that Cooley (1987) rightly abhors when he calls for technologies of information rather than automation. As I write this in 2023, Twitter now filters top tweets by default, making them more prominent and thereby hardening the soft process of discovering interesting tweets. Although all tweets remain available to those willing to look for them (and those who know the extremely arcane spells needed to disable the automatic filtering and sorting), it is significantly more difficult to do so. Twitter thus partly dictates how people use it and removes some of the decisions that they formerly had to make, piping the "naturally" ordered list of tweets into a filter that, though not eliminating choice, makes some choices far less likely. We are all becoming increasingly familiar with the risks that such automation can bring, from filter bubbles (Pariser, 2011) to effects on election results of entire countries by actors bent on manipulating the algorithms to their own benefit.

The lessons of Twitter should not be lost on educators who seek to increase adjacent possibles. Just as the addition of well-chosen hard technologies softened the technology for its users, so too teachers (including autodidacts) can aggregate different technologies to support learning. From active hyperlinks in online presentations to uses of YouTube videos in classrooms, the possibilities opened up by automating parts of the pedagogical process are manifold. Moreover, they lead to new adjacent possibles—flexible paths for learners, integration of online and face-to-face activities, and so on—that create the potential for aggregation with new and different pedagogies that would be impossible had those steps not been taken. Equally importantly, it is not necessary to eschew the benefits of hard technologies in order to gain those of softer ones.

The key is in the assembly, not in the parts assembled. Building technologies out of small, well-defined, connectable, replaceable pieces is a powerful design pattern that brings with it the benefits of both the soft and the hard. However, as the increasing intrusiveness of Twitter's sorting and filtering algorithm shows, it is easy to harden too much. Even when all that we do is make something a default, it can radically affect behaviour. In my own research (Dron, 2006), I discovered that 99.15% of over 6,000 courses in my institution's LMS accepted its default landing page of course announcements. This presents a much harder and teacher-centric view of a course than, say, one that presents discussions or student blog posts first. Most of the exceptions that presented a softer perspective were my responsibility as either course or program leader. This was the case even though it easily could be changed with "only" a few clicks of a mouse button. Following up on these findings, I discovered that, even among the presumably computer-literate teachers of the Faculty of Information Technology, over 78% did not know that this could be changed, and on being informed of it over half said that they might change it in their courses, with over 15% saying that they definitely would do so.

My intervention that informed them of the possibility softened the technology for them, though no change occurred in the underlying platform. The power of defaults runs deep and broad. Most of us normally read books in sequential order of pages, most of us sit in chairs when they are provided. There are seldom rules that force us to do so, but in general there are what Gibson (1977) describes as "affordances" (what I prefer to think of as "propensities"), the likely ways in which we will interact with technologies thanks to features of their design. It typically takes effort and creative thinking to depart from defaults, and for the most part most of us have insufficient time, attention, energy, or desire to behave otherwise. As a computer programmer, I could, in principle, make a computer do anything that it is capable of doing, but it would be crazy for me to rewrite the operating system or build a new word processor.

Softness and Creativity

It is not a coincidence that all the technologies of arts and crafts of all kinds are inherently soft: they are about filling gaps. Similarly, it is a feature of the vast majority of social technologies that they are fundamentally at least fairly soft. In most circumstances, it would make no sense to automate dialogue and social engagement, though we can and do shape and channel behaviour in many ways to affect the forms and outcomes of social interaction, often with a clear purpose. For example, the StackExchange family of sites is built to provide reliable answers to questions through a process of dialogue, based upon the assumption that some answers will be more useful and reliable than others. It thus makes use of user upvotes and downvotes, as well as "karma" ratings to assess the reliability of those providing answers, in order to shape the dialogue visibly. Even when shaped this way, the system affords great flexibility, and the capacity for better answers to bubble up to the top is one of the major benefits of systems such as StackExchange, SlashDot (which uses multiple dimensions of ratings to indicate, say, humour, accuracy, and so on, as well as sophisticated mechanisms randomly to allocate temporary moderator roles to those with sufficient karma points, thus avoiding persistent power relationships), or Reddit (which uses simple star ratings that express only likes or dislikes but requires all Redditors to have earned their own ratings to give them to others). Social technologies (by their nature) allow people to communicate and thus negotiate processes and meanings, to add further parts to the assembly that allow people to change the rules, methods, and procedures.

Our softest technologies of all—such as language, writing, and computers—unfold into an infinitely rich range of new and enriching technologies and artifacts that bring usefulness and value to human lives.

Unfortunately, the effort involved in their operation, while making them deeply human, also makes them slower and more prone to error compared with their harder cousins performing similar tasks (notwithstanding the fact that they can become or be part of harder technologies). However, leaving aside the manufactured ready-made objects beloved by Warhol or Duchamp (where it is not the object itself but the concepts with which it is assembled that make the work), I would normally prefer a portrait painted by a three-year-old child than the perfect lines of an automatic drawing machine that uses a photo as its basis. Some things simply should not be hardened because they are ways of expressing and communicating our individual creativity and invention. These are things that define and fulfill us as human beings. In art, we do not need nor should we normally seek perfection from the point of view of the viewer, reader, or listener. It is precisely because of individual interpretation and invention that artworks have value, so, if we take that away and harden it, then there is nothing of any value left. Film, poetry, music, painting, sculpture, or fiction leaves spaces to be filled by the viewer, listener, or reader, a notion taken to its extreme in John Cage's $4'33''$, (almost) nothing but silence, and that is the point. It requires listeners to pay attention to the sounds around them, to orchestrate their own experiences. The techniques and inventions that fill the gaps in soft technologies also fill the gaps between us.

Soft technologies are innately accommodating of diversity: because they are open to the future, they can play out in myriad ways. Softer technologies can have infinitely many uses in an infinite number of technologies. But, as always, it is important to remember that all soft technologies involve at least some hard technologies, that softness can be achieved by assembling harder technologies, and that, in many cases, those harder technologies in the assembly are what make creativity possible in the first place.

Hardness and Creativity

Soft technologies are innately rich in creative potential, whereas hardness by definition provides none. However, hardness is no barrier to creativity as long as it is part of an assembly that is or can become softer. Almost all soft technologies have harder elements integral to their assemblies, whether they be techniques, physical or virtual structures, or rules.

Sometimes, even as they reduce freedom, harder technologies can provide boundaries and obstacles that act as stimuli to creativity (Boden, 1995). If technologies were entirely restrictive, dominative, and prescriptive, then we would have no means to be creative, but creativity can emerge whenever there are gaps that can or must be filled. More often than not, we find ways of assembling hard technologies with other technologies to make them softer, a creative process that might not occur if the technologies were overly soft in the first place.

For instance, a teacher faced with the need to fill an hour of time allocated to a lesson, with a predetermined curriculum that needs to be addressed, might find it easier to do than to imagine how learning can happen with no constraints, and such constraints certainly will help learners to focus on goals, and means of achieving them, no matter what happens in that allotted slot. We are finite beings with finite attention spans, and constraints, up to a point, can help us to structure our thinking. Of course, we have limitations that vary considerably according to task and context. Although it might be useful sometimes, the requirement to fill an hour (no more, no less) is an almost completely arbitrary constraint that often can be the opposite of liberating.

When technologies are too soft, we have nothing to kick against, no reason to choose between a potential infinity of options. Too many choices are as bad as no choice at all (Schwartz, 2004). An excess of softness is what causes the tyranny of the blank page as much as it leads to the increasing challenges of information overload that modern networked societies face. Even the technologies involving the stick on the ground have harder parts—methods, techniques, rules, and so on—that, though flexible, provide some level of structure and replicability.

As Brown (2009, loc. 233) puts it, "without constraints design cannot happen." The principle of the adjacent possible is not just an opening out of opportunities but also a channelling, creating an ever-growing supporting structure of foundations upon which to build, a pattern of path dependencies that, as we have seen, can play a hard and structural role, though what led to them in the first place was anything but.

Although a certain amount of constraint can support creativity, when it gets in the way and prevents us from doing what we would like to do, a hard technology can become positively harmful. It acts as an obstacle, an authoritarian channel that determines what we can and cannot do whether we like it or not.

The worst hard technologies are not only restrictive in themselves but also demand high levels of dehumanizing skill to operate them. They are dehumanizing because they entail the loss of free will in determining how they will operate. Implicit in this behaviour is the fact that, in bowing to the will of the machine, people are bowing to its creators, owners, or managers. This is the kind of technology that many—such as Ellul (1970), Franklin (1999), Mumford (1934), and Norman (1993)—rightly despise. Such technologies are often associated with inequalities and power relationships because what is automated is often for the benefit of the creator or owner of the technology rather than the person who must become a part of it. A production line is for the use of its owners and shareholders, not for its producers who enact the technology. The orchestration, the phenomena, and the use are all for someone else, so humans are nothing but parts in the machine, providers of phenomena orchestrated and assembled by the machine's owners to achieve their own purposes.

The creators, owners, or users, though, can be us. We use countless hard technologies for our individual or social benefit. Egg timers, practice regimes, meditation rituals, telephone numbers, and computer backup applications are at least as hard as any factory or bureaucratic system, yet they appear mainly to benefit their end users. As always, perspective matters: the issue here is not so much whether a technology is softer or harder but who controls its use and whose purposes it serves. Often such control can be shared. For example, though I may choose to use my fitness watch and benefit from the control that it gives me over my exercise regime, its creators can impose ways of using it on me (e.g., nagging reminders to jog) that I might not want or even loathe (I do). Hardness is a continuum, not an absolute binary distinction.

It is critical to understand that prescriptive and dominative hardness matters only to an individual whose choices are forcibly limited by the hard technology and that this is not necessarily a feature of the specific technology itself but of the socio-technical context in which it is applied: of the whole technology and (most significantly) the use to which it is put, not just the parts of the assembly around which we choose to place our boundaries. More often than not, the problematic aspects of any given technology are the rules, norms, and constraints overlaid on the parts, not the parts themselves. What makes examination systems or classroom attendance requirements hard is the fact that they are assembled with further technologies—sets of rules—demanding that their users obey them, with significant penalties for those who do not comply. There is nothing wrong with any of these things if they are freely chosen by people who must play their fixed roles, with nothing further riding on them. Many of us enjoy taking quizzes and tests of our competence when it is our choice to take them and nothing much depends on our success. There is a vast industry of quiz books, sudoku, crosswords, jigsaw puzzles, and so on that gives great pleasure to many. They are parts of different assemblies, with different boundaries, than the same quizzes and tests used to judge other people. Boundaries really do matter.

For those who have control of them, hard technologies can do a great deal of good. For instance, automated light rail transit and personal accounting systems typically are fairly hard technologies for end users, who have to play well-defined and invariant roles that can liberate far more than they inhibit because the end users can choose whether or not they have value and whether or not or when to use and participate in them. They are part of an assembly that, as it grows, becomes as soft or as hard as needed. It would be unwise to underestimate the value of delegating control to someone or something else in order to free ourselves to have more control, more capabilities, more options, greater comfort, greater safety, greater convenience. We harden technologies for good reasons most of the time, and, as long as we are aware of and not required to conform to their demands, they do much good.

Indeed, when a system is too soft, we tend to create our own boundaries to give us something to hang our ideas on or to kick against. For instance, to overcome the tyranny of the blank page, we might use ritual boundaries, such as introductions, conclusions, or the accepted formal structures and phrases used in letter writing to help give a form to our writing. As long as the signals that emerge through the boundaries have value to us, boundaries are essential to creation and critical in enabling us to function in our environments. Without boundaries, nothing would exist, or, if it did, then there would be no means to distinguish one part of it from another.

Technique, Soft and Hard

We can now examine more closely the notion of technique, first discussed in Chapter 3. Techniques, the ways in which things are done by people, invariably have some harder elements that might be described equally as methods or procedures. There are techniques for strumming guitars, for drawing, or for developing photographs, and all of them refer to the hard roles that we play as part of a hard technology: they are methods that can be codified, mechanized, repeated. However, as alluded to earlier, there is also an idiosyncratic element to virtually all techniques: even on and off buttons can be pressed in different ways (though it might not make a lot of difference to the operation of the technology of interest). Although we might talk of "perfecting" our technique, the reality is that it is often impossible and, as we will see in detail in Chapter 8, might be positively undesirable. It is highly unlikely that Leonardo da Vinci, gazing at the finished *Mona Lisa*, believed that his painting was an example of technique that could be improved no further. And, of course, it was not, no matter what we might think of the painting as a whole. And, though we might be deeply impressed with the hard skill of a photo-realist artist in producing paintings or drawings indistinguishable from photographs, normally the compositions and contents rather than the fine attention to detail move us.

Most of us would rather view the wild, organic, chance-filled brush strokes of Vincent van Gogh than a painstaking replica of the same subject traced from a camera obscura. Technique, in softer technologies, is infinitely or at least indefinitely malleable. It is always capable of refinement, and it is always capable of reinterpretation and re-evaluation in the light of the ever-unfolding adjacent possible. Soft technique is not quite the same as creativity, though it might be an engine that drives it. Soft technique is often born from imperfections and inadvertent mistakes. They can then become discoveries that we can use to ends that perhaps we did not seek, but that we find in ourselves and our creations, from which subsequently we can build new creations.

This is as true of teaching as it is of fine art. We can learn and refine harder techniques—how to pace a lesson, how to sequence activities, and so on—but how we teach, perhaps more importantly, is an ever-unfolding result of how we react to and use the "imperfections" in our enactment of those techniques, the ways that we adapt as we learn them. We make (often unintentional) variations into something of our own, in constant and never-ending conversations with what we do and what we learn from what we have done. More than anything, these idiosyncratic habits, these deviations from a described method, lift our technologies from realms of the predictable to realms of the human, the situated, the individual, the complex, and—when it works—the beautiful and divine. Without soft technique, there could be no art, no meaning, no communication, no creativity, no progress beyond that of the slow march of evolution. Without it, we would not be recognizably human, and there would be no meaning. We will return to this notion in more detail in Chapter 8.

Baby Bear's Bed

Hardness brings efficiency, ease of use, scalability, and freedom from error, whereas softness supports creativity, flexibility, and diversity. Both are necessary for different reasons, and virtually all of our technologies are a rich and complex mix of soft and hard, with few at either extreme. What matters is not whether a given technology is hard or soft but whether it is sufficiently hard or soft for the case in question and at the boundaries that we choose to consider.

This is true as much of pedagogies as it is of other technologies. Harder pedagogies—more prescriptive ones—can be extremely useful. Prescriptive scripts, for instance, can be helpful to temporary teachers or beginners, providing a recipe or pattern that can be followed until they are sufficiently adept at designing the process themselves. Pedagogies that are hard for learners (dictating methods and processes that must be followed) can be the most effective ways of learning some hard skills.

Spaced practice, interleaving (which implies at least some spacing), and other hard, repetitive approaches to learning, for example, can provide essential foundations for further learning. Moreover, at least some degree of hardness is usually a good idea when encountering something truly novel: offering choices makes no sense unless the person making those choices has enough knowledge and skill to make them (Garrison & Baynton, 1987), so it is worthwhile for beginners to delegate control of the process to someone or something else until they have those skills, as long as they are free to regain control at will. Softer pedagogies, those that provide only rough guidance and principles, whether they are soft for teachers or learners or both, better allow for adaptation to learners' needs and creative and divergent approaches. They provide learners a sense of being in control, which can greatly aid motivation (Ryan & Deci, 2017). Yet we should always remember that soft is hard: the more freedoms are required (not just allowed), the more effort and thought are needed to choose what to do. Choosing which parts to harden and which parts to soften is one of the key activities of teaching.

A blend of hard and soft is almost always not just desirable but also necessary. For example, gamification (in the proper sense of the application of game-inspired approaches to learning, not the pointsification that mars too much of the genre) often involves some hard processes, from the point of view of the learner, including the requirements to follow rules, to aim for fairly rigid and unambiguous goals, and to submit to a great deal of teacher/designer control of the process. However, done right, it offers great softness in places that traditional education makes hard. In particular, effective gamification almost always makes a virtue of failure, allowing learners to try and try again until they succeed, to experiment with different approaches each time around, and to develop hard techniques through repeated practice in multiple, variegated contexts that allow them to build competence at a pace that suits them, without fear of judgment.

The only time that a technology is too hard is when it prevents us from doing what we want to do, when it curtails our freedom at points that matter to us. Prescriptive, dominative technologies are often bad for this reason: they limit our capacity to act as independent, creative human beings. Sometimes this can be insidious, such as the use of leading defaults, or the appearance of control afforded by algorithmically filtered search results, a problem to which we must remain alert.

The only times that a technology is too soft are when it makes things too complex, difficult, slow, inefficient, or prone to error. This can be equally constraining and at least as harmful as too much hardness. Many learners feel disempowered when faced with choices that they have insufficient knowledge or skill to make, to the point that they might give up or be put off learning something for life.

In any given context, for a particular individual or group, from a particular perspective, at a particular scale, there will be a perfect sweet spot. Like Baby Bear's bed in the story of "Goldilocks and the Three Bears," the sweet spot is not too hard, not too soft; it is just right. What is just right will always vary according to context, purpose, and individual needs or wishes. This is the essence of why teaching, of necessity, is a soft technology. It is about building the right assembly, with an effective orchestration of the correct phenomena in order to create a learning experience not too hard, not too soft, but just right.

Summary

This chapter has wound around some of the complexities of our intimate participatory relationships with technologies and the relative merits of performing our own orchestration or allowing parts of our technologies to be orchestrated for us. Almost all technologies are somewhere on a spectrum between soft and hard. Table 2 shows some dichotomies that characterize some of the commonly seen features of each, any or all of which can be found in a technology as it is instantiated.

However, points of view and the overall orchestrated assembly around which the boundaries should be set can affect deeply how we view their pliability, so this should be taken only as a rough guide for identifying relative softness or hardness, a means to establish rules of thumb rather than hard and fast laws. These are not definitional features so much as aspects that help to identify technologies as more part of one family than the other, in accordance with Wittgenstein's (2001) use of the term "family resemblance" (*Familienähnlichkeit*).

Table 2. Patterns of Family Resemblance in Soft and Hard Technologies

Soft pattern	Hard pattern
Aggregation	Replacement
Signposts	Fenceposts
Freedom	Constraint
Flexibility	Efficiency
Bricolage	Engineering
Networks	Hierarchies
Open	Closed
Creators	Users
Distributed	Monolithic
Dialogue	Structure
Complex	Complicated
Searching	Filtering
Pliable	Reliable
Irregular	Regular

The hard–soft spectrum allows us to view our learning technologies, from pedagogies to international education systems, in a different light. First, it emphasizes the role of the human participant, too often ignored. Second, it allows us to define more clearly a technology in any given instance as something highly situated, rather than as a generic label, where the boundaries that matter extend beyond the most obvious components and tools to include all aspects of the assembly. And third, it makes it easier to understand education as a highly distributed (not just decentralized), collective endeavour—as a gestalt that is emergent and greater perhaps, but certainly different from, the sum of its parts—that teaches us and of which we all are parts. With this in mind, in the second part of the book, I use the participatory model to help examine and explain why this matters to how we learn, and I extend it to explore how we are not just participants but also, in any learning context, co-participants in the construction of technologies.

PART II

EDUCATION AS A TECHNOLOGICAL PHENOMENON

In the previous section, building mainly upon the work of complexity theorists such as Brian Arthur, Stuart Kauffman, and John Holland, I developed a theory of how technologies work, using a model of technique that describes the different ways in which we participate in technologies as softer or harder. My purpose was to lay the groundwork for understanding the nature of education as a technological phenomenon, to which we now turn.

In this section, I build upon this groundwork to develop a theory of teaching, which I describe as a co-participation model. In this model, teaching is seen as a massively distributed technology in which we are all teachers of ourselves and others, in which our technologies are not just means but also parts of ends, machines that form part of our cognition, within our individual minds, beyond our minds and bodies, and tangibly intertwingled with the minds of others.

Chapter 6 is about the technologies that we label pedagogies and how they fit into broader technological assemblies. I use the word *teaching* in its title rather than *learning* because teaching (in some of its most significant aspects) is technological, whereas learning is not, and almost all acts of intentional learning (and many that are unintentional) are also acts of teaching, whether of self or of others. Thus, though framed as a theory of teaching, it is at least as much about how we learn as it is about how we teach. This learning is a massively distributed process in which what we learn is as much embedded in as it is enabled by our technologies, in which our technologies become part us as much as we become part them, so we are part of a collective, cultural, and species-level intelligence, and that collective intelligence is an inherent, indissociable part of each individual intelligence.

Above all, it is a vastly complex, dynamic, ever unfolding, always situated, and deeply human intertwingularity (Nelson, 1974) that makes us who we are as much as our hearts and limbs. The theory explains the nature and value of soft and hard pedagogies, how they develop, how they bridge gaps between us, and when and where they are used. This is not a description of psychological mechanisms, still less of changes in the brain. It is a different level of description altogether. When I describe the creation of machines in our minds, I make no assumptions or assertions about how they are instantiated.

Chapter 7 examines a range of popular families of educational theory—–described here as objectivist, subjectivist, and complexivist—in the light of the co-participation model, showing how they are more closely related than their proponents might care to admit.

Chapter 8 delves into what it means to be a co-participant in the technology of education, examining the nature of technique, on the one hand, as the development of hard skills to use or enact a technology and, on the other, as the soft, idiosyncratic, ever-situated expression of our individual hearts and minds. Hard and soft techniques are inseparable twins: hard techniques provide technologies that connect and extend our collective minds, making us capable of greater physical and cognitive activities; soft techniques provide the engines of passion, creativity, adaptation, and inspiration. The chapter goes on to use a lens of literacy (defined as the hard skills needed to participate in a given community) to gain a richer picture of the connection between technology and culture.

6 | A Co-Participation Model of Teaching

We get schooled by the people around us, and it stays inside us deep.

—George P. Pelecanos, (2003, ch. 19)

Having established some broad features of technologies in general, I now examine more closely a particular kind of technology: pedagogies. Our ways of teaching are of great significance in understanding the larger educational machine because they are the *sine qua non* of all educational interventions. Without them, there can be no education. There are many other things that an education system does, from weeding and sorting to feeding industry, not to mention maintaining social stability, keeping children out of harm's way, enabling non-profitable but important avenues of research, and providing a home for thinkers and dreamers who otherwise would starve. But, at its heart, an education system is a system for teaching.

Pedagogies as Technologies

"Pedagogies," as I use the term here, are replicable processes, methods, designs, models, theories, and principles used to help people learn. If this does not accord with your own definition, then you might prefer to substitute "pedagogical methods, theories, models, and designs" when I use the term, but this seems to be a bit unwieldy to me. AECT's definition of educational technology from as early as 1972 as "a field involved in the facilitation of human learning through the systematic identification, development, organization, and utilization of learning resources and through the management of these processes" (1972, p. 36) or, more recently, its definition as "the study and ethical practice of facilitating learning and improving performance by creating, using, and managing appropriate technological processes and resources" (Januszewski & Molenda, 2008, p. 1, quoted in Hlynka & Jacobsen, 2010) makes it clear that the processes, patterns, and repeatable elements of instructional design have long been thought of as educational technologies, so my claim that pedagogies are technologies is far from controversial. Pedagogies are orchestrations of phenomena that include stuff such as our beliefs about how people learn, the means that we use to instantiate them, and the nature of the competences that we are trying to gain in order to achieve learning.

It might be useful to clarify what I mean by the term "pedagogy," because it has multiple layers of meaning and a certain amount of fuzziness in its application. To say that pedagogies are technologies is not the same as to say that pedagogy is technology. The *Oxford Dictionary of Sociology* fairly accurately describes *pedagogy* as "the science or art of teaching" (Scott & Marshall, n.d.). It is a field of study related to a set of practices, attitudes, and approaches rather than just the methods used. Pedagogy as a field is not the same thing as a pedagogy. The matter is confused further when we talk of pedagogical purposes, pedagogical value, or even, poetically, pedagogical love (Vandenberg, 2002); the term is simply a means of describing a relationship of teacher to student or, more generally, to signify some kind of teaching and learning focus.

It might be simpler to describe pedagogies in languages other than English. Friesen (2007) observes that the English language fails to distinguish pedagogics from didactics (in German *didaktik*). Didactics is concerned with a consistent and intentional method used for teaching, whereas pedagogics is concerned with the theory, models, and principles behind that teaching. Although, as we have seen, there are good reasons to believe that theories, models, and principles are also technologies, they are fundamentally different kinds of technology. This is thus a potentially useful distinction that, though not unheard of in educational theory circles, is not commonly applied in educational practice in English-speaking countries. In this book, I assume the more common and broader distinction that (for English speakers) a pedagogy is a technique, method, structuring principle, guiding model, or theory for teaching, thus encompassing both didactics and most (but not all) of the denotation of pedagogics.

Pedagogies are repeatable and communicable sets of processes and techniques as well as higher-order principles, theories, and models that structure and constrain those processes, and all are technologies. "Pedagogical" pedagogies are ways that we structure and understand the processes and phenomena on which they act. They are technologies to explain and inform "didactic" pedagogies—meta-pedagogies perhaps. For the sake of simplicity, the meaning that I use here is the one that might be assumed if we were to ask a teacher to describe the pedagogy in a particular intervention and the one implicit in a large number of educational research studies that describe interventions in terms of actions performed, methods used, techniques applied, and principles followed. A pedagogy is a way of teaching, how it is done. Whether we are describing a detailed learning design, a methodology, a theoretical model upon which our design is based, a broader principle, or the activity of teaching, it is still a technology.

Didactic pedagogies are essentially algorithms for teaching or, bearing in mind that they typically can be used by learners as much as by teachers, more accurately can be described as algorithms for learning. Although commonly associated with the fields of mathematics and computing, an algorithm is simply a set of rules that describes how something is done. In some countries, algorithms are patentable inventions, in recognition of their inherent technological nature. Whatever the practical or moral implications of treating algorithms as intellectual property, it is hard to argue that they are not designed, constructed, and implemented for some purpose or purposes. They are both inventions and technologies.

Pedagogies are technologies of process and method more often applied by human beings than by machines. However, like many other processes and methods, many are technologies that can be embedded as easily in hardware and software as they can be enacted by people. We do not have to go as far as explicit instantiations of pedagogies such as Skinner's (1960) teaching machines or educational adaptive hypermedia technologies (Brusilovsky, 2001) to see examples of this. Pedagogical theories (implicit, valid, or not) form part of the design of lecture theatres, exam rules, and even the time allocated to classes, not to mention more complex orchestrations such as learning management systems (Lane, 2009). All such things are based upon assumptions about the uses—parts of the assembly—to which they will be put, supporting some methods of teaching more easily than others and preventing or strongly discouraging other methods of teaching. Sometimes explicit pedagogical methods can be built into regulations: requirements for courses to have textbooks, for example, or homework, or standardized curriculums often cemented by standardized tests or other assessments that strongly determine not just what is taught but also how it is taught. In extreme yet all too common cases, they can even be imposed in the form of lesson plans, scripts, and learning designs to which teachers must conform.

Pedagogies, Softer and Harder

Like all technologies, pedagogies are soft for their creators. For the teacher in the classroom, even when that classroom, regulations, expectations, and other extrinsic constraints are taken into account, often great flexibility is possible in the format of the lesson and great scope to develop and use a personal technique. For students in that classroom, the teacher's (combined with the institution's) control of the space might leave little scope for flexibility while the class is in progress, but students may yet make important choices about how and whether to pay attention, and of course many other choices can and will be made before and after the event that might help or hinder learning in the classroom. Students also have pedagogical techniques. As always, it makes a huge difference where the boundaries of the technology are placed—and from whose perspective— regarding whether the overall assembly is seen as softer or harder. In all cases, though, the real-world enactment of any learning technology can and must include the orchestration performed by learners, and it makes a big difference whether the pedagogies that they use are part of someone else's orchestration or something that they orchestrate themselves.

For a teacher, pedagogies can be more or less hard. At the extreme soft end of the scale, the pedagogies might offer little more than principles to guide creative teaching. For example, Chickering and Gamson's (1987) popular "seven principles" have more to do with attitudes and values than with directing which methods a teacher should use.

1. Encourage contact between students and faculty.
2. Develop reciprocity and cooperation among students.
3. Encourage active learning.
4. Give prompt feedback.
5. Emphasize time on task.
6. Communicate high expectations.
7. Respect diverse talents and ways of learning.

These principles leave almost nothing but gaps for teachers to fill with technique and invention, offering minimal guidance on the form or content of interventions. They achieve this by shutting down harder paths as much as they increase the adjacent possible. Teaching approaches that follow these principles are constrained—conventional lectures, for instance, rarely fit well with this model—but within their boundaries endless different methods and other technologies can be used.

In the middle range of the spectrum, for example, Gagné's (1985) equally popular "nine events of instruction" specify a sequence of actions and activities that should be followed and provide an algorithm for teachers seeking to structure a lesson or course design:

1. gaining attention;
2. informing participants of objectives;
3. stimulating recall of prior learning;
4. presenting the content;
5. providing learning guidance;
6. eliciting performance;
7. providing feedback;
8. assessing performance; and
9. enhancing retention and transfer.

Although prescriptive, on a spectrum of soft to hard, even this hard formula offers huge gaps that must be filled by the teacher in countless different ways. The method almost guarantees the use of lectures, presentations, or similarly teacher-driven ways of presenting content, but there is almost infinite variety in how they can be developed. Similarly, the popular "compliment sandwich" approach to feedback, in which problems with the work are sandwiched between positive and encouraging feedback, is prescriptive, but it offers great variety to the teacher in how it is enacted. Technique is overwhelmingly more important than method.

At the extreme hard end of the scale, a lesson script that the teacher is required to follow offers little choice, but even so there can be opportunities for a teacher to diverge (e.g., when students ask questions), different ways of expressing what is written in the script (vocal emphasis, facial expression, etc.), and some interpretive flexibility, depending on how rigid the requirements are to adhere to the script. Rules requiring adherence to the script, or timetabling constraints that inhibit divergence, can make this a lot harder. The hardest of all pedagogies are those embedded in the tools, media, rules, and artifacts used in the assembly. If a textbook is used, say, or if the teacher is tutoring someone else's online course (or even the teacher's own if prewritten), then the teacher might have no control over an essentially fixed technology that forms the main motif of the activity. As always, however, it is possible to add parts to the hard assembly in order to create something softer. Teachers can recommend or emphasize different parts of a textbook, tutors can add explanations and interpretations of course materials, and so on. Largely, therefore, pedagogies tend to be soft for teachers, even when they seem to be as hard as they can be.

For students, a certain amount of softness is always available in the pedagogies that they themselves apply to the assembly. Even when a teacher controls every second of a lecture that students are forced to attend, with rewards and punishments driving their attendance, they may still use note-taking techniques, daydream to associate ideas freely, connect what is being said to prior experience, and use many other sensemaking approaches to adapt the teacher's pedagogy to their own contexts.

However, the teacher's pedagogies can be extremely directive and hard, thus playing a huge structural role in setting boundaries that cannot be crossed, constraints on action, and many ways of confining the adjacent possible. In many cases, students might be little more than enactors of a teacher's orchestration. A teacher following, say, Gagné's (1985) model might leave little room for students to diverge from the established path and will tend to emphasize power relationships that strongly militate against student autonomy. It does not have to be that way: Gagné's model is soft for teachers and therefore allows them to give students greater agency, but it is always theirs to give or to take away.

In the middle range of pedagogical plasticity for students are those learning activities that invite participation, from the simple ability to ask questions to seminars, tutorials, and group projects in which the teacher sets tasks, perhaps imposes structure on the form of participation, and establishes goals to be achieved. As soon as dialogue enters the frame, the teacher's control is not as great, and power (and orchestration) are shared among participants. A model like that of Chickering and Gamson (1987), with its heavy emphasis on student autonomy, social interaction, and active engagement, makes softness almost inevitable. However, the teacher might well demand that this softer process is followed, and constraints on fixed learning outcomes and assessments, say, can harden the process considerably. Although students can perform some of the orchestration, the uses to which it is put can remain firmly in the hands of the teacher. If that is what learners need—and if it is their choice—then it can be a good thing, because hardness brings efficiency, replicability, and reliability. For those who do not know how to learn a particular topic or skill, hard pedagogies can provide useful scaffolding so that they have the hard techniques that they need to do so in the future.

At the extreme soft end of the scale, self-directed learning, for example through reading a Wikipedia article and following its links and references, or watching a set of YouTube videos, or following a Khan Academy tutorial, provides a great deal of freedom to learners actively to invent and adapt pedagogies to their own uses, orchestrating what they find in ways that suit their needs, interests, and capabilities. However, even then it is difficult and almost impossible to escape a certain amount of pedagogical hardness, inasmuch as the resources that they use typically include at least implicit pedagogies designed by someone else: the structure of the Wikipedia article (and Wikipedia itself), the explicit pedagogical methods of a Khan Academy or YouTube tutorial, and so on. Soft technologies are always assemblies that include hard components, so this is not unexpected. Importantly, though, self-directed learners faced with a hard tutorial that does not achieve the desired results might stop using it and find a more suitable one, or they might repeat it in the hope of understanding it better, perhaps applying different ways of orchestrating it, and different technologies in the assembly, for instance by making notes, mindmaps, and so on.

Although there is no direct causal relationship between the plasticity of a pedagogy for the teacher and that for the student, there is a tendency for pedagogies that are soft for teachers also to be soft for students. The reason is that softer pedagogies for teachers tend to allow for (at least) a two-way flow between teacher and student and for students to take diverse paths in learning. Perhaps most importantly, soft pedagogies give teachers the flexibility to adapt to what they observe students want or need. Thus, as long as they can be aware of how students are responding, they can take greater control over the teaching process, so that both they and their students gain greater control over the learning process. Conversely, harder pedagogies for teachers also tend to be harder for students because they (rather than the needs of students) drive the process.

Pedagogies in Assembly

Pedagogies are technologies for the same reason that computer programs are technologies, and like computer programs they are nothing without their instantiation: they need a machine to run on, whether that is a soft substrate of human interaction, or an institutional system, or an LMS. Thus, though it is possible to describe pedagogies in fairly abstract terms, they become working technologies only when they are organized with other stuff to attempt to achieve the aim of learning. Teachers do not need to design all the parts. As Hlynka and Jacobsen (2010) observe, "most educators are not in the business of designing or inventing the hardware, cables and connectors. Instead, educators select and evaluate technological processes and resources; they create environments and design learning experiences; they assess learners and deep learning and evaluate the quality of performances. In short, educational technologists are interested in creating and evaluating learning and performances that are more effective or efficient because of the technological processes and resources."

What Hlynka and Jacobsen (2010) leave unsaid is that it is common for some of the parts themselves to include pedagogies, for instance the implicit assumptions of lecture theatres, the multiple pedagogies embedded in textbooks, regulations for exams, and so on. Pedagogies can be instantiated in countless ways as simple as words, gestures, or actions or as complex as a book, computer program, or classroom, with all the surrounding complex interrelations that such technologies entail. Although we might be able to describe it in abstract terms as a distinct tool/method/technique/process/structure/model/and so on, a pedagogy is not recognizable as a technology until it is instantiated, which always means that it is part of an assembly. If we are investigating the effects of pedagogies, then of necessity we are also investigating the assemblies, including other technologies, with which they are orchestrated.

Pedagogies Rarely If Ever Come First

If they are parts of other assemblies, then pedagogies should rarely if ever literally come first in a learning design process. Pedagogies are technologies that orchestrate other technologies and phenomena, and exist within larger assemblies, so these other technologies and phenomena must already exist. More often than not, pedagogies' forms are dictated at least partially by technologies with which they are assembled and by the limits of how they can be orchestrated together. Often the parts with which they are assembled can be harder, and thus more structurally dominant, than the pedagogies themselves, and/or the pedagogies can be part of a larger assembly, such as an educational system. This means that, though it is reasonable for learning designers and teachers to say "pedagogy first" if all that they mean by it is that we should not forget that our purpose is to teach, it is not true if they mean that pedagogies should always come first in the list of procedures and methods used to achieve that end and certainly not if they are talking about the assembly and orchestration used to attain it. Pedagogies are inseparable parts of an educational assembly, but they are just parts of the orchestration of the educational machine. Similarly, a bicycle must have wheels or it would not be a bicycle, but wheels do not have to come first in the design, nor should they always dictate how the vehicle is designed (though they will always impose their own constraints, which can be strong in some cases).

Analogous to remembering that the purpose of teaching is to teach, a bicycle should normally transport its rider from A to B, but cost, comfort, speed, reliability, safety, and so on can be at least as important. Similarly, when designing or performing a learning intervention, costs, timetables, curricular constraints, resource availability, time constraints, tech options, and so on can matter to the designer or performer of them at least as much as the fact that the purpose is to teach and might well come prior to a consideration of teaching methods. Pedagogies are soft. The assembly always matters more than the parts. The parts are significant only in terms of how they relate to the whole. Equally, a student's pedagogies, in a formal learning context, can be subservient to a teacher's pedagogies. Although students can choose to orchestrate different phenomena to help them learn, the range of options available can be constrained. In too many cases, if they diverge too far from those intended or condoned, they can suffer punishments such as poor grades or the censure of the teacher.

Distributed Pedagogies

Pedagogies are not just technologies used by teachers in classrooms. Learners themselves are always the final orchestrators of phenomena for learning, and consciously or not they always apply strategies, techniques, and methods of their own to the process of learning. As Fawns (2022, p. 715) puts it, "students co-configure and co-design as they reinterpret and complete teachers' plans." Although others can strongly influence them, and they are certainly skills that can be learned and refined, a learner's own pedagogies invariably are parts of any educational assembly, and every learner will apply them differently because every learner is different.

But learners and designated teachers are far from being the only orchestrators of phenomena in a typical learning experience.

Beyond the pedagogies supplied by people designated as teachers and learners themselves, almost always, intentionally or not, pedagogies are added to the assembly by many others. Even within the extremely limited context of a conventional classroom, we might find pedagogies commonly used by

- other students discussing what they have learned;
- authors of textbooks writing in ways meant to teach;
- textbook illustrators using visual technologies to explain or amplify;
- textbook editors clarifying language and structure for clearer transmission;
- website developers building information and tutorial sources;
- computer technicians setting up projectors and smartboards who assume how they will be used;
- lab technicians setting out equipment in ways that assist understanding;
- technical authors of instruction manuals, like textbook authors, aiming to help learners understand their tools;
- writers of notices on walls intending to communicate quickly and efficiently;
- designers of school regulations intending to support successful learning;
- creators of timetables seeking appropriate times and durations for learning;
- librarians helping learners to learn how to find resources as well as finding resources themselves;
- classroom designers and architects whose assumptions about the teaching program influence their designs, and hence affect which teaching methods can be used effectively;

- purchasers of classroom furnishings assuming how they will be used;
- makers of exercise books assuming generic features of pedagogically useful note taking (e.g., flexible organization or margins); and
- curriculum designers operating sometimes at a national level.

All of these actors make decisions based upon (often tacit and sometimes erroneous) assumptions about their probable effects on learning and/or the teaching and learning methods that they will support, and all can have a greater or lesser effect on student learning in the classroom. Most can make all the difference between successful and unsuccessful learning. Invariably, there are countless co-participants contributing processes and structures that affect learning, for better or worse. There is often a recursive and complex relationship between these co-participants. For example, designers of classrooms (hopefully) will be influenced by what they imagine students and teachers in those classrooms will do, which in turn will influence what they actually do, which (if it differs from the program intended by the designer) will influence future designs.

Beyond the Class or Course

Learning does not begin or end in the classroom. Even if we confine ourselves solely to the subject of a lesson, it will also be affected by news articles read before and after the lesson, movies, Wikipedia articles, discussions on social media, conversations around the dinner table, a large number of objects, and interactions with other people before and well after the class, months, years, or decades in the future, all of which embed methods of passing on knowledge and skills. We place convenient boundaries around the time, the place, and the actors in a learning transaction, but those boundaries, in real life, are extremely fuzzy, permeable, and wide. What and how we learn become both grist and mill (Heyes, 2018) for future learning, and neither the "what" nor the "how" remains static. Knowledge and skills—including the skills of learning—are not saved to our brains like bits on a computer storage device but participate as active, constantly renewed, constantly transformed elements in our cognitive toolchest. When educators claim that students have achieved specific learning outcomes, they are referring at best to a snapshot of an ever-unfolding process that will continue indefinitely, whether gaining in richness or being forgotten (usually a bit of both). At least some of my teachers of 50 years ago continue to teach me today, for better or worse, persisting (with countless others) as co-participants in my ongoing learning journey.

Perhaps the majority of acts of communication are intended to affect the knowledge and behaviour of those with whom we communicate: in effect, to teach. As Dewey (1916, p. 9) put it, "not only is social life identical with communication, but all communication (and hence all genuine social life) is educative." To communicate, we must make assumptions about how our messages will be understood by others, and we must make decisions about how to express them effectively: in other words, we apply pedagogies. Most intentional communication is meant to bring about learning, whether or not we intentionally aim to teach. There are some possible exceptions, including performative utterances such as "I do" in a wedding ceremony (Austin, 2013), phatic expressions such as small talk (Zegarac, 1998), discussions of dinner plans, and so on. However, a great deal of what we try to express in language, image, video, sculpture, dance, and so on teaches, or attempts to do so, even if it is only an attempt to express how we feel, to impart information of transient value (e.g., how to get to one's hotel room), or to reinforce something already known. Even a poem—if it affects us—teaches us. It changes how we think, feel, or perceive. In fact, even phatic communication is usually intended to affect: to cement a relationship, acknowledge a connection, signal a willingness to communicate, and so on. It might not contribute directly to our long-term learning or ability to adapt, but it can be an important component of an assembly that does, supporting necessary bonding social capital for trust building and relationship forming between learners and between learners and teachers.

At the fuzziest end of the teaching spectrum, pedagogies can be found embedded in many structures and technologies, from classroom designs to learning management systems (the software as well as the contents that it displays or the interactions that occur within it). At the least, designers have some general scenarios and uses in mind when they are built that can reinforce some behaviours (e.g., tiered seating to support lectures) and inhibit others (e.g., user roles and permissions in an LMS that prevent exchanges between different courses, needlessly perpetuating a path-dependent design pattern of classroom walls invented solely to solve problems caused by the limitations of physical spaces).

Designers of technologies, buildings, furniture, and even clothing typically attempt to teach users about their purposes through the designs themselves, using obvious and subtle cues to invite people to use them in their intended ways. Even those that deliberately make their purposes obscure—hidden doors or safes that look like cans of beans—invite reflection on why that is. Books are made to be read, cups to be held and drank from. The neck of a guitar invites a particular kind of grip, and its frets invite a certain kind of finger placement. Symbols and labels tell us what buttons or bottle caps are supposed to do. Metaphors, conventions, skeuomorphic designs that recall prior technologies, and countless other acts of communication fill our designed world. We design things to be used, and in so doing we make assumptions about how people will learn to use them. In structuring our world to be intelligible, we are also making decisions about what makes it intelligible.

Cyborgs and Collectives

Even in the most highly structured and constrained circumstances, teaching is always a highly distributed technology, orchestrating many phenomena at many levels and in many assemblies, involving multiple pedagogies as well as other technologies, enacted by many different co-participants, each of whom, directly or indirectly, affects others in the assembly.

The many teachers who, intentionally or not, contribute to any learning that we accomplish can be thought of as a gestalt, as a distinct (if fuzzily boundaried) entity, a collective intelligence composed of purposeful acts of teaching, engagements with others, embedded learning in our technologies and artifacts, reified teaching in our communications, and active pedagogies in processes or methods that we have learned in the past. Each part contributes to the assembly through which we learn and with which we think. From words to textbooks, from theories to desks, from whiteboards to windows, the act of deliberate teaching is a largely unwitting cooperation between myriad teachers, all of whom are co-participants in multiple technologies.

Franklin's (1999) conflation of culture and technology acknowledges the fact that we and our technologies are inseparable parts of the same entangled coalition. Our technologies are a fundamental facet of what it means to be human living among other humans. Our technologies are what provide intellectual and creative potential that far exceeds that of any other known species. To live as a human being in a human society is continually to invent and instantiate soft technologies, as well as to incorporate the hard inventions of others into our own thinking, in an ongoing process of assembly and orchestration. The intelligence that results is only partly human. It is also partly something emergent, different from and perhaps greater than the sum of its parts, an entity in its own right, a collective. Indeed, it is a lot more than a single collective: there are many layers of emergence, many collective entities that make a difference, from groups to cultures to networks of people whom we know, along with the artifacts that they create (Davis & Sumara, 2006).

It is not unreasonable (if a little uncomfortable) to see ourselves as cyborgs, partly composed of technology (Haraway, 2013), but being a cyborg is an important part of what makes us distinctly human. Equally, though, and perhaps more interestingly, it is possible to see our technologies as cyborgs, partly made of us, partly made of one another, each part of the assembly perhaps another cyborg, a collective made of collectives. Without our technologies, we are just smart, social, and not particularly effective apes. Technologies embed as well as support pedagogies, and they mediate the collectives that learn, linking our cognition with part of a dynamic whole distributed in time and space. Humanity can only be understood properly as not just a collection of organisms but also the artifacts and processes that those organisms create and share.

Technologies—and our roles as co-participants in them—are what make us as individuals smart and what make our species collectively (and as a collective of collectives) intelligent or, as Cohen and Stewart (1997) put it, extelligent. This is not the same kind of smartness possessed by an individual human, and almost certainly it is not sentience or consciousness in any form that we would recognize. Intelligence, more generally, can be seen as the ability dynamically to adapt to and survive in an ever-changing environment: the evolution of species and even evolution itself (constantly evolving greater evolvability), in this sense, can be seen as an intelligent process (Watson & Szathmáry, 2016). Intelligence results in, and draws from, learning, but the learning does not have to be embodied in a brain. A brain is just one bounded emergent entity among many. Which entities we choose depend on where we draw the boundaries and what level of emergence we choose to observe. Davis and Sumara (2006, p. 86), for example, distinguish between species-level learning and individual-level learning: "Most dogs will instinctively leap back when encountering a snake or a snake-like object. Such an action is clearly an intelligent one, and has no doubt preserved the existence of many canines. However, it would be inappropriate to attribute the intelligence to the individual animal. Rather, this instance of smart response operates at the species-evolutionary level. The species selected the response, not the individual."

Collectively intelligent behaviours cannot just be ascribed to us as individuals, but seldom do they operate at a species level like the instinctive behaviours of dogs. We work and learn only with the technologies—tools, methods, artifacts, structures, and so on—that we encounter in our lives, only with a small subset of them, and only in a limited number of ways. There is thus a great deal of local variation in the skills and knowledge of a given network or community operating at multiple scales.

Given the massive spread of communication technologies, combined with the enormous networks of trade and travel that have featured in our evolution, what we have encountered for thousands of years, and at a vastly accelerating rate in recent centuries, has included technologies from around the world, leading some to suggest that what results is a worldwide collective, akin to or in some way implementing a global brain (Bloom, 2000). This might be so, in a broad sense, though it is not at all like a single, thinking, purpose-driven mind with its own will and consciousness. A large part of the reason for this is that none of us can ever see more than a fraction of it, let alone understand it in its entirety, any more than individual termites understand the complex mounds that they build or the collective behaviours of their colony. The parts in which we co-participate involve local, not global, action, and there is differentiation at an indefinitely large number of scales, from our personal networks or families, to the geographical communities that we inhabit, to our cultures, nations, religions, and many more smaller- and larger-scale clusters. One group, network, or set of people and its shared objects (cognitive and physical) can differ considerably from another, forming differently boundaried extelligences, though, just as each individual connects to every other, so too all connect at some level and thus co-participate in one another and ultimately with all others.

The various collective entities that we participate in, in some though not all ways, might be smarter than us as individuals: they certainly know a lot more, but they can act more intelligently too. Collectively, for instance, we have created many extraordinarily complex technologies without any individual actually understanding them. As Derex et al. (2019) demonstrate, the accumulated improvements of technologies made over generations can lead to technologies based upon poor causal reasoning (individually) but that nonetheless embody far more complex causal relations. For example, to create optimal bows and arrows from scratch would require multidimensional causal thinking—including knowledge of things such as gravity, inertia, and stored energy—that would have been impossible for our forebears. However, thanks to improvements made over many generations, using incorrect causal reasoning, bows and arrows used by our ancestors were as highly optimized as any that we could create with our more advanced knowledge of physics. In effect, by embedding the learning of many individuals, our technologies can become smarter than us as individuals, and thus we, as participants in them, become smarter too. Perhaps as interestingly, we (and the word *we* speaks volumes) have now developed the cognitive technologies to understand the complex design issues involved, at least in part thanks to the examples provided by such technologies. Technologies are not just the results of intelligence but also participate in it, because we participate in them.

We are not at all like *Star Trek*'s Borg, in the sense of being one vast collective entity with a single and centrally managed will. Instead, we interact with people and artifacts around us, which in turn interact with others, and so on, each making its own interpretations and transformations, in ever-spreading, scale-free networks that cluster around us and that unfold continuously into the world. In this sense, we are somewhat like ants or termites, communicating stigmergically with one another through the signs that we leave in our environments (Dron, 2004). Like ants and termites, mostly we see and communicate only with our immediate environment (people, groups of people, and their artifacts), and we have a dim idea, at most, of the whole. Unlike termites, through our technologies we can come to know any part of the whole.

Technologies enable us to achieve goals more quickly, more easily, without needing to learn the knowledge that they embody, and to move on from there. Johnson (2012, Section 2, para. 10), for instance, describes the near-miraculous safe landing of a stricken plane as "a kind of duet between a single human being at the helm of the aircraft and the embedded knowledge of the thousands of human beings that had collaborated over the years to build the Airbus A320's fly-by-wire technology." Notwithstanding the effort that might be needed to learn to use them, hard technologies often eliminate the need for their users to go through the sometimes gruelling and, for any moderately complex system, impracticably lengthy process of learning the same things. They are co-participants in both our actions and our cognition, extensions of our minds that overlap with extensions of other people's minds, in a rich and ever-shifting tapestry of shared cognition.

This is the essence of the dynamic of socially distributed cognition: the learning of others is a part of the objects, buildings, and other stuff they create. It is what makes the human race smart (Henrich, 2017), far more than the individual intelligence of its members. We are able to affect our environment massively, in both negative and positive ways, because we do not have to rely on our own intelligence, or even that of those in the vicinity, but can incorporate the combined wisdom and reified knowledge of countless others, including our forebears, into our thinking and use the technologies that others have built (cognitive, physical, or whatever) in our activities. Any individual intelligence that we possess is almost entirely founded on our collective intelligence as cultures and societies.

My cognition is partly shared with yours, and partly with anyone (though likely not everyone) else's on the planet, including many of those who lived before us. We are able to use and participate in technologies that we have learned from others to orchestrate other technologies around us, in order to think and act intelligently ourselves, in ways that can be used and orchestrated by others. When we enact hard technologies, we are just part of that orchestration, but when idiosyncratic technique and creativity come into play, especially when others must perform acts of interpretation using their own extended minds, our collective mind adapts to the world that it both invents and inhabits. The technologies are not just extensions of our own minds but also the means through which our minds become intertwingled with those of others.

Given these multiple layers of bounded learning systems in which we participate, learning can be understood properly only as a distributed function, and teaching can be seen only as a collective pursuit in which we are at once co-participants and co-beneficiaries. This is one of the reasons that learning with, from, and through others is such a good idea. There are richly recursive feedback loops that are filtered through and orchestrated by those involved, all of whom see different parts of the whole, and that make the whole much greater than the sum of its parts. Teachers do not just teach individuals in a class: they teach the class itself, and the class teaches back. Classrooms cannot and should not be seen as disconnected entities, however. All members of the class are part of many cultures, large and small, partly defined by common technologies—at least vocabularies, norms, and shared communication tools—that participate in our learning and our thinking.

Given the irreducible complexity and extraordinary scope of the phenomena that must be orchestrated, not to mention the vast range of possible orchestrations, the chances of two particular assemblies—two instances of learning—ever being more than a bit similar are remote. The fact that the larger and slower parts of the system will likely result in some recognizable shapes and patterns when viewed at a coarse level hides a wealth of detailed differences. The chances that they are identical are zero because the world (as experienced) is constantly unfolding and always experienced differently by each person at a particular place and time, each with unique histories interacting with countless other unique histories. It is no more possible to repeat a learning experience than it is to restore prairies or woodlands to their historical states (Katz, 1992), because the unique complex phenomena that led to those states can never be the same twice. To learn is to change in ways that have never happened before and will never happen again in the whole history of the universe. Although an individual teacher might precisely replicate a method, or it might be recorded through a replicable medium, teaching, viewed as a distributed technology involving countless phenomena, including those provided by the learner, is therefore always a creative act that can never fully repeat itself, any more than one meadow or forest can ever be identical to another, let alone to one in the past. Parts can be the same, but the whole never is. Just as we have seen how computers and many other technologies should be treated as different technologies according to the boundaries that we choose and the points of view that we take, so too pedagogies that we apply as intentional teachers can only ever be part of a much larger assembly. And, as for the computer, the pedagogies that such teachers intentionally use can be among the least significant parts of the technology that brings about learning. They are not, however, unimportant.

The picture that I have painted of a massively complex, only partially designed gestalt might seem to leave little room for education systems and formal teaching. However, like all complex systems, the harder, larger, slower-moving parts have large roles to play in giving shape, purpose, and structure to the overall system. Just because teachers, education systems, and all their associated methods do not lead to predictable, deterministic results (and, even if they do, invariably they lead to others unintended) does not mean that they lack value or influence.

The Value of Education

Education (in its broadest sense) brings stability or—if it works well—metastability in society, a state of continuity that, like human bodies or ecosystems, maintains its identity but constantly adapts to changes from within and without. Education is concerned with enabling us to operate as humans in a human society, co-participating in its many technologies, and thus for society itself to adapt to its needs and to operate effectively. Without education, societies as we know them today could not exist or, at best, would be horrifically unstable and weakly adaptive. Education is for the benefit not just of individual students but also of everyone in a society. The kinds of knowledge enabled through education systems make it possible for each of us not only to operate the technologies of our societies and cultures successfully but also to play our roles in making them work for everyone. The numerous technologies and the great complexity of this collective endeavour thus provide a good case for moderately consistent, fairly hard education systems, albeit that institutions of the sort with which we are most familiar might not be the only or best solutions to the problem. Excessive hardness—where everyone is forced to learn the same things in the same ways—creates far bigger problems than those that it solves, however. If the needs of society are solely for people to play their roles in predesigned hard technologies, then such uniformity might have some value, though the value of such a society itself might be limited, unless you happen to be one of the few who has control over those hard technologies. Societies that can adapt to changing conditions need people with soft skills who can orchestrate technologies creatively, flexibly, and well, not just correctly. Systems that seek to inflict hard pedagogies on teachers and/or students, especially at scale, run a huge risk of training a population to be part of a large, inflexible machine, adept at performing large-scale coordinated tasks, capable of solving known problems, but less able to adapt to new ones. Given the inevitable expansion of both the adjacent possible brought about by our technologies and the problems that they in turn cause, which consequently have to be solved by counter technologies, an overly hard educational focus is unlikely to be the best way forward in the years ahead.

The technologies of institutional education can make designated teachers among the harder, more influential parts of the educational assembly. In sharing received wisdom they tend to act as preservers of relatively invariant cultural knowledge. However, as teachers, in our pedagogical designs and methods, we must be aware of the gestalts with which they are combined; we need to remember that we must be responsive to the effects that our interventions have when assembled with countless other interventions; we should be prepared to adapt or at least to acknowledge ways that our plans can and will be subverted, transformed, or distorted by the whole. The deeply complex interweaving of technologies in which we are co-participants means that outcomes can be very different from, and almost always far richer than, those that we intend. Teaching changes the extended mind in which we are co-participants, and thus it changes (or should change) us and our teaching in an ever-repeating and complex recursive cycle.

Teaching, done right, is learning. Pedagogies are soft technologies in which we constantly reinvent, transform, and embroider the coarser and harder methods from which they are assembled, in ways never to be replicated again. As we do so, the fabric of knowledge and skills woven takes on a character and form that no one can predict with any precision but that, acting locally and seeing how it changes, we can build upon and influence. Often we can take the mistakes, the serendipitous emergent forms, or the unexpected patterns and turn them into something closer to what we aimed for or (perhaps) into something new and more wonderful than what we planned.

Teaching is a form of distributed, partly emergent, contextually situated bricolage in which our designs are assembled with as well as from other pieces, so we must be aware of and responsive to all those pieces, including those provided by the learner, if our designs are to be successful.

The in-person teacher can use any of an almost infinite variety of technologies, including pedagogies, as part of the bricolage and can observe the learning behaviours of students closely as long as there are not too many of them. However, being aware of the parts is perhaps even more important when we have limited opportunities to interact with our students, such as when teaching asynchronously online or dealing with large classes. Because we cannot be as directly responsive, and because students will inevitably learn independently no matter what we might plan, our designs need to acknowledge the distributed teacher, to provide freedom to diverge. We need to design ways to observe and, if possible, to engage with that distributed teacher.

Pedagogical technologies that reveal the process such as shared reflective learning diaries (blogs, wikis, etc.), shared discussion spaces, as well as shared products of learning (assignments, essays, projects and other shared inventions and discoveries) can help to reveal many of the other participants in the gestalt. We might not be able accurately to plan everything that will happen, but we can respond to what does happen and, in so doing, help to guide the process. We are more like sailors or balloonists, seeking the winds and using them to guide us, than like drivers of trains, guiding machines along well-defined tracks.

For those of us who are employed as teachers in an institutional learning environment, the realization that we are not in control, that we are part of a collective, and that teaching is a soft technology enacted by many people apart from us comes with the critical proviso that we must stay close to our students in order to understand how they are navigating this complexity.

7 | Theories of Teaching

> *Whenever a theory appears to you as the only possible one, take this as a sign that you have neither understood the theory nor the problem which it was intended to solve.*
>
> —Karl Popper (1972, p. 266)

In this chapter, I situate the co-participation model in a broader field of educational theories and models, using the participatory distinction between soft and hard technologies to shed light on families of existing teaching approaches that are typically seen as mutually exclusive, and I suggest ways in which they can usefully connect together. Viewed as technologies, pedagogies are parts of assemblies and composed of other parts and other assemblies. It is possible therefore to think differently about disparate learning and teaching models not as fundamentally irreconcilable perspectives but as components that can be used to more thoughtfully construct learning events, activities, and environments.

Pedagogical Families

Terry Anderson and I (2011, 2012) divided the field of distance learning into three distinct (but persistent and nowadays coexistent) generations defined by the dominant pedagogies of successive historical periods. The first we originally described as behaviourist/cognitivist, though recently we have preferred the term "objectivist" (Dron & Anderson, 2022) because what binds such pedagogies is not a set of methods or common theories but the assumption that there is an independent true body of knowledge to be learned and an optimal set of methods to learn it, whatever that might be. Some prefer the term "instructionist" (e.g., Johnson, 2009), which effectively captures the pedagogical emphasis of such approaches, but I am reluctant to fully endorse the negative attitude that it implies, and it is equally applicable to learners who apply such methods themselves.

The second generation we originally described as social-constructivist but now prefer to label as "subjectivist" (Dron & Anderson, 2022), reflecting its epistemological underpinnings that focus on how subjects construct knowledge (not normally that reality is subjective). Subjectivist pedagogies assume that knowledge is individually and socially constructed rather than (or, more often, in addition to) being independently true. Typically, subjectivist teachers adopt a softer set of pedagogies such as problem-based, inquiry-based, and other more student-directed active learning techniques. Some, such as those of Papert (Papert & Harel, 1991) and Piaget (1952), focus mainly on individuals' learning, whereas others, such as those of Dewey (1916) and Vygotsky (1978), treat learning as fundamentally social in process and substance.

The third generation we (Dron & Anderson, 2011) initially labelled as connectivist (with a small c to distinguish it from the specific theory of that name) to describe models of learning developed in an age of information plenty. We now (Dron & Anderson, 2022) follow Davis and Sumara (2006) in describing this generation of models as "complexivist" because all share the common feature of seeing learning and the processes of learning as complex adaptive systems, many predate Connectivism, and the term better reflects the diversity of the field. Complexivist models treat knowledge as distributed, situated, complex, emergent, as much embedded in the networks of people and stuff that surround us as in our own brains.

Although our model was used to examine the history of distance education, it has broader applicability as a means to distinguish all families of pedagogical theory. In brief, objectivism is concerned with theories of teaching, subjectivism with theories of learning, and complexivism with theories of knowledge. Thus, they can be seen as orthogonal views of the same basic phenomena, and, as I hope to show, they are not mutually exclusive. Each can play a complementary role in the educational technology assembly.

Objectivist Pedagogies

Objectivist pedagogies typically consist of a fairly hard series of steps to be followed, by both teacher and learner, to achieve a specified predefined learning goal, with clearly defined objectives and clearly measurable outcomes. There are two broad families of objectivist theories, typically labelled as behaviourism and cognitivism, both of which look to reductionist studies of how humans learn for their foundations. Behaviourist pedagogies focus on discovering causes and effects in behaviour, deliberately ignoring whatever goes on in learners' minds because (practitioners believe) they are not observable and therefore not susceptible to scientific study.[4] Cognitivist pedagogies build models of mental processes borne out by empirical studies and theories of mind and use them to identify ways of teaching that effectively bring about learning. Both families, however, are focused on finding the most effective ways to engender established skills and knowledge: to bring about specific changes in learners.

These transmissive pedagogies, explicitly or not, have dominated formal education for much of its history, right up to the present day. The teacher-dominated model that an objectivist view embodies has often played roles of indoctrination, preparation for factory work, training for military engagement, and so on, to support a particular powerful organization (religious, commercial, government, or military) that requires uniform knowledge, skills, and understanding in its subjects. Objectivist pedagogies are well suited to preparing individuals to act as cogs in a machine. Although uncomfortably extended into softer domains, this remains a central motivation for objectivist teaching, in which education systems are primarily seen as incubators for roles in industry, commerce,

---

4 This approach fails to acknowledge the inconvenient fact that underpins this book: the ways in which we educate people are technological inventions and thus might not represent generalizable phenomena that apply in every imaginable situation, unlike the learning of rats and chickens that underpins many of the most foundational models on which behaviourists rely.

and service. Such pedagogies were also popular in the early days of distance learning because the non-pedagogical technologies for distance learning available at the time did not make two-or more-way communication easy, fast, cheap, or effective, if it was even possible. The adjacent possibles for the uses of more social, open-ended, discursive pedagogies were limited and, when available, were expensive, unreliable, and awkward to use, so, regardless of a particular teacher's beliefs about the nature of education, they were largely off limits. Inevitably, objectivist pedagogies tend toward hardness and the invention of methods to efficiently transfer the knowledge of the teacher to the heads of the learners. It is also noteworthy that this model is focused on individual learning and pays little or no attention to the learning of groups, collectives, or other social wholes. Although, in assembly, objectivist pedagogies can support softer learning, and many profess to achieve softer outcomes, by far their most natural application lies in the development of hard skills, memorization tasks, and easily measured competencies.

Subjectivist Pedagogies
Subjectivist methods are based upon the assumption that perception and understanding involve an active process of construction in which individuals are not blank slates on which knowledge can be inscribed but active creators of meaning, connecting prior (and sometimes instinctual/innate/epigenetic) knowledge with new learning to bring about something unique and situated within a context. Social constructivist models, typically (albeit often loosely) based upon models and ideas proposed by Dewey (1916) and Vygotsky (1978), see this as a fundamentally intersubjective and social process, whereas cognitive constructivist models focus more on an individual's construction of knowledge. Whichever flavour is dominant, most subjectivist teaching methods involve group processes, dialogue, problem solving, and relatively free-form inquiry or exploration.

There is great variety in subjectivist pedagogies, ranging from Piagetian models that focus on the role of the teacher to andragogical models (e.g., Knowles, 1975) that primarily emphasize the role of the learner. Pedagogies informed by subjectivist principles are usually much softer for the learner because the learner must actively construct knowledge in a flexible and unpredictable social environment in which change and diversity are valued features rather than obstacles to overcome. This applies to method as well as to outcome. Flexibility and the need for learners to invent and apply their own pedagogical methods to make sense of phenomena are perhaps their most defining features. They are also much softer for the teacher, who must fill the gaps with reactive and proactive pedagogies to sustain learner interest and focus. Although they might specify broad processes to achieve learning, subjectivist pedagogics are deliberately loose and rely on creativity and active involvement in all the parties involved. Subjectivist approaches are inherently soft, situated, and (in the case of social constructivism) co-constructed, acknowledging the contributions made by both learners and groups of learners to the process and accepting that different learners and their social groups—typically classes, tutorial groups, and so on—will follow diverse paths toward shared goals. However, in formal education, those goals are usually specified in advance, with measurable outcomes that are tied to assessments. Although learners in a subjectivist system orchestrate much more of the process than those taught using objectivist pedagogies, the use to which it is put is usually strongly determined by teachers and institutions.

Complexivist Pedagogies

In recent decades, the huge amount of information available on-demand through the internet, combined with the rich networks of people that form the read-write web, combined with a growing understanding of the significance of complex systems, combined with increasing recognition of the distributed nature of our cognition, has opened up new adjacent possibles into which complexivist models of learning have evolved. These models often occur in informal or non-formal learning, though they are common in MOOCs and, increasingly, in formal learning. Most complexivist models have emerged only in this century, including networks of practice (Wenger et al., 2011), Connectivism (Downes, 2008; Siemens, 2005), rhizomatic learning (Cormier, 2008), and heutagogy (Hase & Kenyon, 2007), though similar ideas can also be found in earlier models and theories such as distributed cognitive apprenticeship (Collins et al.,

1991), communities of practice (Wenger, 1998), and distributed cognition (Pea, 1993; Saloman, 1993). The co-participation model presented in this book is also part of this complexivist tradition, though—as I hope to show in this chapter—it is a more holistic model that equally encompasses earlier generations.

Complexivist models typically involve little formal teacher control. The teacher is just one well-connected or influential node of a broader distributed network, or a catalyst to action, but not the primary orchestrator of learner activities. Complexivist approaches tend

- to have vague or general pre-stated outcomes, often shaped by themes that emerge through interactions of individuals in the network;
- to celebrate serendipity, path divergence and diversity of views;
- to be highly situated in practice, not just within a formally constituted group of individuals but also in a broader social network;
- to have no formally constituted groups, with no formal leaders, limited formal rules, and often indistinct time frames and schedules;
- to have limited predetermined resources and to rely more heavily on those shared by participants (everyone is a teacher and a learner);
- to not be explicitly assessed or to make use of expansive, non-predetermined, open-outcome forms of assessment, often through fuzzy measures such as reputation or approval of peers;
- to acknowledge that each individual will learn differently (unlike constructivism), learn different things than every other, and then share that knowledge within their networks;
- to be highly focused on action and enactment—doing stuff, with stuff, in concrete, unique, unrepeatable, socially rich situations.

Complexivist pedagogies evolved thanks to the vast expansion of available information and connection with others enabled by the internet. This is qualitatively as well as quantitatively different, because artifacts created by and interactions between learners, by default, are reified persistently.

Thus, the process of learning becomes part of the substrate for further learning. A typical traditional in-person course (whether objectivist or subjectivist) is designed by one teacher or a small group of teachers (notwithstanding the many contributions of others), and then the course runs, interactions occur, work is done, and the course is gone with barely a trace left behind. Teachers can modify their approaches in the next iteration, and individual students can keep their work for later reference, but otherwise a course tends to be an ephemeral occurrence that lives only as an episode in the memories of participants. In online complexivist models, things shared, and discussions that surround them, can persist for many years and continue to play significant roles in the learning of those who come later, providing in MOOCs what Cormier (2014) refers to as "zombie courses." This is an evolutionary process, with emergent structures and patterns constantly unfolding, branching, and coalescing. The environment of learning itself evolves as a result of the learning that occurs within it. As a result of all these dynamics, complexivist approaches tend to be extremely soft.

Assemblies of Pedagogies

I have presented these paradigms of pedagogical theory in order of harder to softer: objectivist, subjectivist, and complexivist. In distance education, this is also the order in which they emerged, largely because of the constraints imposed by the communications technologies with which they were assembled, path dependencies caused by what was inherited from in-person education, and the affordances of new inventions such as the internet that created adjacent possibles into which they could evolve. However, though often presented as competing models or successive generations, the reality is far more complex. Far from competing, it is normal to find all coexisting in any given learning trajectory, each playing a different but complementary role in the process. Indeed, there are arguments to be made that this should be so, because each speaks to different aspects of the educational assembly.

Objectivist (behaviourist and cognitivist) pedagogies are usually fairly hard, from a learner's perspective, and often prescriptive. However, bearing in mind the inherently distributed nature of teaching, pedagogies are soft for learners as well as their ostensible teachers, so the reality has always been that learners under such conditions seldom follow the rigid paths determined for them by instructional designers (Haughey & Muirhead, 2005). Although the norm in distance learning, this is even true, to an extent, in tightly controlled traditional classrooms. In a fascinating in-depth study of a small selection of learners in a conventional classroom, Nuthall (2005) found that they had critical learning experiences because of their own self-designed experiences and resources (from 6.5% of the time for the lowest achiever to 13.1% for the highest), and all learned through interactions with others (from 6.5% to 14.8% of the time, similarly related to lower and higher achievement), and that was not counting occasions when the teacher gave them choices that made them partly autonomous by design.

Asynchronous learners who work independently, of necessity have more choices than synchronous learners in a classroom—because a teacher does not directly control any moment of the activity—so the overall technology of learning is therefore, at least for the duration of the formal teaching process, almost invariably softer, regardless of the teacher's intentions. For students trapped in a physical classroom, though they will construct their knowledge differently and play some of the teaching role for themselves, the pedagogy used by the teacher, especially when following a typical lecture format, may be considerably harder than it would be for students watching (for example) a videotaped lecture online, which they can pause and rewind or play at a different speed as needed. Notwithstanding a reduced capacity to interrupt to seek a different explanation (something that normally demands assembly with other technologies, such as discussion forums in a distance setting), the online learner usually controls the pace, the place, and the time of learning and typically is more able than an in-person counterpart to take divergent paths not planned by the learning designer. There are distinct limits to this autonomy. The fact that the almost ubiquitous focus on set outcomes and the assessment of those outcomes makes the distance teacher's control strong and places fixed limits on how far a learner can diverge, so detracting significantly from learner autonomy, but (compared with an in-person classroom context) there is always greater freedom to follow alternative paths to achieve the same goals. Objectivist assessments have a tendency to focus on those fixed outcomes, and it is not uncommon to find the use of objective tests, the hardest of all assessment technologies, playing a significant role as well as other mostly hard assessment tools such as written exams and quizzes. For distance learners, given the absence of classroom roles that emphasize the dominance of the teacher, these are often the primary means by which teachers assert control over the learning process.

Whereas objectivist models are explicitly concerned with teaching or training, subjectivist theories are primarily concerned with learning. This means that teaching processes do not arise directly from theory but are developed with a learner model in mind and assembled responsively as that model changes. Subjectivist pedagogies thus tend to be softer than their objectivist counterparts, requiring learners to engage creatively with problems, discussions, arguments, and constructions, each learning in unique ways because part of the process is enacted explicitly by the learner in interaction with others. This has led to some criticisms. Some have noted that subjectivist approaches tend to be time consuming, inefficient, and expensive (Annand, 1999, 2019), and this is indeed what lies at the root of what Daniel et al. (2009) describe as the "iron triangle" of access, cost, and quality—the need for skillful technique and constant adaptation makes subjectivist approaches expensive and unreliable. Others object to the softness itself.

It is precisely that softer lack of prescribed process that Mayer (2004) finds objectionable about pedagogies based upon subjectivist principles. If learners are left entirely to their own devices and have insufficient skills to add their own pedagogical processes, then the results might be (and often are) relatively poor when measured by predetermined outcomes. Equally, if unskilled teachers fail to provide the necessary scaffolding and support, then there is a good chance that their efforts will fail. However, though such instances can and do occur frequently, Mayer is wrong to dismiss subjectivist methods altogether. First, the notion of the unguided learner who makes discoveries alone is a myth: we have already seen that there are always other teachers, and this is explicit in social constructivist pedagogies. Second, a lack of prescribed process does not mean a lack of process: it is just a softer technology that leaves plentiful gaps to be filled, and therefore demands active creation and refined technique by its instantiators, who might do it well or not. Because they are soft, subjectivist methods usually require responsiveness, skill, and talent from a teacher (especially when learners are inexperienced in the method and/or subject area), who must responsively adapt and invent pedagogies to address changing needs and concerns as individual and group problems are addressed. This is both the biggest weakness and the greatest strength of such pedagogies, inasmuch as a poor (or time-poor) teacher will do much worse and a good (or time-rich) teacher will do much better. In social constructivist approaches, there are likely many teachers, further softening the overall assembly.

Effective subjectivist methods are not free, however, of cognitivist or even behaviourist pedagogies. Every participant in every group of learners has a model of how others learn that is brought into play during interactions with them, and this is especially true of one playing an explicit teacher role, who may use any number of different pedagogies along the way to help support learners in their discoveries. Simply explaining the process, even if it is thereafter very hands off, demands at least a rough model of how best to impart information in a manner that will be understood, remembered, and utilized by the learner (and is often one of the ways that it goes wrong). Objectivist pedagogies are therefore unavoidable. However, the difference between subjectivist and objectivist models tends to be not that subjectivist teachers avoid objectivist approaches altogether (which would be absurd and inefficient) but that, they are assembled as needed, often on demand, rather than being dictated in advance by an outcomes-focused teacher.

Complexivist models, notably in their most archetypal form of Connectivism, are not quite theories of learning nor theories of teaching but theories of knowledge. Their various forms explain how knowledge comes to emerge in individuals and in networks or groups of connected individuals and the artifacts that they create. Common to this idea is that bounded systems—from cities to ecologies to termite colonies to human brains—learn in analogous ways, adapting and accommodating change through similar processes. Therefore, the boundaries of the "system that learns" are not necessarily drawn around the learner. The learner is one significant bounded element of the process, recursively a part of a whole taught by the whole. As Davis and Sumara (2006, p. 15) put it, "the physical or conceptual boundaries of a complex/open system are always contingent on the criteria used to define or distinguish the system from its backdrop." They explain that, "in complexity terms, learners can include social and classroom groupings, schools, communities, bodies of knowledge, languages, cultures, species—among other possibilities" (p. 14). In such a system, technologies are not just reflections or products of cognition but also active participants in it.

Given that the self-organized emergence of order in richly connected systems is central to all variants of the complexivist model, and that intentional design tends to take a more reactive, partial, and (if visible at all) structural role, complexivist pedagogies, such as they are, are thus so soft that they might provide little or no process guidance beyond dictating a theme or general principles of assembly. This is particularly significant when we remember the mantra that soft is hard, and hard is easy. As we move away from objectivist teaching methods, learners have to make more and more creative decisions, to be active creators, not just users, of the pedagogy. Because pedagogies (to the creator) are soft technologies, it is possible to create them and use them with greater or lesser expertise. In complexivist accounts, this relates not only to individuals but also to the social networks, groups, and sets of which they are parts, to which it is rarely easy to ascribe volition, let alone intention or design. Nonetheless, collectives (emergent entities formed from local interactions of independent agents), as well as designed technologies, more formal groups, and their processes, play important roles in shaping the behaviour of self-organizing systems. Locally, at the level of an individual learner, hardness can start to creep in through both intentional design and unintended emergent structure.

Achieving the right balance between soft and hard is important, and it is not enough simply to assume that the right help is a click away. Learners must be able to choose when to choose, because choice alone does not give them control (Dron, 2007). Once again complexivist accounts might explain how knowledge emerges, but, beyond some broad patterns of role modelling and engagement, they do not predict in any detail how to make learning happen, let alone what will be learned. It is not a totally self-organizing free-for-all but a richly connected assembly of both intentional and unintentional interactions and processes. This itself is in keeping with a complexivist account given that complexity-driven explanations invariably recognize the emergence of different levels of explanation according to the boundaries that matter at any given time. Although there might be important and interesting commonalities (e.g., that they obey laws common to all scale-free networks), there is a need for different kinds of explanation of, say, the structure and dynamics of social groups or organizations than of, say, the exchange of chemical messengers in cells, neural networks, the operation of the endocrine system, or the formation of network cliques.

In both complexivist and subjectivist accounts, guidance can come from any of the many teachers in a learning transaction, but especially and most effectively it is best when it comes from the learner. Thus, for subjectivist and, especially, complexivist models of learning to work well, support is needed to allow learners to gain expertise in learning itself, to become effective users of pedagogies, not just to become proficient in the subject of what is being learned. This is an assembly that grows more by accretion than replacement. The assembly leads to greater overall softness, but the parts themselves can be hard. We still need to learn, for instance, hard, human-enacted technologies such as spelling or the actions needed to submit a blog post. One interesting feature of such phenomena is that the pedagogies used by learners typically, at the finest granularity, tend to be objectivist. It would make little sense for them to be anything else, though multiple scales of assembly can make it fairly common for subjectivist pedagogies to be assembled from other subjectivist pedagogies too.

Subjectivist and complexivist learning technologies are therefore assemblies constituted largely by objectivist pedagogies. Where they differ from purer objectivist pedagogies is that, to a greater or lesser extent, learners themselves perform much of the assembly, rather than their teachers, and (at all scales) the various participants have greater freedom in their choices of pedagogy than those following a more objectivist approach. In the case of complexivist models, it is assumed that there will be many teachers, including those that are non-human (software, texts, and emergent collective entities), and that learning will occur at a system-wide level as well as in the individuals of which the system is composed. Subjectivist and complexivist approaches have many advantages, not the least of which are the fact that learning is tailored to the learner and integrated with a learner's existing knowledge and the fact that hard prescriptive pedagogies forcefully applied by someone else are demotivating for the same reason that all prescriptive technologies sap motivation—they reduce control. However, their major disadvantage lies in the expertise needed to instantiate those pedagogies effectively. The enactment of an objectivist method demands relatively little skill, once it has been expertly designed. Objectivist pedagogies can be designed largely in advance, whereas subjectivist and especially complexivist pedagogies must be developed, or emerge, on the fly.

Because of their innate softness, to both learner and teacher, a teacher (including a learner) who wishes to use subjectivist or complexivist approaches needs to provide, discover, or invent support for the process. Technique is critical. In a subjectivist approach, this support typically takes the form of scaffolding, of creating tasks that gently lead learners outside their comfort zones while providing feedback, encouragement, and support, answering questions, prompting reflection, and critiquing methods. In a complexivist approach, it typically means modelling good practice, exposing ideas, providing opportunities and support for active creation, discovery, and curation of knowledge artifacts, revealing interesting and diverse resources, and helping to aggregate a strong network of interested people and artifacts they find or create around a topic. Often such support is emergent, for example through the sharing of useful ideas or resources that, if useful to more than one or two people, will be reshared and recommended by enough people to allow learners to assume some value in them. Digital tools for aggregation and discovery usually play a significant role in this process. Despite such possibilities, one of the most common criticisms of subjectivist and especially complexivist models is that learners can receive insufficient guidance. They can be set adrift, fail to notice important facts, take suboptimal learning journeys, or shuffle a limited range of ideas.

The social context often can work against them. As Kay (1996) explains, simply putting a piano in a classroom without support for learning it leads to a chopsticks culture in which little progress is made. The blind lead the blind. Although, especially in a complexivist model in which online resources play a significant role, the social environment can afford both exemplars and direct tuition, this can be haphazard, incomplete, and inadequate for individual needs. Although it is great to be exposed to diverse ideas, and to be afforded the opportunity to discover the best that the world has to offer, it is easy to learn falsehoods, or to learn ineffectively, or to learn too little. Much of my own early research was devoted to finding ways around these problems through software that supported the collective organization of resources, as summarized in Dron (2007). The challenge is to influence the development of the collectively generated, emergent structure so that it is more likely to support learning, with a focus on connections and the signals that pass between them. Analogously, just as the signals that pass between termites and their environment have evolved to support the building of intricate, air-conditioned towers that support the colony's well-being, so too it is possible to support signals that pass between learners to support effective learning.

Objectivist, subjectivist, and complexivist accounts of learning and teaching differ mainly in the relative softness or hardness of their orchestration. On closer examination, however, and from the perspective of a learner, the lines are blurry, and there are few hard and fast distinctions between them. When successful, objectivist models benefit from softening; likewise, complexivist and social constructivist models benefit from hardening. Although they might be the creations of their participants, the softest Connectivist MOOC (cMOOC) is filled with hard elements, and the hardest objectivist course, at least for mature and wise learners who exercise their autonomy, is as soft as it needs to be. Unsurprisingly, as Hattie (2013) notes, there turns out to be little difference in learning outcomes on average no matter what pedagogical method is used, but of course the devil is in the detail, and virtually no learner is average. For instance, when discussing the surprisingly minimal effects of class size on learning outcomes (measured in achievement), Hattie observes that different approaches are needed for different numbers of students, but it appears that a great many teachers adopt the same approach for all, thus negating any potential advantages or disadvantages of a particular class size.[5] Just because a particular set of pedagogies is used does not mean that it is used well. Pedagogies and other technologies have to work together if they are to be effective. Unfortunately, such issues are seldom examined with the care that they deserve in reductionist studies of educational interventions.

Mitra's Holes in Walls

Sugata Mitra's (2012) Hole in the Wall project affords a useful example of the interplay between different pedagogical models in a real-life setting. The project provided (and, at the time of writing, in some places continues to provide) internet-connected computers in open spaces, designed (through placement and positioning as well as software and design) so that only children would be likely to access them. In a loosely complexivist account of learning, Mitra writes of the remarkable way that what he describes as "self-organized learning" emerges as small groups of children gather around machines, without apparent guidance, and learn to operate them. As a result, they learn to use the machines to learn more, making and sharing discoveries with one another, co-creating learning strategies that result in all learning together in a virtuous circle of ever-increasing knowledge and understanding.

In keeping with complexivist accounts, Mitra (2012) puts this down to the combination of computers and the emergent processes of groups of children interacting with them and one another. The computers themselves are not the technologies that do the teaching: largely, the software

---

5 The kind of knowledge matters too. Interestingly, Taft et al. (2019) find that for distance learners larger class sizes are better suited to hard, foundational, factual literacies, whereas smaller class sizes are better suited to higher-order thinking, mastery, and skill development. Given the greater likelihood of hard, objectivist pedagogies in larger classes, and the greater chance of softer, social constructivist pedagogies in smaller groups, this accords well with the predictions of the co-participation model.

and content that they provide do the work, along with the interactions of the children with one another. The computers are filled with reifications of knowledge and ideas, myriad small, hard pieces that can be assembled together, each containing knowledge and learning, each filled with implicit ways of understanding the world. Some are objectivist tutorials, help files, and other deliberate acts of teaching, others are simply things to interact with and, in so doing, to learn from, in the subjectivist tradition. Attached to the internet, the kids have access to a countless number of teachers, including those who have embedded many intentional teaching processes as well as a vast amount of reified knowledge that, intentionally or not, informs, inspires, influences, and explains. Rather than having a single teacher, these children (potentially) have millions of them as well as (in a somewhat more self-organizing way) one another.

The internet links and connects them, cross-referenced and infinitely varied, the embodiment of the augmentative, cognitively enhancing Memex imagined in the mid-20th century by Vannevar Bush (1945). Through mistakes and accidental discoveries, amplified through implicit pedagogies employed by the children as they explore together, thought processes shape themselves around and with those offered by the machines. Beyond that, to use a computer means having to think, at some level, like the designer of the hardware and software that it uses. The user has to interpret both the explicit metaphors provided in an interface and the mental models of its designer. We do not necessarily need to be taught this by someone else, or to share the same models, as long as those whom we work with understand our meaning. Mitra notes that children create their own vocabularies for things such as icons and cursors in an act of sense making shaped around and by the machines.

What is less clear about the allegedly successful Hole in the Wall project is whether the pedagogies that emerge as children engage in constructive dialogue with the thought processes embedded in the machines are particularly efficient, effective, or useful: soft is hard. The pedagogies that children encounter are many and varied, and not all are of equal quality. They appear to work sometimes, and sometimes well, but this might well be a result of high motivation (the relatedness, control, and competence aspects that underpin intrinsic motivation are extremely high) and consequent time on task rather than innate value in the pedagogies that children encounter.

There are clues in Mitra's (2012) work that things are not quite as self-organizing as he suggests. In fact, even in the early interventions, there were pre-installed training programs provided by one of the project sponsors (a commercial learning technology company), each of which strongly embodied intentional teaching, though it is not clear to what extent they were used by the children.

In later studies, Mitra and his team have discovered that the addition of an adult mentor to help children focus more on specific tasks can increase the effectiveness of their learning by a considerable amount. The pedagogies employed by such mentors harden the assembly a little and, in so doing, increase the efficiency of the process, the focus, and the equity of use. The mentors play a guiding and moderating role, helping the children to discover things that might be more useful. Most of the computers provided in recent years have not been out in the open but in controlled spaces such as school playgrounds. In these later iterations of what Mitra (2012) somewhat misleadingly christened as SOLEs (self-organized learning environments), the pedagogies are far closer to subjectivist methods used in much traditional teaching than to a complexivist model, though they do benefit from the vast web of knowledge with which learners are connected.

Indeed, without mentors, things did not go well. Mitra sometimes leaves it unsaid that the original Hole in the Wall experiments were not a long-term success. After the researchers stopped paying attention, the holes in the wall soon succumbed to misuse and abuse, with larger and more assertive children dominating the process, great gender inequalities, vandalism, and lack of educational benefit. There was a great deal of game playing that might not have been particularly educational, notwithstanding whatever the kids learned by playing games and engaging in "negotiations" to use the machines (De Bruyckere et al., 2015, pp. 158–160).

The vast majority of the original holes in the wall are now simply that—holes in the wall. Having millions of teachers might seem to be a wonderful thing, but it is just as important to have the power to choose between them (Garrison & Baynton, 1987) and the support to discover their value.

It is not the specific methods that matter as much as their appropriate uses at the right times, and how they are assembled, that make a difference.

Using the Right Technologies

There is a place for more or less any technology, model, principle, or approach in any educational assembly as long as it works with the rest of the parts. If a designated teacher has not considered the process from the multiple perspectives implicit in objectivist, subjectivist, or complexivist models, then chances are that, somewhere in the assembly, they will occur anyway because each represents a meaningful and useful way of coming to know something. Designated teachers do not need to do or enable all of this, but they do need to be aware that it is happening. This is necessary because it is also important to ensure that one model does not inhibit or crowd out the others. Complexivist or subjectivist approaches are virtually useless without at least some objectivist teaching, whether it comes from the designated teacher, one another, the internet, a book, or a friend. Equally, an objectivist approach is virtually useless without careful consideration of the social context and the ways that hard skills and knowledge will be applied: at best it will demotivate, at worst it will be bypassed altogether (e.g., by cheating or dropping out). Without an authentic, meaningful, socially beneficial, and personally relevant context of application, without being put to uses that matter, the machines constructed in learners' heads will break, be forgotten, or, worse, be instantiated at a cost—in attitudes, values, and beliefs—greater than the benefit derived from them. Similarly, the goal-driven nature of subjectivist and objectivist models can blind both teachers and learners to the many other important effects and learning that result, and emergent effects of complexivist behaviours can create barriers or brakes on intended outcomes. Above all, therefore, there is a need for all teachers in the process—especially the learner and (where applicable) the designated teacher—to be aware of how, why, and for what purposes teaching occurs, from whatever sources it derives. If you learn anything from this book, then at least learn this: teaching must incorporate learning about whoever or whatever is learning. Even when we let go of the learning process, it is important to stay close to the learner.

8 | Technique, Expertise, and Literacy

It's not just learning that's important. It's learning what to do with what you learn and learning why you learn things that matters.

—Norton Juster (1962, p. 229)

Beyond broad pedagogical principles and theories, a co-participation perspective allows us to think differently about how learning occurs at individual and social levels and how teaching can affect it. It allows us to see that one part of the educational process is concerned with constructing "machines" in our (individual and social) minds. Hard technologies such as rules of arithmetic or grammar are clearly analogous to their physical counterparts, as are the methods and procedures that we must learn in order to participate in other hard technologies. It also allows us to see that soft techniques—how we use such hard knowledge—are equally if not more significantly developed by educational processes and are the main reasons that we create those hard machines in our minds in the first place. We do not just learn to be like machines in order to behave as cogs within them. We normally learn to be like machines so that we can use them to do more, do better, do differently.

If a significant part of learning is concerned with the creation of technologies in our minds, then it seems to be reasonable to suppose that those technologies will behave in the ways that, as we have seen, all technologies behave. In this chapter, I discuss some of the ways that this plays out in practice.

Hard Skills, Soft Skills, and Technique

The hard skills required to enact even the softest technologies demand what we commonly refer to as "technique," by which I mean how something—a method—is done by a human being. Machines do not have techniques, but people (and perhaps some other animals) do. A technique is a way of doing something: holding a pencil, moving a bow over strings, giving constructive feedback, and so on. Viewed at a fine-grained level, techniques are methods, but they are more than that. They tend to be idiosyncratic, seldom if ever recur in the same way twice, and evolve over time as we become more proficient.

People can develop and hone their technique, and, if a technology is even moderately soft, they can improve it indefinitely. For instance, if our intention is to write a sentence with a pencil, then we need hard motor skills to hold the pencil and to control it on the paper; we need to know about spelling, syntax, and semantics; we need to know the alphabet that we are using; and so on. The letters that we write must be sufficiently similar to their numerous archetypes to be legible. There are hard techniques of handwriting that must be performed correctly. However, there are only fairly soft and diverse rules about what "correct" means, and the chances of writing even a single letter in the same way from one word to the next are slim: handwriting is highly idiosyncratic, as are styles of writing. It is therefore possible to express much more than the words that we write in how we write them: handwriting can convey mood or personality as much as it can represent words. Given that the majority of our uses of writing have a softer purpose, we also need to be able to use the words that we write creatively, to express our thoughts, beliefs, and arguments, each of which demands a host of both softer and harder skills and techniques: uses of metaphor, knowledge of different ways of structuring a narrative, and so on, not to mention knowledge of phenomena such as what is acceptable to an audience, what is expected, and which effects we want to achieve. The many phenomena orchestrated range from hard rules that should not be broken (e.g., application of APA citation rules) to much softer ones that can be broken with impunity and used with virtually limitless creativity, such as

where

to

break

a line of text.

It can take time to learn how to use both soft and hard techniques, but the human role differs in each. Soft techniques can be complex. Skill is needed to use them well. Hard techniques can be complicated. Skill might be needed to enact them correctly, but, no matter how complicated they can become, there is still one and only one way to enact them.

Soft techniques take form, in part and sometimes in whole, in the human mind (however we conceive it, extended into the world or the body). They become softer the more we use them because our minds change by using them, and, recursively, we change the enactment of the technologies as a result. As we learn more, more adjacent possibles emerge, paths that were not there before, because each new capability that we develop offers opportunities for further capabilities to emerge. For the most part, this is an additive process: what we learn does not replace what came before it, so it increases our potential to do more. The technology itself plays a part in our cognition, often leveraging our thinking to new and different levels. In effect, the technique becomes softer as it and we evolve. This is mainly why we practise: to become more skillful and more capable of a wider variety of things. Although we might get pleasure from the practice itself, its purpose is usually to perfect (or, more precisely, to aim for perfection in) the hard techniques required to make the technologies soft: to become better practitioners. From playing a violin to drawing, from writing to playing chess, each new technique that we learn expands the adjacent possible. We can not only to do what we could do before but also new things that, in turn, make further things doable. It is a powerful learning process or, more accurately, part of an assembly that leads to learning.

Techniques assembled in this way are aggregations that are adapted and refined as we learn more. The more we know, the greater the adjacent possibles, the softer the technologies become. Just as physical machines and devices evolve through assembly, so too techniques join and merge to create something new, with different parts often enriching others. For instance, we might apply tactics from one game in another or approaches to learning one musical instrument to a different one. Pedagogical methods, in particular, tend to be highly assemblable with others, and thus they are highly transferable to different contexts. We can learn ways to learn. Sometimes we invent new techniques. Technologies therefore learn, and, because we are part of them, as well as affected by them, we learn too. Echoing Clark's (2008) notion of the extended mind, learning is in the system, of which we are part (including our bodies), not just in our heads.

Soft techniques are an embodiment of Culkin's (1967, p. 70) dictum that we shape our tools, and our tools shape us. Technology emerges through complex and ever-evolving interactions between us and our tools (Orlikowski, 1992). We build technologies, and not only do they help to shape us but they are, in part, made of us.

Although a skill such as carpentry becomes softer with increasing proficiency, this does not make carpentry a particularly hard technology for the novice. It is just one that offers fewer adjacent possibles than it does for the veteran. Unskilled users of a soft technology learn from their errors, experiment and adapt, in conversation with the technology, not just as users of it. They can also learn from others, directly or indirectly, or they can gain inspiration from models and designs and strive to improve. To an unskilled carpenter assembling a piece of IKEA furniture, it is a hard technology. The pedagogies that teach us how to assemble it are also hard, in the form of precise numbered visual instructions, all of which must be obeyed. A great deal of thought and pedagogical design normally go into making this as clear and foolproof as possible, so that we can play the role of a production line or machine in bringing it to fruition. However, because we enact it, we can change it. Indeed, there is a whole movement of IKEA hacking, as can be found at http://www.ikeahackers.net. So, though the technology of IKEA superficially might resemble a poorer version of an assembly line, it contains within it a deferred (Patel, 2003) but perhaps limitless potential that an assembly line cannot achieve.

The hardest technologies do not have this capacity. We can learn to use them correctly, but once they are learned there is no more correct way of using them. For example, a machine to manufacture electronic components might require a great deal of learning before it can be operated effectively, but once the skill is learned it will never do more than manufacture the same electronic components in the same way. Perhaps aspects or components of the skill are of more generic use, but the skill itself is perfectible. Skills needed to be part of hard technologies can be perfected (in principle and sometimes in practice), whereas skills needed to operate soft technologies seldom if ever are. We can aim for perfection and achieve high levels of proficiency in the hard skills that form part of their assembly, but not in the assembly itself. There is no fixed point, say, at which one can say that one knows everything there is to know about using a guitar, language, computer, or even screwdriver. The same is true of the use of any pedagogical method. Although the hard techniques that might be part of its assembly—for instance, clear handwriting or diction or accurate marking of tests—can be measurably correct, there is no perfect standard for setting a challenging assignment or encouraging recall, no point at which it can be said that it can't possibly be improved.

Honouring Error

"Perfect" hard technique is not always desirable and, in many cases, might mask what we value most in soft technologies, or worse, as in the case of prescriptive copy editing, the rigid application of a technique might render an authors' sentences unreadable, meaningless, or ambiguous. In artworks, for instance, we typically value the differences that give particular artists their style. Although it could be argued that this might stem from their invention of techniques that differ from the norm, it is at least as often in the gaps between intention and execution that the most interesting things can be found, because they open up new potential, different opportunities, new adjacent possibles. Brian Eno, in collaboration with painter Peter Schmidt, once created a deck of cards to be used as inspiration in the creative process that summarizes this aspect of technique well. Among many pieces of good advice, one card simply read "honor thy error as a hidden intention." For example, as a presenter (despite a huge amount of practice and a love of public speaking), I tend to stutter, fumble words, "umm" and "ahh" constantly, forget words, forget whole concepts, repeat myself, and so on. I sometimes make weird gesticulations and expressions, jump around a lot, and generally distract my audience in ways that, were I to design the presentation in advance, I might be circumspect about trying. Occasionally—and unfortunately beyond my conscious control to repeat—I get into a flow and reel off long, dense, and at least superficially erudite phrases at great speed with barely a pause. This is probably just as bad as my fumbling, if not worse. I have a tendency to diverge. The gap between intention and execution is usually vast. However, and notwithstanding the many times that I have failed to interest or inspire my audience (these are soft technologies that demand constant invention and can easily fail), none of that really matters. My numerous flaws might be weak components when viewed individually, but in assembly they sometimes work well, achieving a wide range of desirable effects, from gaining audience sympathy to allowing time to absorb a message. All are deeply affected by my perception of my audience, the richly interwoven ways that we interact with one another, and above all the narrative flow in which each sentence, gesticulation, or movement builds upon and incorporates those that came before it. I am usually aware of and reactive to my errors, which then become part of the tapestry that I am weaving (and often components that I might use later in a different assembly). At least some people like it at least some of the time. I have watched countless speakers who do this better than I, whose "flawed" delivery actually gains effectiveness from its imperfections. The same essential dynamic is true of almost all music, dance, and visual art, not to mention philosophy, critical analysis, and the writing of books. We shape ourselves, as well as what we create, in the act of creation itself, often without prior intention. As Richard Powers (2006) said in an interview, "I write the way you might arrange flowers. Not every try works, but each one launches another. Every constraint, even dullness, frees up new design."

Conversely, most of us have had to sit through somebody reading from notes (worse still from slides), perhaps with something close to "perfect" diction, intonation, and phrasing, while we have struggled to stay awake. Perfect hard speaking technique does not necessarily equal perfect teaching technique, because it eliminates the human, the possibility of being affected by feedback, the conversation with the unfolding process. It hardens something that (arguably) should be soft. On the whole, I would rather read what someone has written or at least listen to a recording that I can pause, rewind, and fast-forward. Some public speakers can sustain both exceptional hard technique and exceptional expression, and their oratory seems to be almost superhuman, yet they remain engaged with and responsive to their audiences, and with their own narrative flows, throughout. Indeed, most of us, with enough practice, and like actors, can learn and deliver a speech with "perfect" technique, but some fantastic speakers can do this on the fly, including in their responses to questions from audiences. They might well be employing some preplanned intentional hard techniques (e.g., use of pauses, dramatic inflections, narrative devices, and so on) that can help a lot, but for the most part it is their on-the-fly soft technique (unique to them and every situation), which includes engagement with their audiences and with what they have already presented, that impresses. They have at their disposal a toolbox far bigger than mine at least from which to assemble new and impressive works. Although few of us will ever become as skilled as Winston Churchill, Oscar Wilde, or Groucho Marx in this regard, we can all learn to improve our technique, through methodical and reflective practice. Indeed, there are techniques for learning techniques: we can become better at learning. Repeated practice, when we reflect on it and observe its effects, at least enables us to become better at dealing with and responding intelligently to our flaws. This is how we develop a distinctive style, and even flawed techniques can achieve effective or even brilliant results.

Great hard technique can make a great artist greater, but relatively poor hard technique does not preclude the potential for great artistry. Indeed, I am fond of some punk music that makes a positive virtue out of poor hard technique—it is part of the raw energy and a major contributor to the emotional impact of the genre—and there is much outsider art that displays weak technical skills but great expression. Technique and creativity are not causally related, and, though a certain amount of technique is usually essential to create anything at all, too much focus on perfecting a technique can limit creativity. It is not the fact of it but the focus that is problematic. It is normally worthwhile to practise, reflect, and constantly seek to improve one's hard technique but not at the expense of sucking the life out of the finished performance or product. Excessive focus on hard technique, in effect, can strip away some or all of the softness inherent in the activity by imposing constraints and boundaries that do not need to be imposed. Few of us are sufficiently talented or creative to pass through such boundaries, though when such a passage occurs we tend to notice it. The genius of, say, Glenn Gould (whose timing while playing Bach combined perfect technique with superb expression) demonstrates that sterility is far from a necessary consequence of perfection, but for most of us an excessive focus on becoming more technically proficient puts us at risk of forgetting the things that we value most in the technology. This is nowhere more true than in the act of teaching, in which personal technique cannot be developed fully in isolation but must conform and adapt to the learning needs of (potentially many) others. We must observe, be aware of, and reflect on the effects of our actions if we are to be successful.

Machines Pretending to Be Human

Technique can be emulated by machines, sometimes convincingly. Even when unconvincing, they can be useful. As a musician, I abhor drum machines because they eliminate (or, worse, emulate) the imperfections in technique that express the nuanced humanity of the performer. A perfect beat (to me, though you might think differently) is a rigid, unadaptive, soulless taskmaster, robotic and devoid of the life that makes music meaningful to me, and emulated imperfections seem to express emotions that no sane human could feel. Likewise for voice autotuners. Nonetheless, thanks to the power of assembly, they can be used to create great art. Great musicians have used the phenomena that I normally loathe to create magic.

For those who are time poor and/or cannot develop such skills themselves, it can be useful to automate hard techniques that usually would be enacted by humans. It can provide a means to produce something more pleasing to the ear or eye than what they could produce otherwise or to provide scaffolding for the learning process, and, if that is the intended use, then this is an effective way to achieve it. Despite my abhorrence of drum machines, occasionally I use one myself while practising an instrument. It is good enough to allow me to develop some (but far from all) of the skills needed when playing with a human drummer, and it is far better than a metronome for keeping time. Significantly, even when such technologies are used to produce a finished product, they seldom completely remove the need for skill. Some creative decisions must still be made, even if they largely involve picking an item from a list. It is about as creative as sharing a meme that someone else has made, but there is a place for that. In fact, it is much like a tried and tested approach to course development that, at my university, we describe (scathingly) as a "textbook wraparound," in which course authors add little to a textbook other than instructions to read particular chapters and to perform particular exercises. It might not be pretty, it is certainly not great art, it is hardly inspiring, and we try to discourage the approach as much as we can, but (at least when a good textbook that embeds effective pedagogies is available) it has proven to be a sufficient learning technology for thousands of students over the past few decades. We are co-participants in the technologies of education, but this does not necessarily require us to be creators and leaders of everything that they involve. In fact, we cannot and should not even attempt to be so, because it is a waste of the teaching gestalt, and none of us has enough time to achieve expertise in all things. There is a great deal to be said, for example, for the use of open educational resources (OERs), especially in subjectivist or complexivist approaches, because they can fill gaps for different learners in different and often better ways than we could manage for ourselves. In the process, we often learn to be better teachers, because we see other ways of teaching that we might not have imagined.

It is also possible to convincingly simulate a human teacher using software and hardware, at least when the scope is sufficiently limited. Goel and Polepeddi (2018) have successfully fooled many students into thinking that they were being helped by human assistants, that were actually chatbots built using IBM's Watson AI engine. The machine—under the pseudonym Jill Watson—only answered questions that it could, with some assurance, answer. Humans answered the rest, and their answers were in turn used to improve the machine's training. Jill Watson did not depart from the confines of a limited data set of problems with well-defined answers within a particular course, almost all of which related to course procedures and rules, not the subject of study. Despite appearances of softness, this was a hard technology used in the service of the hard technology aspects of the teaching process—assignment deadlines and formats, schedule issues, and so on. At its most refined, the technology was able to field about 60% of all questions (though work continues on improving this percentage, and I have heard from Goel himself that it can now effectively answer 90% of the questions). It is unclear to what extent these answers furthered student learning, though no doubt there were benefits in relieving human tutors of some of the need to repeat mechanical answers to questions that had nothing to do with the subject being learned. However, something important was lost. When humans interact with other humans, there is at least a chance that they might understand contexts, motivations, needs, fears, and hopes of one another, whereas chatbots, including those based on large language models like GPT or LaMDA, understand nothing of them.

Education is about learning to be human in a human world, with all its complexity and intertwingularity (Nelson, 1974), so there are firm limits on how far this kind of technology should be taken. Even in this limited context, Jill Watson failed in some disturbing ways to answer questions that any human would understand. For instance, though it recognized a question about procedures from a male student who was about to become a father, it failed to recognize a similar question from a female student who was pregnant, thanks to the predominantly male demographics in the computer science course from which training data were taken (Eicher et al., 2018). As Shulman and Wilson (2004, p. 504) observe about classroom teaching, but that could be applied to the whole educational endeavour, it is "perhaps the most complex, most challenging, and most demanding, subtle, nuanced, and frightening activity that our species has ever invented." This is undoubtedly a gross exaggeration, but, notwithstanding the remarkable achievements of large language models like ChatGPT or LaMBDA in simulating human behaviour, the kind of artificial general intelligence (AGI) that might cope with its complexity is at best a long way off, and there is a good chance that it might never occur at all (Goertzel,

2014). If it ever comes close to happening—when machines themselves truly can be soft partners in harder technologies—then I might need to rewrite this book. I doubt that I will.

Machines may increasingly easily fool us, for sure, but the gap between current technologies and a machine that understands what it is to be a human, living in a society of other humans, is hardly any less vast than it was 70 or more years ago. The use of generative AI is and remains that of the humans who create or deploy it, not of the machine. Machines are not creators of technologies but instances of them. Though sometimes closely resembling human users of soft techniques in what they produce they are not fillers of gaps so much as generators of them. Their participant roles are as hard parts of our own soft assemblies. This is probably a good thing, because there is something deeply distasteful about a process through which we learn to be human that is managed by a machine. This is not to dismiss or diminish the enormous changes wrought by generative AIs. By mixing and remixing vast swaths of our own creations they vastly expand the adjacent possible in unforeseeable, excitingly disruptive ways. But, though their seeming intelligence derives from the works of countless humans, they are not and cannot be human, or anything like it.

Even and perhaps especially when such a machine represents the "best" of us—when, like recent large scale large language models, it may appear to be tireless, supportive, friendly, or even compassionate—its very lack of foibles makes it a poor role model. This is not to mention many concerns about whose idea of best is being imposed, whether it ossifies systematic biases, some individual's concept of best is programmed into it, or it blandly averages out what it learns from its vast dataset, like a mediocre filter bubble the size of the internet.

There is a creepy dystopian aspect to accelerating trends in the use of generative AI to mimic human behaviours. This may be blatant, such as in the way that Jill Watson was designed to incorporate a random (but never long) delay in its answers in order to appear "more human," or in "companion" AIs such as Replika, which is described by its makers as "the AI companion who cares" (https://replika.com/). However, mimicry of humans underlies most uses of such tools for everything from cheating in colleges to generating books or lesson plans. When expectations of being human are learned from a (hard) machine, and when emotional attachment and belongingness depend on something not quite human, they are the start of a slippery slope that will not end well for any of us. Such machines currently learn by ingesting vast amounts of data from human interactions and creations: their seeming humanity derives directly from average behaviours of actual humans and, for the most part, the outputs are therefore very average: good, but not great. Before long, a significant number of those interactions and creations feeding the machines will (if trends continue) be created by such machines, so subsequent generations of machines will learn from them, and we will learn from them, in a slow cycle of decay or stagnation, with all the creative softness and humanity taken out of it. But, even if it ends less dystopically, the underlying values that it represents remain deeply problematic. To teach using an artificial human is underpinned by values that treat education as nothing more than a mechanical process of learning facts, hard techniques, and cognitive tools. Such elements are indeed parts of an educational process, but they are not the reason for it. They are the means, not the ends.

Humans Pretending to Be Machines

Those who practise a musical instrument in order to play a particular piece "perfectly," or who copy famous artworks as precisely as possible, appear to be replacing human creativity with harder processes. If that is their sole intention, then indeed they are enacting a hard technology, and in terms of performance it probably would be better automated, for instance using a pianola or similar device. However, that is seldom the use to which the orchestration of phenomena is applied. Sometimes we might simply find joy in overcoming a challenge. In this case, the purpose of achieving perfection is personal satisfaction, not replication of a perfect method per se: we orchestrate the orchestrations that we enact in order to please ourselves or to impress others. It is important to remember that there can be value in acting like or as part of a machine. Mastery of a human-instantiated technology, whether soft or hard, can be very supportive of intrinsic motivation, whether or not it leads to further capabilities (Deci & Moller, 2005, Ryan & Deci, 2017). Conversely, sometimes we practise to meet the demands of someone else, such as a music teacher or examiner. This can be very antagonistic to intrinsic motivation (Ryan & Deci, 2017).

More often than not, though, we practise a piece of music or copy an artwork in order to become proficient in our own right so that we can become more effective creators. If we need to participate in a hard technology in order to enact a soft technology, then it matters that our hard techniques are well honed. Our hardest human-enacted technologies are nearly all prerequisites for assembling softer technologies: we need to become parts of a hard technology in order to make it a soft one. The purpose of repeating a musical scale until something like perfection is attained is not normally to reproduce perfectly a musical scale but more quickly to gain the ability to play more complex pieces and often to be able to be more creative. Practice is rarely an end in itself but a pedagogy intended to change us in positive ways.

We can see this in even sharper relief in common join-the-dots pictures used to teach children a range of skills, from manual dexterity to visualization. These are puzzles with a purpose, which is not the production of a picture but the development of mental and motor skills. This relates significantly to the nature and role of technologies in learning and especially to technological literacies, to which we will soon turn. There are significant differences between how and why we acquire hard skills than softer ones, and the kinds of pedagogy that work for one might be inappropriate for another. There is a large difference between this and a dominative or prescriptive technology demanding that we play a particular role, inasmuch as (unless coerced by teachers) we choose to do so. We are intentionally (and perhaps even creatively) building the cognitive tools that we will later assemble into something else, and like most technologies there are better and worse ways to build them.

It is also important to be aware of more than the obvious façade of a technology, because many technologies do more than what it says on the tin. Take handwriting, for instance. Viewed as a hard technology, a handwritten letter is no more than a vehicle for conveying words from one person to another. In many ways, such a letter lacks the efficiency, speed, and clarity of an email (especially if your handwriting is as poor as mine), so it makes more sense to use email or a typewritten letter for many purposes. However, a handwritten letter's meaning extends far beyond the mere communication of words between one person and another. In part, this is because of the non-verbal things that handwriting communicates, especially in terms of mood. The tear-stained email has yet to make the mainstream, and it is difficult to see whether something has been typed passionately. It might be partly that we write differently (though not often better) by hand than by computer (Bangert-Drowns, 1993). However, the act of handwriting itself—the physicality of it, the layers of meaning stretching back for millennia, the gifting of an object, and so on—creates something much more than a medium for transferring words.

The simple fact that a piece of paper has been handled by another person lends it a different meaning: this is why even cheap and mass-produced artifacts formerly owned by famous people or related to auspicious events command high prices in auctions. More than that, other information can be imparted. Seely Brown and Duguid (2000) describe a researcher who, investigating an archive of letters from the 19th century, sniffed each letter that he handled. When asked why, he replied that he was seeking the smell of vinegar, a widely used means of disinfecting letters sent from cholera-afflicted areas. Knowing these circumstances, he was able to read between the lines of otherwise cheerful letters and to extract layers of meaning that otherwise would have been hidden. When we talk of the utilization of phenomena to particular uses, we must always be alert to the possibility that those uses can extend far beyond their most obvious utilitarian functions, and the phenomena can involve far more than what we focus on most easily.

Failure to recognize hidden utility lies behind many problems with hardened technologies, especially in the field of education. For instance, when early e-learning adopters wittingly or unwittingly replaced lectures with web-based resources, they neglected to observe the value of shared schedules for sustaining motivation and engagement; of meeting others outside a lecture hall and learning with them (often serendipitously) simply as a consequence of being there; of myriad small acts of communication (not always with the lecturer) that occur in even the driest of lectures; and of the flexibility in form possible in a live performance, including opportunities for dialogue. There are plentiful ways to avoid such traps, and many ways to use online learning that are more effective than most lectures, but it is all too easy to focus on obvious functions to the exclusion of things that really do matter. To this day, far too many online learning solutions replicate the veneer of the lecture—its information-imparting function—while neglecting the vast web of benefits that surround it in in-person learning.

The COVID-19 pandemic revealed this in sharp relief as many in-person teachers attempted to replicate the methods and motifs of their classroom teaching using technologies such as Zoom, Webex, Adobe Connect, or MS Teams, and either they were overwhelmed by the effort of trying to sustain the human connection, or they failed to adapt to the distinctly different affordances and limitations of the technologies, leaving students adrift and unsupported. Lectures work as solutions to problems of in-person teaching for many reasons, including the salience of travelling to them, the affective presence of others in the room, opportunities for engagement when leaving them, and much more. They are not great ways of imparting information at the best of times, but without these vital elements they are nearly worthless, and much else needs to be done to make up the shortfall. It is interesting, though, that the overall system sometimes found ways to adapt. Students with supportive families and friends, for example, were able to fill the gaps more easily than those without them and, in the process, amplified inequalities and weaknesses already endemic before the crisis began (Darmody et al., 2021).

Humans Made to Act like Machines

Uncreative participation in hard technologies does not have to be a bad thing, as long as we have chosen to participate, and we can choose not to do so. However, it is important to be able to diverge. Those of us who have sat on, say, exam boards or university committees can almost certainly remember countless occasions when unrelenting rules determined the behaviour of otherwise rational humans in completely irrational ways, when divergence was frowned on or prohibited. I have sat in meetings at which motions failed to carry because of the incorrect application of Robert's Rules, despite nearly unanimous assent by all parties present.

Although pedagogies are inherently soft, human-enacted hard technologies are often found in the practice of teaching itself. Schwartz (2015, p. 42) provides a sample of a script issued to a teacher in America:

> Script for Day: 053
> TITLE: Reading and enjoying literature/ words with "b"
> TEXT: The Bath
> LECTURE: Assemble students on the rug or reading area. . . .
> Give students a warning about the dangers of hot water. . . . Say, "Listen very quietly as I read the story." . . . Say, "Think of other pictures that make the same sound as the sound bath begins with."

Schwartz observes that the script that the teacher had to follow was twice as long as the book that she was reading. This is an extremely hard technology, which seems to be dominative and prescriptive, as much as possible reducing the human within it to a cog in a machine. In fact, that is precisely the intent. As Schwartz notes, "scripted curricula and tests were aimed at improving the performance of weak teachers in failing schools—or forcing them out of teaching altogether" (p. 45).

This is not a new phenomenon. Among the earliest and most influential proponents of this approach, Pestalozzi (1894, p. 41) wrote that "I believe it is not possible for common popular instruction to advance a step, so long as formulas of instruction are not found which make the teacher . . . merely the mechanical tool of a method, the result of which springs from the nature of the formulas and not from the skill of the man who uses it."

The underlying assumptions—that most teachers are average or below average, that there is a "right" way of teaching, that uniformity is an equalizing force rather than a driver of mediocrity, and that method can be divorced from technique—remain strongly embedded in education systems. Such beliefs are much of the reason that textbooks, reusable learning objects, open educational resources, and MOOCs are seen to be beneficial, inasmuch as (though capable of achieving many more benefits) they allow a weak or overworked teacher to be replaced, in part or in whole, by better, tireless teachers. The same is true of many applications of AI, from automated tutors to learning analytics tools.

Because such hard technologies are enacted by people, there is a lot of scope for error, inefficiency, and interpretation, so not only is it dehumanizing and demotivating, but also there is a good chance that it can fail to work as intended. From my point of view, as one who sees education as archetypally human, fundamentally soft, and essentially liberative, this appears to be a horrendous distortion of all that learning with a teacher should be. However, thanks to creative human nature and the many cracks in the technology through which softness might shine, and especially since a hard pedagogical method like the aforementioned script can be used as part of an assembly rather than as the sum total of the activity, it is not doomed to fail. Indeed, it is unlikely that—unless acting under obscene coercion or monitoring—many human teachers would take this script as anything more than (perhaps strongly) advisory. Furthermore, there are occasions when even a champion of teacher freedom would find it justifiable to use such a hard, human-enacted technology—for example, if someone without any training as a teacher and virtually no knowledge of the subject had to step in temporarily to lead a class, then this kind of script might be useful. The fact that education is and must be a soft process does not preclude there being hard components of it. What matters is whether the degree of hardness is appropriate to the situation. The situated nature of all learning means that there can be occasions when even the inhuman, the sterile, and the mechanical are useful. Like practising scales, this can help us to learn or at least explicitly to take advantage of the distributed teacher in order to teach better than we could alone. As ever, we are co-participants in the technologies of education, not just users of them. It is fine to be part of the machine if that is what works and if we do so willingly.

Appropriate Roles for Hard and Soft Pedagogies

Hard technique is needed to operate any hard technology, be it a form or a vending machine. Equally, virtually all soft technologies demand at least some prerequisite hard skills to enact them: the ability to spell accurately, form handwritten letters correctly, draw lines with a pencil clearly, place fingers on the fingerboard of a violin accurately, pronounce a word properly, and so on. Likewise for "facts" (knowledge of previously defined and classified information) that might be needed to support them. This dependency—and the fact that learning the hard skills must precede or at least coincide with learning the soft skills—tends to lead to the perception by both teachers and students that education is concerned most significantly with enabling learners to replicate hard skills and knowledge.

The tendency is reinforced by the relative ease with which hard skills and knowledge can be assessed. If something can be done correctly (as opposed to well), then normally it is not too difficult to measure the extent to which it is done incorrectly. It is in principle and usually in practice much more difficult to measure soft skills, or knowledge production objectively, because there is no end to the number of ways that they can be expressed or enacted. This is not to suggest that they are totally unconstrained: a soft technology allows a move into the adjacent possible, not the impossible, and all are rich in path dependencies, not least those imposed by the hard technologies, skills, and structures that provide their foundations. Nor is it to suggest that judgments of soft skills are particularly difficult, especially when a soft technology is used with the intention of bringing about specific aims, such as teaching someone a hard skill or making a comfortable chair. Furthermore, there tends to be a lot of agreement between evaluators of even the softest pieces of work. However, there is always room for interpretation, surprise, and invention that teachers have never thought of. The hardness of a poorly designed marking scheme might make it difficult or impossible to award marks, but creativity in execution is always possible when using soft skills.

Learning technologies intended to teach hard skills, such as most Khan Academy tutorials, or many adaptive hypermedia lessons, and much institutional learning, deliberately focus on the inculcation of habits and behaviours that allow a learner to be part of or enact a machine. Such things matter greatly, as parts of a learning technology assembly, but it is all too easy to confuse the parts with the whole and to forget that the main reason we need hard skills is to react, adapt, and act creatively in the world. Hard skills are a non-negotiable part of what we learn, but they are only ever a part.

Harder pedagogies tend to be more effective—or at least more provably so—when learning harder skills than when learning softer skills. There is a circle here, though. They are more provable precisely because they are hard: the fact that orchestration, phenomena, and uses are well defined and replicable makes comparisons possible in ways that make no sense when every instance is invented anew. Repetition, drill and practice, spaced learning, interleaving, behaviourist techniques, and many sequenced pedagogical methods from Gagne's (1985) nine events to Direct Instruction (Stockard et al., 2018) can all be provably effective means of achieving a tightly specified outcome, even though they might offer far less value and even be counterproductive in achieving soft skills with expansive, fuzzy, or open outcomes. They might not even be particularly effective for learning hard skills, especially if coerced by teachers. Softer methods are more variable, more dependent on skillful technique, and thus more likely to be done badly, so on average they might not seem to be so beneficial. However, though hard pedagogies likely will form part of an assembly, they should rarely, if ever, form it all. At the least, they will be more effective if they are aligned with authentic, personally relevant learner needs or interests, or they are applied in a meaningful and, where appropriate, authentic context.

Although harder techniques will be needed to enact virtually all soft technologies, subjectivist pedagogical methods, such as problem-based, inquiry-based, or other more open-ended complexivist learning approaches, tend to be necessary parts of the assembly when softer skills are to be learned. By definition, softer skills require invention and creative choices to be made, which means that (among other things) they always contain the capacity to surprise, and that success rarely can be accurately quantified, whether or not human markers agree substantially in their evaluations. Because softer skills can always be improved, no matter the level of competence, the notion of achieving 100% in a test makes little or no sense: 100% of what? There are also far more likely to be outcomes that were not pre-specified but that can have great value. Some subjects are inherently soft: creative writing, art, design, some aspects of architecture, computer programming, philosophy, and so on can barely be conceived in terms of hard skills alone (though many hard skills are needed for all of them), so more open, expansive pedagogies are par for the course.

The need for soft pedagogies might be less obvious in the case of "right answer" harder subjects such as math, physics, engineering, and computer science, but we should remember that the main value of such subjects lies in their application, not in accomplishing accurate replication of their mechanical parts. The occupations, for instance, with which they are associated tend to be anything but hard, demanding great creativity, problem solving, and adaptability. This is equally true when they play a subsidiary but still prominent role in other assemblies, from social contexts such as barroom arguments, to critical or reflective writing about their roles in society, to their use in the construction of other technologies. All have deep and complex ethical dimensions and greater or lesser relevance in forming personal identity and meaning. Also, notwithstanding the great pleasure gained from solving a right answer problem or doing something well, many hard pedagogical methods, especially those focused on repetition or replication, can be boring. Pragmatically, therefore, as well as pedagogically, it makes no sense to teach them as though they were purely hard skills, separate from their context of application.

This is all the more important in applied areas such as medicine, architecture, or computer programming. It is important that doctors know the names of all the bones in the body, because they must work with other doctors as co-participants in the same machine, and may not always have time to look it up in a reference source: unless all agree that this bone is a radius and that one an ulna, or that this medicine is a statin and that one an anti-inflammatory, the consequences for patients can be dire. However, though it makes sense for there to be some means of judging whether they know enough, this does not imply that mechanistic means should be used to train doctors or to judge their competence. Hard skills alone are useless: no practising doctor in the history of medicine has had to identify all the bones in the body under test conditions, so it is odd that doctors often have to do so as a rite of passage toward becoming doctors in the first place. It is far more important that they can apply such knowledge in an authentic setting or one that closely resembles it (bearing in mind the risks to patients of learning on the job). It also matters more that they have learned appropriate methods to continue to learn throughout their careers, because new knowledge and new technologies that replace as well as augment existing approaches are constantly being developed.

The machine is not static, and learning does not end when programs and courses end, in any subject. Tellingly, it is rare for practising doctors to memorize new knowledge in the same way that they are expected to memorize body parts for tests. Rather, they remember new things because they are useful and necessary in practice, and/or they know where to look things up when needed, and we would judge their success as practitioners according to how well they used that knowledge. Why would we do any differently in an academic setting? It is worth remembering that this kind of hard knowledge can deteriorate too. If the names of bones are not used in practice, some might well be forgotten. As patients, we care mainly about the soft technology of medical practice because that is what makes us well, not the hard parts assembled to achieve that.

Hard Technologies as Part of Our Knowledge and Skills

The fact that much of what doctors "know" is actually where to find the information that they need (or the people who have it) points to another important aspect of learning. Hard technologies embody the learning of those who contributed to their creation and thus become part of our own: our minds extend beyond our bodies into the objects and people around us.

Many human-enacted hard technologies, on some occasions, can do more than just embody the learning of others: the learning that they embed can rub off on us. They can provide a scaffold for us to be supported in learning for ourselves, a support on which we can build and develop our own independent skills. This is true, for instance, when we practise scales and arpeggios on a musical instrument or learn to play a piece of music "correctly." Whether or not we learn from hard technologies, at least sometimes they can give us a boost. Their patterns embody the creative thoughts of another person and let us begin close to the point where they left off, or to take what we need and branch in another direction. The same is true of teaching. We can learn to teach ourselves in part as a result of having been taught. As Cuban (1986, p. 59) puts it, "teaching is one of the few occupations where practically everyone learns firsthand about the job while sitting a few yards away, as students, year after year. We all have absorbed lessons on how to teach as we have watched our teachers."

We acquire many useful habits of learning this way. Of course, if we are badly taught, then we might learn bad ways of teaching ourselves. This is a highly significant issue when we are taught through conventional methods by teachers who do not understand the processes that they use to teach. I sometimes describe myself as an unteacher because many of my students, through hard technologies of objectivist, carrot-and-stick teaching, have learned that learning is about being told something and having to perform in some extrinsically defined way to prove that they know it. My job, in part, is to unteach them so that they can unlearn their preconceptions derived from objectivist approaches.

There can be disadvantages to leveraging the learning of others. There is a virtual industry of books and articles bemoaning the dumbing down of society and especially the effects of the internet on learning (e.g., Brabazon, 2007; Carr, 2011; Keen, 2007; Vaidhyanathan, 2012). As I write this, only months after the launch of ChatGPT, a plethora of similarly fearful nostalgic authors are lamenting the ease with which cognitive tasks can now be performed by machines, and predicting dire consequences. It is true that, among the myriad technologies that have become available through the internet, many sometimes cause harm, including those that mostly cause good. Postman's (2011) Faustian bargain remains ever present. It is also true that we (and our brains) are changed by the things that we do in the world, especially those that we do a lot. The fact, say, that taxi drivers' hippocampi (on average) are different from those of most of the rest of us (Maguire et al., 2000) is because habitually they have been used differently.

Whether our increased reliance on digital technologies is harmful or not remains an open question, and the answer is almost certainly different for every person. Those who rely on such technologies might be less able in some respects but (thanks to our ability to access and process more information) more able in others (Pinker, 2010). We gain cognitive prosthetics that let us do more complex things. In fact, Johnson (2006) makes a compelling argument that the (inevitable) rise in the complexity of media has made us smarter than we ever were, albeit that there is some evidence that the Flynn effect—a general tendency for average IQ scores to increase over time—upon which he based his arguments might have plateaued or even be in decline (Uttl et al., 2018).

Whether or not the average effects are positive or negative, when techniques are hardened into the mechanism of a machine, it can come back to bite us later. For instance, when we fail to learn how to land a drone manually because there is a button provided for it, a gust of wind or the appearance of an unexpected obstacle can leave us ill prepared to take on a skillful role in operating the device. Similar concerns apply to a dependence on internet resources as a prosthetic memory, or our inability to light a fire without a lighter or matches when neither is available, or even when our car breaks down in the middle of nowhere, especially if highly hardened technologies such as microcomputer controllers are essential to its operation.

When hard technologies fail, we might regret not learning the hard skills that they replace, and we might regret not having the skills that they embody. Yet, in many cases, we would not be able to achieve the heights that we have achieved if we learned those skills at the expense of others that incorporated more orchestration. It seems to be entirely inappropriate, for instance, even though it might be true, for Socrates to complain that writing provides only a semblance of knowing (Plato, 360 BCE), and thus represents a retrograde step in our development, because reading is one of the most central foundational technologies upon which much of our extelligence (Cohen & Stewart, 1997) as a species rests. If we had not invented it, or something like it, then we would not (for better or worse) be the smart species that we are today. And it is highly significant that it seems to be natural to use the word *we* for the inventors of these technologies. Language and its associated technologies of reading and writing were and are continually reinvented as a collective enterprise. Almost all of us are not just users but also creators of and participants in the evolution of these technologies, in smaller or larger ways.

Whether contributing small pieces to a softer assembly or acting as forms around which we can learn more, harder technologies allow us to leapfrog parts of the journey and to get to points farther along the path, letting us grapple with more complex and (sometimes) interesting and useful problems sooner. Beyond that, if people are involved in the enactment of those hard technologies, such as when following a recipe or repeating a phrase in a foreign language until it sounds right, then those technologies can allow us to develop habits of mind and increase our expertise to the point that we can become creators and inventors. From a learning perspective, we should wish for hard technologies. They do restrict what is learned and how it is learned, but in many cases that is precisely why they are useful.

The Technological Nature of Literacies

Until the close of the 19th century, to be literate simply meant that one was educated and well read (UNESCO, 2006). Its meaning has evolved since then to mainly signify that one can read and write, though shades of the original meaning remain: it is possible to be more literate, implying not just a greater vocabulary but also familiarity with more literature and all the learning that it implies. In recent decades, the word *literacy* has been hijacked by a great many academic communities to stand in for any group of skills that seems to be relevant to the topic of interest for researchers or teachers, such as media literacy, network literacy, digital literacy, music literacy, health literacy, and even hip-hop literacy (Richardson, 2006), to name but a handful of the many uses of the word. To the creators of such uses, a notable benefit of using the word is that it makes an area of interest seem to be more important than one defined simply by the need for a set of skills. I am uncomfortable with such uses.

The reason that literacy itself is important and deserves a name of its own is that the hard skills of reading and writing are essential foundations that every individual needs to participate effectively in any modern industrialized and technologically complex society. The ability to operate the hard technologies of vocabulary, grammar, syntax, and writing is a prerequisite of the soft techniques of reading and writing (or close analogues), without which it is difficult to perform any useful role in a developed society or to partake fully in it. Many societal roles would be impossible without literacy. Likewise for numeracy: it is difficult to operate in a society without some grasp of how to manipulate numbers, though the ways in which they can be used once such hard skills are learned are innumerable. There are plenty of other essential skills in most modern societies, from shopping to paying taxes, from following the rules of the road to dressing appropriately. However, though necessary, few are foundational, in the sense that other skills depend directly on them.

We might need food, say, to do pretty much anything else, but it does not form a part of most other activities beyond cooking and eating, and often cooking can be delegated. For most skills that might be thought of as similarly foundational as reading and writing, notwithstanding that they can be improved through explicit tuition or intentional study, it is normally easy to acquire them by imitation, practice, or simple instruction: politeness, say, or manual dexterity. If not, then we can employ others to provide them—accountants for our taxes, lawyers for legal help, and so on. Reading, writing, and arithmetic differ insofar as they are extremely difficult (or impossible for many people) to learn without a deliberate and fairly prolonged process of instruction, and they cannot be delegated easily. The hard skills needed are complicated and arcane. As Steinbeck et al. (2003, p. 123) put it, "learning to read is probably the most difficult and revolutionary thing that happens to the human brain and if you don't believe that, watch an illiterate adult try to do it."

Plenty of other skills have little to do with reading, writing, or arithmetic but also demand deliberate instruction, such as music. I strongly value musical skills. I think that music has immense cultural and social significance and should be taught to all. However, it would be hard to argue that skills in music are necessary for effective participation in most societies. They are essential for some musical subcultures, for sure, and can matter to many people, but they are not of general concern as a crucial set of techniques for survival within a modern society, and, more significantly, musical literacy is of relatively limited (though not zero) value as a means of learning other things. Moreover, though it is easy enough to identify skills of reading and writing, and they remain moderately (though far from wholly) consistent across most contexts, the skills needed for music vary considerably more than those for reading and writing. The ability to read musical notation and turn it into beautiful sounds matters greatly to a classical musician but is irrelevant, for example, to most blues musicians. For modern pop musicians, technologies such as autotune and sampling matter more than a grasp of musical notation.

Although there are many culturally specific forms of writing, and a world of difference between, say, reading a legal document and enjoying poetry, the hard, technical differences are nowhere near as vast as those between different musical cultures because the foundational hard skills (reading and writing) remain consistent. For musicians, the instruments, scales, rhythms, need to learn hard skills such as reading a manuscript, and almost every other aspect, beyond the fact that all involve the production of sound, differ radically from one culture, instrument, or genre to the next, notwithstanding substantial overlaps between many. Mastering each genre, instrument, scale, and so on is not like learning a new language but like learning a new way of thinking. Similar concerns relate to many of the x-literacies that have been invented: they have value in specific cultures, but few if any matter outside a narrow range of cultural contexts.

Digital and Other Technological Literacies

In most modern societies, it might be argued, and many have done so (e.g., Gilster & Glister, 1997; Koltay, 2011; Lankshear & Knobel, 2006; Potter, 2013; Rivoltella, 2008; Sharkey & Brandt, 2008), that skills in the use of digital technologies are as fundamental, widespread, and complicated to learn as reading, writing, and arithmetic. Indeed, it can be complicated to use some digital technologies, and increasingly they are essential for everything from shopping to watching TV. However, some critical differences are worth noting. First, as digital technologies evolve, many techniques that apply to older generations become irrelevant. Whereas the skills of assembling letters to write words and deciphering them to read change fairly slowly and normally last a lifetime, those needed to deal with modern technologies are ever more transient, thanks to ever-expanding adjacent possibles.

Although spelling, grammar, and vocabularies do constantly evolve, they are sufficiently stable that we would have little difficulty deciphering what someone wrote 200 years ago or more, and (ignoring terms and uses of terms that might cause trouble) vice versa, but someone born 20 years ago would be flummoxed by a computer from even 30 years ago, let alone 40 or 50 years ago. For most modern digital technologies, notwithstanding their gradual evolution that assembles old with new, their value beyond a particular time and/or place is often negligible. They become stale. Once upon a time, it was useful to know how to deal with config.sys and autoexec.bat files in a DOS or Windows system if one was a user of an IBM-compatible PC, and any definition of computer literacy in those not-so-far-off days would have included these competencies. Now, my ability to navigate the original Netflix web app only partly transfers to operating the Apple TV version of the app.

Second, the issue is made worse by the fact that a large amount of the development of digital technologies is concerned with trying to make them easier to use by hardening aspects of software that formerly demanded hard skills, from managing file systems to producing well-exposed photographs to parking cars. Ongoing and burgeoning hardening and automation render previously useful skills useless or at least relegate them to minor roles about which few people need to care. Much can be lost in this process. For example, in old-school photography, it is still useful to be able to manipulate apertures, shutter speeds, film types, lenses, and focus. There are many ways that we can soften the technology to produce exactly the effect that we seek, albeit with the usual costs associated with a soft technology. Nowadays, though, we can let the camera focus, choose a film speed, an aperture, and a shutter speed, because it does so better than all but expert photographers.

Hard is easy, so we do not have to think about it anymore. This brings some benefits. As a result of such mechanisms, we are freed to more easily consider composition, timing, lighting, and other factors that (in most cases) matter more when producing a photo. Sometimes even experts can capture moments that they might have missed while adjusting settings manually. Automation can liberate as well as dominate. More of us can participate effectively, without the limitations of simplified cameras that could capture only a fraction of possible photos well. And, in fairness, the capabilities of modern image editing software can bring even greater softness in post-processing than we had in the past, without any of the dangerous chemicals and expense. However, they also bring additional ways to harden. The ubiquitous filters on photo upload sites that make any photo look "artistic" offer such "skills" to anyone, including my cat. Some digital cameras can even take the picture for you, choosing a moment according to predefined algorithms that take into account composition, movement, and the expressions of subjects. Whether this is good or bad in the grand scheme of things is open to argument. However, the overall trend is toward hardening, automation, and deskilling, in everything from cameras to operating systems to help systems to automated teller machines to learning management systems, reducing or eliminating our need to learn hard techniques to use them.

Recognizing the transience and cultural specificity of modern "literacies," some have sought underpinning commonalities that are more persistent and relatively unaffected by constant change around us or that seem to matter more in this shifting landscape. For instance, Jenkins (2006) identifies a range of what he describes as "New Media Literacies" that include play, performance, appropriation, judgment, negotiation, and multitasking. Although these are all aspects of an individual's competence that can be improved through instruction and practice, and they often come with (typically culturally specific) techniques that can be used in their enactment, they are not techniques like reading and writing, but attitudes and aptitudes that we value in individuals in order for them to do pretty much anything in a society, including reading and writing. Equally, reading and writing are potential causes of such qualities, not types of the same kind of thing. These skills are not about being literate; they are about being human. Children are usually pretty good at playing, for instance, and do not need to be taught explicitly to do so, albeit that there might be many technological skills involved. It is a misappropriation of the term, though, to call them "literacies," and it confuses the issue. Attitudes and values are important parts of many competencies, and we need to cultivate them (usually through applied techniques), but that is exactly the point: attitudes and values in themselves are not competencies.

Despite these reservations, the term "literacy" might have some value as a shorthand for the set of hard techniques that is a prerequisite for any human system for which we can identify boundaries: in other words, for any culture. Such techniques are what we need to operate the technologies of a culture, from the smallest clique to the largest nation and beyond, whether it is transient or stable. Different hard skills are needed to be part of a culture of academics or hipsters, a family, a religion, a country, Twitter users, researchers in learning technologies, and often subcultures within those cultures or that cut across them. Each culture has its own literacies, its own suite of hard techniques (including structures, methods, principles, skills, strategies, and so on), that must be mastered to participate at a minimum level and that are prerequisites for using the soft technologies that help to define its values and purposes. We can identify these technologies by considering what is required of an outsider to become a participant and of a participant to become a full member of a culture.

The culture is not wholly defined by such techniques: usually, there are common values, attitudes, and shared context that are at least as important and often more so. But every culture demands a set of hard skills and knowledge of the technologies and structures that matter to it. "Literacy" seems to be as good a term as any to describe that set, and it is in keeping with its more conventional meaning. There are, though, millions of these cultures. The Reddit site provides a useful function that Usenet newsgroups or, before the internet became popular, bulletin boards used to play in the past of allowing such cultures to be reified. As I write this in March 2023, according to Business of Apps (https://www.businessofapps.com/data/reddit-statistics/) there are over 2.2 million subreddits (representing topics of interest), of which over 130,000 are active.[6] Each subreddit not only reifies a culture but creates a new culture of its own, shaped by its moderators, having explicit rules and expectations of behaviour. This is just the tip of the iceberg, inasmuch as there are cultures in every organization, community, and household distinct from any other. All demand literacies of greater or lesser complexity.

---

6 https://www.businessofapps.com/data/reddit-statistics/

Soft and Hard Illiteracies

There are two distinct forms of this broader technological definition of literacy that relate to our abilities to use different technologies, and they are revealed when we consider what it means to be technologically illiterate. The first is when we are part of a hard technology and fail to play our role correctly (e.g., pressing the wrong buttons at the wrong times, overwinding a watch, or filling in a form incorrectly), in which case the technology simply does not work as it should. The second is when we are not sufficiently able to fill in the gaps in a soft technology (e.g., not knowing how to draw a picture of a hand, play an instrument, or compose a sentence), in which case the technology does not work well. We might characterize these as hard illiteracy and soft illiteracy: in the case of hard illiteracies, the technologies fail to work at all, whereas in the case of soft illiteracies we can see different degrees of skill, and better or worse techniques, ranging from hardly any (e.g., a toddler's first attempts at drawing) to a lot (e.g., a professional artist's skill in illustration).

Programmers have an acronym for everything, and there are plenty for user "errors": PICNIC (problem in chair not in computer), RTFM (read the fucking manual), CBE (carbon-based error), or TSTO (too stupid to operate), for example. I teach my programming students that, if they ever need to invoke such acronyms, the problem is with their program, not with the user. Although it is easier to blame the user, hard illiteracy might be seen equally as a failure, or at least as an opportunity for improvement, in hard technology design. This is particularly true in anything mediated by a computer program, especially since most code in a modern computer is dedicated to making software error-proof. It makes no sense to devote hundreds or more hours to building software and then to require users to play roles that the software could perform just as easily, and far more efficiently, accurately, and speedily.

Anything that can be performed better by a machine or uncritical process probably (or at least normally) should be: this is where automation can have great value. However, this comes with a big proviso that inordinate care needs to be taken to ensure that hardening does not come with unwanted constraints or hardens things that should not be hardened. It is important to bear in mind that virtually all technologies involve costs as well as benefits, all have side effects, and, most importantly, sometimes the obvious use is not the only one that matters. Dishwashing, for instance, in most ways is done better by a dishwashing machine, which is more effective, faster, less environmentally harmful, and so on. However, there are social aspects of the hand-washing process in many families, there is a sense of pride in accomplishments that some people experience, it is far more convenient when camping, it is essential in the absence of electrical power, and so on. The uses to which we put technologies can extend far beyond those that give them their names.

It is especially important to be aware of what we are hardening and why. For instance, designing an assignment submission system that does not allow for the possibility of late submissions normally would be a bad idea, though it does happen. "Assignment submission" is not just what it says on the box. In fact, it is part of a much bigger assembly of complex processes, which includes mitigating circumstance processes, methods of dealing with broken systems, teachers' knowledge of students, and much more. Our failure to acknowledge such factors is a classic example of our common failure to understand technologies as situated, deeply connected systems in which the boundaries that matter are seldom those of a labelled technology: assignment submission is a synecdoche for many processes, not just the thing itself.

It is also important to recognize the value of some "mindless" processes, from sawing wood to cleaning to giving lectures, that often have purposes and physical, social, or psychological benefits that go beyond their most obvious functions. Many technological activities that we do for pleasure are concerned with a great deal more than the labelled activity itself. Nonetheless, from a design perspective, if we are creating any sort of technology, then it is normally a bad idea to force humans to play fixed roles simply to make a hard machine work, and (at least when the activity is performed regularly) efforts should be made to reduce the need for it. Students should not need to learn too many esoteric and situated hard skills for submitting assignments in a specified format if they are learning, say, to write creatively, unless such esoteric skills are an authentic part of the process of being a creative writer.

Regardless of our preferences or needs, or the many unwanted consequences for many people, it seems that, from a broad perspective, fewer and fewer hard skills are required of people in a modern society, and, with some exceptions, most of those needed are ephemeral. On the whole, hard illiteracy should be designed out of a system because hard literacy is dehumanizing. With a few exceptions, it should not be possible to be illiterate in hard skills if (and only if) all that they achieve is the correct operation of a machine, because machines can replace us more effectively, efficiently, and reliably and because being nothing but a cog is (in itself though not necessarily when viewed as part of an assembly) debasing. It is important to be clear about what I am claiming here. This is not an appeal to embed all hard skills in machines, by any means. It is about doing so only for those things that fail to provide any extra value to any of us (beyond extrinsic reward) and where we provide insufficient value in our role in the assembly in any way that could not be performed just as well or better by a machine. Speaking to the socio-technical perspective of soft and hard technologies, it is about reducing the need for us to be part of dominative and prescriptive technologies.

Soft illiteracy should never be designed out of a system, even though the technologies that we might use can evolve over time or be replaced by better ones. To make creative use of most technologies, there are virtually always hard skills to learn, in both senses of the word *hard*. For example, to form written sentences, we need to learn how to form letters that are intelligible to others, as efficiently as we can. We need vocabularies, a grasp of syntax, understanding of approaches to rhetoric, knowledge of punctuation, and many other hard skills. On their own, hard skills usually can be (and have been) programmed into machines, but in assembly they become part of something deeply soft: they offer the means to create new technologies, from forms to poems, to reports to shopping lists to dictionaries. They provide us with the tools to be more human, to be our best selves. Relatedly, language learning, at least in some of its most important aspects, is hard learning: notwithstanding the great artistry involved in rhetorical and poetic skills, it is fundamentally concerned with repeatable habits that should be replicated reasonably precisely; otherwise, they become unintelligible. Indeed, language learning is one of the few contexts in which harder methods such as drill and practice, spaced learning, and computer-based training show unequivocal benefits (Chang & Hung, 2019). Harder pedagogies may support skills as diverse as kicking a football, performing calculations, or making a valid argument. But what matters is the value that they bring to us as creative, social, engaged, motivated human beings, to expand our horizons, to open ourselves to one another, to make the world a better place (for people, not for machines).

It is not coincidental that pedagogies used to develop hard literacies are often hard themselves. Where we must be enactors of hard technologies in order to be participants in soft technologies, it is important that we play our roles correctly, and that often means "programming" ourselves to behave like machines. To be more precise, we are not programming ourselves (as a whole) so much as parts of ourselves that we can assemble with parts of other technologies to do something else. The word *programming*, as I use it here, is decidedly metaphorical. We are not programmable in remotely the same way that computers are programmable, but there is value in the metaphor inasmuch as it serves as a reminder that, just as computers can run many programs and subroutines, so too our thinking can be composed of many parts necessary in the enactment of the whole. Whenever we make changes in our brains (i.e., when we learn), unlike when we program a computer, those changes are seldom if ever localized, are always connected with other knowledge, cannot be switched on and off or loaded and unloaded at will, and can affect and be affected by many other aspects of our thinking.

If we unlearn them, we do not so much erase them as add alternative paths. In effect, as discussed in Chapter 6, we are building small and large technologies in our minds that we can assemble in different configurations and incorporate in infinite varieties of other technologies to achieve our purposes. This is a massively recursive process in which we create technologies in our minds that in turn alter our minds, enabling us to do things, change things, change ourselves, and form our identities in the world. The assemblies and assemblies of assemblies used together in a vast network or interlinked technologies lead to a vast range of possible combinations, almost all of which will never combine, so creativity, uniqueness, and selfhood emerge as inevitable consequences (Hofstadter, 1979).

Further evidence that at least part of our thinking is composed, in some ways, of technologies comes from the fact that the technologies that we build in our minds obey the same general rules and patterns of other technologies: the large and slow changing affect the small and fast changing more than vice versa, and they develop through a process of assembly of hard and soft parts. This is not to suggest in any way that our brains are physically organized like technologies: the technologies of the mind exist at a different level of explanation than the connections and networks of which our thoughts consist physically. Computer programs written in a high-level programming language similarly bear little resemblance to the machine code that runs inside their microchips, though there is a direct correlation in computers that might not be present in brains: computer code, can be decompiled to reveal much if not all of its original code, whereas there is no good reason to believe that this might be possible for thoughts.

The Double-Edged Sword of Expertise

Boundaries matter when considering hard literacies because skills are aggregable. For example, once we have developed the skill of repeating a common phrase, to a large extent it can be seen as a single harder assemblage that henceforth can be treated as an atomic unit (or at least a subroutine) in further technologies—to use the phrase in a conversation, for example. This effect has been well researched in chess playing in which it has been found that expert players do not consider each possible move and its detailed consequences but recognize patterns (Chi, 2006), thus allowing them to disregard those not likely to be useful. They have pre-orchestrated significant parts of the assembly, making them harder, thus faster and more efficient, and they can chunk them together to achieve more than those of us who must figure out those patterns anew. In some ways, expertise can therefore be seen as a reduction in knowledge (or at least a reduction in information)—we do not need to concentrate on irrelevant or distracting details—rather than an increase in it. In effect, we black-box some of the machinery in our minds in order to achieve more complex ends. Many of us can remember the early stages of learning to drive a car or ride a bike, when each action required thought and attention, and the result was clumsy, unreliable, and a little embarrassing. As we develop the necessary habits, such actions become second nature: hardened pieces that then can be used in a bigger assembly, allowing us to perform skillfully in order to use them in many different ways, as soft technologies. This hardening, however, can be a two-edged sword.

Experts no longer need to think of the smaller details, which means that they "know" what is wrong and "know" that some patterns are not worth pursuing. This works well as long as the aggregated models that they are using are valid and the conditions surrounding them do not change too much. Unfortunately, those models are sometimes wrong, or incomplete, or fail to adjust to external changes. Not all of our habits make sense, and not all such learning remains useful forever. Sometimes habits of thinking can become counterproductive. Having lived in a country whose citizens drive on the other side of the road than the country in which I grew up for well over fifteen years, I still have to think about where to look each time I cross a road, and my early skills in procedural programming have not served me well in object-oriented let alone more recent coding approaches. Most technological skills are ephemeral, but they can be harder to forget than to learn.

It is significant that a disproportionate number of major innovations and breakthroughs in many fields are accomplished by the young, because they do not necessarily know what is impossible and do not have so many ingrained habits to unlearn. They can assemble the more atomic skills differently because they have not developed habits and knowledge orchestrating coarser, larger patterns. Shirky (2007) describes this as the Bayesian advantage of youth. Although, in a large percentage of cases, those who lack expertise will come up with poorer solutions than experts, big breakthroughs often occur precisely because of that lack of expertise. As always, soft technologies provide greater flexibility and the potential for creativity. If we lack the "subroutines" gained through expertise, then we have to make them up ourselves, usually based upon our incomplete knowledge. On the whole, we will do so less well and with greater effort than we would, or will, when we have learned to do them "properly"—soft technologies tend to be inefficient, inaccurate, slow, and difficult to implement. But sometimes we will wind up inventing something better than the "proper" way of doing it. Such examples, though rare, are important. Teachers (including when we teach ourselves) should be aware of what and how learners are learning and seek misconceptions and errors in order to correct them. However, it is always important to look at such deviations with a critical eye to see what might be good or even better than what we believe to be correct. Teaching is and must always be learning.

PART III

APPLYING THE CO-PARTICIPATION MODEL

This section returns to the observations and anecdotes of the first two chapters of the book and, as promised, explains them in the light of what has come in between. Although it has taken most of the book to explain it, the basics of the theory probably can be expressed in a couple of paragraphs, which I now attempt to do.

Technology is concerned with the organization of stuff to do stuff, then organized with other stuff to do even more stuff. Pedagogies are part of both that stuff and its organization. We are co-participants in a deeply intertwingled technological system of learning, through which we learn from and with one another. We all teach, and most of what we create teaches too, participating in our cognition as not just an object of learning but also an inherent aspect of it. We are part technology, and technology is part us. How we do things—the techniques that we use—fill the gaps that other technologies leave, and they fill the gaps between us, connecting us with one another as much as they connect the stuff that they assemble. Each use we make is itself an organization of stuff to do stuff: a technology. Sometimes we are just part of the organization, doing what has to be done for the technology to work, but the more of the stuff that we organize for ourselves the softer the technique and the less predictable its unfolding.

Most technologies, as we enact them, are at least a little soft, and all can become so in the right assembly. Soft technologies are idiosyncratic, never repeating, always moving into the adjacent possible, often revealing who we are, and affecting both us and those around us in unpredictable, unprestatable ways. The hard techniques and the stuff that they assemble are critical to this unfolding, without which we could not progress at all, but they are not predictive of it. The relationship is one of enablement, not entailment and, though harder structural elements do strongly affect how the gaps between them can be filled, there are always different ways that we can arrange them, always new stuff with which they can be assembled to do something not hitherto imagined, always new ways that they can interact with the complex whole of which they are a part.

I might have missed a few crucial steps, but that's the gist of it and I believe it explains many phenomena and addresses a wide variety of problems and confusions in educational research and practice. This section provides examples of how it may be applied.

Chapter 9 discusses the anecdotes from Chapter 1, showing how the vastly distributed nature of teaching and learning can explain many real-life phenomena that otherwise might be puzzling or go unnoticed.

Chapter 10 delves into the reasons behind the observations made in Chapter 2, explaining various problems or phenomena that have challenged generations of educational researchers and practitioners, such as the no-significant-difference phenomenon, Bloom's 2 sigma challenge, the lack of value of learning styles in teaching, and the inherent motivational shortcomings of in-person formal education.

9 | Revealing Elephants

My dad always taught me that, when there's an elephant in the room, introduce it.

—Randy Pausch (2008, p. 16)

In the first chapter of this book, I provided a set of anecdotes that I claimed were closely related and that illustrated a few of the elephants in the room that, in education systems, we often fail to see or, perhaps worse, try to ignore. This chapter revisits the anecdotes in the light of the co-participation model and includes a number of suggestions and practical advice on how to overcome the problems that ensue. There is a great deal more to be said on the subject of each—a whole book could be (and, I hope, one day will be) written about this. My interpretations and recommendations are only a few among many, but this is exactly what the co-participation model suggests should be. We are in the realm of soft technologies with all their indefinitely large and perhaps infinite adjacent possibles.

Revisited: "You're Not Teaching Me"

Summary: a student claimed to have learned more on a course than in any other despite complaining bitterly that he was not being taught.

Of all the teachers involved in any learning activity, the most important is the learner, who performs most of the orchestration that leads to individual learning. When we talk of being "learner centric," we appear to acknowledge this fact explicitly, but too many of us fail to heed what it implies. Too often we worry about adapting our teaching to a learner's needs, but it is still our teaching, and we are still talking about things that we do to or on behalf of the learner. If we truly take learner centricity on board, learning must be driven by learners, personalized not by teachers but by learners themselves. Teachers in an institutional setting can and should play a big part in that, of course, but they should harden their pedagogies only when that is what learners actually want or need. Good teaching therefore typically involves being aware of how the learner is learning, and how teaching is working, in a conversational process ultimately concerned with supporting a learner until the learner is ready to let go and with being there to help when things get too difficult. In the course that my student was complaining about, I was trying to let go as early as possible. This was for many reasons, not the least of which a belief—which this book reinforces and doubles down on—that one of the most critical and basic needs for learners is to be in control, to feel a sense of autonomy. I was giving the students choices. However, choice alone does not give autonomy, and, at least in the student's initial perception, perhaps I had gone too far, notwithstanding the apparent effectiveness of the approach.

To give some context, this course adopted a hybrid subjectivist/complexivist approach. There was explicit use of many teachers, though I was the only one directly paid in that capacity. Online technologies, one or two of which I had written with pedagogical intent, helped to aggregate and use the combined discoveries of the students to create a crowd-sourced structure for a knowledge base (Dron, 2002). I seeded it, but it was mainly populated by the students. It was a rich assembly, the organization of which I did not pre-orchestrate. Each resource from the internet had been assembled and orchestrated by someone, however, normally with the intention to impart knowledge. The topics were moderated by me, but they were mostly chosen by the students, and thus the organization was a little haphazard.

Timetabled "lectures" were not exactly lectures; after the introductory session, they were opportunities to discuss things that students had found through their activities and engagements online, to learn from one another, to allow me to intervene in misconceptions or fruitless branches, and to plan future activities (what came to be known, in later years, as flipped classrooms). Instead of PowerPoint slides, wiki pages were projected onto a screen that started as outlines and that we generated collaboratively during classes (though I was the one who chose what to record and how to record it: my role as guide and expert mattered here). These outlines helped to provide focus and grew to include dialogues and student edits that developed over the ensuing week. No grades were given in the course until right at the end, though there were opportunities for discussions of what students were doing. There was no textbook and only broad learning outcomes to provide focus. I did do some didactic teaching, including brief lectures, but only on demand and ad hoc. In brief, the course was extremely soft both for me and for my students.

As the student's initial complaint reveals, this was not a huge success with everyone. The vague and flexible process left more than a few students feeling rudderless. Without more than a smattering of process-oriented instructions, only a vague fixed body of knowledge and skills to learn, and an open set of intended learning outcomes that might appear to be extremely subjective, it was not unreasonable that a student, who had learned that teaching is about someone else taking strict control of the learning process, might find it unsettling. In fact, in attempting to give them control, I was leaving at least some of them feeling lost and rudderless, because choice is not the same thing as control: if we lack the knowledge to make good choices, then we might as well flip a coin. It probably did not help that soft is hard: some of my mini lectures might have been good, but I am certain that not all met the higher standards that might have been possible had I designed them in advance (though I did have a sizable stock of predesigned notes to use when needed, so I was frequently assembling harder pieces on the fly rather than trying to perform them from scratch).

In the end, though the course had some ups and downs, and some students still felt lost, on average it worked out well. Many students liked the freedom and camaraderie, external moderators were deeply impressed with the quality and depth of their work, and I enjoyed it, though it was terrifying and exhausting at times. But there is no doubt that it caused more anxiety than the average course for all concerned. For me, standing in front of a class of expectant students with an almost blank wiki was a frightening experience because of the enormous uncertainty about whether anything good would happen; it was extremely soft and therefore very difficult. Whenever I do something similar, it takes a leap of confidence for students to feel assured that I know what I am doing, especially since, in all honesty, I have only a rough idea at the best of times.

My course was not an isolated learning technology: as a course in a program within a university, it was part of a larger technology. When we focus on a given set of interactions, it must always be understood in the context in which it occurs. In this case, the break with expectations (accompanied by my failure to help students come to terms with it) led to problems. Just using learner-centric pedagogies that provide learners with choices does not put them in control. We have to empower them to make those choices. Equally, since students did bring prior habits and expectations, and were driven firmly by the need to achieve grades, they were enabled to fill some of the gaps that I left: it was not just me and the students themselves but also (at least) a whole institution that was teaching them.

Although the general method might be reused (and I have done so), this particular set of activities cannot ever be repeated. There were countless pedagogical methods used during that class, only some of which were mine and most of which I probably did not even realize. This kind of process places much onus on the teacher to be extremely responsive, able to change direction, adapt, and (sometimes) massage the process for it to work. It requires the teacher to be unusually aware of how the students are learning and of the effects of each intervention. It takes a lot of time, effort, and energy. With a different teacher (or me on a different day) and different students, in almost every way it would be an entirely different experience, sometimes better, sometimes worse. This soft approach to teaching illustrates the point well that the less tightly we specify the process—the softer our pedagogies—the more we have to do to fill in the gaps. Each time I do something like this, I am surprised by new and unexpected ways that it plays out, and I still fail on a regular basis. It is one of the great pleasures of being a teacher that teaching is a constant process of learning.

My student initially failed to realize that he was being taught because he was expecting me to orchestrate the entire process. This was a failure of my teaching; I should have worked far harder to make the approach much clearer at the start, and, in more recent attempts to do similar things, I have started with activities that allow learners to figure this out, both through explicit discussions and through small, "safe" activities that help them to take ownership of the idea themselves. All of my (online) courses now have a "Unit Zero" that unteaches preconceptions and teaches how learning happens in the course in a variety of ways. As Deslauriers et al. (2019) observe, students who have learned to learn in objectivist ways tend to believe that they are learning more than through subjectivist or complexivist methods even though, when challenged, they tend to reveal the opposite to be true. It is therefore important to shift perceptions of what teaching means before this becomes a problem. Making such things explicit is not always enough—constant reminders are needed, ideally built into the process so that they take ownership of it, for instance through reflective learning diaries—but it certainly helps.

It is always important to be aware of all the teachers in the system, including those who have led students to believe that teaching is something done to learners, not by them, as well as all the institutional processes, norms, assessment regimes, and so on that reinforce such beliefs. They are as much parts of the assembly as the teaching process itself. Teachers can and should let go but only when they have clear and unequivocal evidence that learners are ready to swim and only when they have the time, the energy, and a sufficiently effective process of feedback so that they know when to provide support. I am still learning how to do this. At best, I get better; I seek but never achieve perfection, nor do I expect to achieve it. Teaching is a soft technology.

Revisited: When Good Teachers Do Bad Things

Summary: my colleague was a brilliant teacher despite using what appeared to me to be appalling methods.

This bit of cognitive dissonance was perhaps the first time that I clearly saw one of the largest elephants in the room that inspired this book. It was at this point that I grasped the simple truth that the most elegantly designed, pedagogically perfect teaching method was trumped almost every time by technique applied by a passionate and caring teacher, with a love of the subject matter and a deep desire to support the success of their students. Just as a great artist can sometimes produce wonderful paintings with poor tools, and even what others might see as poor techniques, so too a great teacher can use the worst pedagogies yet still contribute enormously to the learning of students. In fact, in some cases, the constraints that poor pedagogies impose can provide a creative impetus to overcome them and to excel.

Although my colleague described his teaching process as lecturing, in reality (and despite lacking a formal named model to follow) his approach was closer to direct instruction (Klahr & Nigam, 2004), involving a carefully constructed process to ensure that he was aware of how and when students were learning, with plenty of formal and informal feedback loops, thoughtfully designed challenges, and a clear plan for remedial action. As well as taking great advantage of the softness of the lecture format, he had softened it further by making himself available outside the lecture theatre: this was both a sign of how much he cared for the students and an indicator of his enormous energy and enthusiasm for the subject. It also allowed him to use more methods of teaching than those employed in the classroom itself. His teaching extended far beyond the timetabled events and classroom walls that appeared to bound it, allowing it to be far more personal than it appeared at first.

The fact that good teaching does not necessarily imply good teaching methods—at least not those easily described by simple labels—is explained easily by the co-participation model. Despite apparently poor methods (the harder elements of his pedagogies), my colleague's success as a teacher was the result of a soft combination of technique, artistry, and compassion. His technique was strong, given the limited tools that he chose to use, and it was backed up by genuine care for his students, along with a highly creative and energetic approach that effectively masked, indeed positively transcended, any underlying methodological "failings" of his teaching methods.

Even his apparently scathing attitude toward students who did not put in the effort or make the grade revealed underpinning concerns about their well-being and success. With a positive attitude and a boundless willingness to help them learn, to become (by his criteria) better learners, the result was that his teaching was what Purkey (1991) describes as "unintentionally inviting." Conversely, my own teaching, which involved a lot of conscious use of what I had been taught and what my studies suggested should be effective methods, was likely, on average, not as good as his. His combination of harder pedagogies and softer techniques meant that, even if he had the occasional off day, the methods gave sufficient structure for motivated students to succeed. Those without such motivation probably suffered, but his use of rewards and punishments (though problematic in many ways, as we will see in the next chapter) probably kept most of them on track.

Revisited: No Teacher, No Problem

Summary: my math class achieved record-breaking exam results despite the absence of its teacher.

As should be obvious by now, many teachers were involved in this class, including the one who was absent. When he left us, we still had some enthusiasm that he had helped to nurture, not to mention cognitive foundations that he had helped us to build. It was probably also materially relevant that we were a streamed class of students who had already shown relatively high proficiency and interest in the subject. Our learning techniques, at least in math, were likely better developed than those of average students. However, what really mattered were five big teaching presences: a classroom, a timetable, a set of school regulations, a textbook, and one another. Each played a significant role.

It was a nice, sunny, purpose-built classroom, on the ground floor at the end of an isolated wing, quiet because it was not close to other classrooms, and it was spacious enough for us to be able to rearrange desks and talk easily with one another without disrupting anyone else's lessons. Since the classroom was at the far end of the school, even the act of getting there helped to prepare us for learning. It made it more of a commitment, and hence more salient, the bodily effort likely enhanced our capacity to learn (Skulmowksi & Rey, 2017), and the increased travel time allowed us to ready ourselves.

The timetable was an anchor ensuring that we all turned up at the same time and did not forget about what we were supposed to be doing: timetables are powerful pedagogical tools for drawing attention to the subject at hand and helping learners to prepare to learn. Even though substitute "teachers" rarely if ever did any active teaching, they still kept a register, in accordance with the school regulations, that likely encouraged many of us to continue to turn up, and that marked a ritual beginning to the process.

The textbook provided us with plentiful information and a process for learning, including many exercises, with useful keys at the back of the book to ensure that we knew what was asked and had answers against which to check our efforts.

And, perhaps most importantly of all, we helped one another, talked about the problems, and worked on them together. We asked one another questions, the answers to which benefited both the questioner and the one giving them. Among the many reasons that teaching is among the most effective ways of learning are that it requires teachers to reflect, to organize their knowledge, and to apply it in different contexts, all of which are good pedagogical methods in their own right and form the basis of Pask's (1976a) "teachback" model. This tended to occur in small clusters determined by the arrangement of desks, combined with the unwritten but surprisingly ubiquitous rule that we almost always sat in the same places for every lesson. My own little cluster consisted of four different people who just happened to gravitate together but, thanks to the classroom layout, stayed that way and formed deeper ties. Our cluster often conferred with the cluster in front of us when we or they ran into contentious or difficult problems. Thus, the group mind of the class evolved as a clustered but interconnected network of problem-solving teams. Complexivist patterns emerged in what had been designed as an objectivist pedagogical process.

The elephant in this room was that, in almost every learning transaction, the "teacher" is not one person but a complex collective distributed among many individuals, their shared artifacts, the processes that guide them, and their environment. In every learning transaction, parts of both the overall assembly and the process of assembly are created by different participants in the transaction. In almost any human context, especially in one of formal education, we are swimming in a sea of teachers.

The math class was so successful largely because rather than despite the absence of a formal teacher. Thanks to the structured hard parts provided by the other technologies of the school, the overall assembly contained all the structures and processes that a teacher might normally provide. The very absence of a formal teacher likely increased the autonomy that we perceived, afforded more flexibility to achieve challenges at a pace that suited us, and the social engagements among us almost certainly had positive effects on our intrinsic motivation, for reasons discussed in detail in the next chapter. As ever it is necessary to look at the entire assembly rather than to focus on one specific aspect of it to understand how it works.

Revisited: An Earth-Moving Learning Experience

Summary: many people made interesting adaptations to their presentations when an earthquake took out the electrical power at a conference, but one delegate attempted to present his slides as originally planned, in a large darkened room, using his laptop on battery power.

The "unsuccessful" presentation was one of the most memorable lectures that I have ever attended, from which I learned more than any other at that conference, even though I remember little if any of the information presented. I did not learn what the presenter hoped that I would learn, but (because I was applying a reflective pedagogy of my own) I got something out of it perhaps even more valuable. There are few technologies or methods of teaching that lead to no learning apart from, arguably, those that cause us to fall asleep. We might not learn what was intended, we might learn falsehoods or bad habits, we might learn to hate a subject, and it is sometimes hard to know whether we learned anything, but few things that we do can be described accurately as negative learning. This is a big elephant in a large and dimly lit room. Simply being human means that we are constantly learning, especially when we find ourselves in a context in which we are expected to learn. We do not learn just facts and skills but also attitudes, beliefs, and ways of thinking. For instance, uninterested teachers do not just poorly teach a topic but also teach that the topic is not interesting, that they don't care much about their learners, and that this is the usual approach to teaching. This was not the case for this presenter. His enthusiasm was palpable, his passion sincere.

Most of my learning was soft: I do not think that I learned any significant hard facts or methods, but the talk enriched what I already knew, reinforced some connections, added salience to them. It helped me to think more clearly, easily, and creatively about the nature of teaching. I learned about the importance of making the technologies fit the pedagogy. I learned a bit about the value of lighting. I also learned about norms and values in the conference community (e.g., the applause was generous, and I wholeheartedly joined in) and how communities can be brought together by shared adversity. I learned about how situation matters: I deliberately attended an event with the intention of learning that put me in a frame of mind for learning. I learned (eventually, not right away, and of course in combination with many other learning events) about what I am writing about right now.

I am often reminded of this when I attend conferences nowadays. One thing that I observed early in my academic career was that full professors, more often than those lower in the organizational hierarchy, almost always carried notebooks with them, which they filled with notes at every opportunity, especially during conferences and workshops. Naively, I used to think that they were making notes about what the speaker was telling them, much as we still encourage students to do. Now that I am a full professor myself, I know that, apart from the occasional reference or pithy quotation, such notes rarely contain much information from presenters. Mostly, I construct my own responses to their talks, often challenging their views, frequently making connections with other things that interest me, and writing down thoughts that have been inspired (often unintentionally) by some offhand comment. My notes are littered with "special stars" next to ideas sparked by (but not directly drawn from) presentations that I want to follow up later or to incorporate into my own writing. Much of this book was developed this way. Often the most effective learning happens simply when we put ourselves in the way of ideas, good or bad, and give ourselves time to think about them. This is a methodical pedagogical process that improves with experience, a pedagogical technique overlaid on whatever pedagogies provide input to it.

The co-participation model applies to a number of aspects of this scenario. The unintended lessons that the presentation taught me result from the fact that I was the primary orchestrator of the learning experience rather than the ostensible teacher. This is generalizable: what we think we are teaching is seldom the same thing as what people are learning. In fact, at the best of times, it is almost never the only thing that we teach and never the only thing that learners learn.

The "failure" of the presentation itself was unsurprising. If part of your pedagogy depends on people seeing your slides, then (no matter how effective the pedagogy might be when well assembled) it falls at the first hurdle if people cannot see them. The phenomena that projectors make available—in the context of a large room–are necessary parts of the pedagogical assembly without which the pedagogy of visual presentation itself is useless. Pedagogies and other technologies must work together if they are to work at all.

Conversely, many of the other presentations at that conference, in which presenters adapted their approaches to accommodate the changed context, were far more engaging than they might otherwise have been. I think that the main reason for this was that they were forced to think about the technologies, including pedagogies, that they were using rather than following the normal PowerPoint-driven reporting approaches most often seen at academic conferences. One way to interpret this is that the constraints drove their creativity. However, it is just as accurate, and perhaps more useful, to see this as a sudden and unexpected increase in the adjacent possible.

Defaults harden, so, when forcibly stripped away, many other possibilities can be revealed. If anything, such stripping away leads to a loss of constraint. Often the things that constrain us are our own habits and the norms to which we feel that we have to conform. Freed from such expectations, we can explore other, and often more interesting, possibilities. Among the new possibilities are that the roles of others—each contributing pedagogy and knowledge—become much more prominent. The social aspect also had value in improving the sessions of the conference later in the day: the fact that presenters picked up ideas and approaches from those that went before is a great illustration of the value of social learning and of the many teachers who contribute to our learning. They were learning ways to teach as well as what was intentionally being taught.

Revisited: Boats That Teach

Summary: using the example of my boat, I showed that learning happens because of how we build the world: the human-built world teaches us and mediates our learning with others.

There are many elephants in this cramped little cabin. None of the former owners or designers of my boat had any intention of teaching me or anyone else, but I learned, and continue to learn, a great deal from them. This comes down to a number of mutually reinforcing factors.

- Pedagogy is embedded in many of the technologies that we use: we learn from others simply by using technologies with purposes that unfold as we use them.
- We learn from the differences between technologies: by seeing how one set of technologies solves problems compared with another, we better understand the problems and the solutions to them.
- Technologies embody learning. They do not just enable it but also do it for us, hardening processes that otherwise we would need to enact ourselves.
- The technologies that we create provide scaffolds and connections that enable and support learning, not just for individuals but also for whole communities. They are not just objects or methods that we construct but also inseparable parts of our learning process and our inherently distributed cognition.

Like houses (Brand, 1997), boats learn, and as they learn so do we. During the writing of this book, my boat has learned to be a fair environment for writing, having grown a folding shelf at a height and position useful for typing and a means to channel wifi to my computer. I have also adapted and developed methods of working in this tight space, including rituals at the start and end of a working session for preparing the space for work.

This participative feature of our constructed environment is particularly significant in the context of internet learning, in which billions of technologies, and people with varying levels of skill, help us to learn and perform the tasks that we wish to perform. Assuming that no great collapse occurs in the technologies and infrastructure of the internet, it is now a significant part of the environment in which we live and learn. To learn without recourse to the ubiquitous tools available to us through the internet—including all the people and systems such as Wikipedia, Reddit, StackExchange, email, and so on—makes no more sense than to learn without the aid of longer-established technologies such as writing, reading, arithmetic, or, for that matter, language. That said, it is worth remembering that old technologies seldom if ever completely die, and it remains useful (at least optionally) to retain the old skills that newer technologies can sometimes make apparently obsolete. There is a good case to be made that at least some of us (and all of us in a culture for which such skills are required) should remember, for instance, how to recite a poem or perform mental arithmetic.

Apart from anything else, without knowing some things, it would be impossible to make sense of others. We need foundations upon which to build, we need tools to examine critically our discoveries, we need methods of effective learning, and there are connections to be made between almost everything. Knowledge is constructed, forms, or emerges only in the context of other knowledge, and the greater our existing knowledge and skills the richer our new knowledge. There is great value in all things, to some people, some of the time, and in some of these things (writing, speaking, etc.) for virtually all people most of the time. However, to require that we learn things simply because they are parts of a curriculum makes little sense and, without due care and reflection, can stand in the way of achieving literacy in things normally of greater importance to most of us.

Distributed teaching occurs simply through interacting with the world, especially the built environment. Every one of our creations can explain things to us, help us to see things differently, connect ideas, mediate dialogue, and more. We never learn alone: we are in constant communication with the makers of all that surrounds us. It is part of our knowledge, part of our means of creating knowledge. We cannot exist in modern cultures without both teaching and being taught by the physical and virtual contexts that we share. As Mitra's (2012) Hole in the Wall project showed, such learning might not always be effective without at least some support, or at least without intention and goal directedness, and it might not be sufficient for those who lack the pedagogical skills (e.g., children) to orchestrate the phenomena effectively. Providing such support remains a useful role for designated teachers. As Bruner (1966, p. 44) put it, "learning something with the aid of an instructor should, if instruction is effective, be less dangerous or risky or painful than learning on one's own." However, none of one's learning actually occurs on one's own. The key to success is to find the right instructors at the time and place that one needs to learn.

10 | How Education Works

> *It is style that gives content the capacity to absorb us, to move us; it is style that makes us care.*
>
> —Robbins (1990, p. 13)

In Chapter 2, I made a series of observations that seemed to me to be odd or anomalous and, like the anecdotes in Chapter 1, seemed to show elephants in the room seldom discussed or even noticed. In this chapter, I explain those oddities and anomalies in the light of the co-participation model. In the process, I hope to elucidate some of the fundamental challenges of mainstream education and research explained by the co-participation model and to suggest ways that they might be overcome. To a large extent, this can be seen as a conclusion of the arguments that I have presented so far, but it too is a technology so it is not a definitive conclusion. Rather, it describes a small subset of entailments that, I hope, helps to illustrate the value of looking at education as a technological system.

Revisited: People Must Be Made to Learn

Summary: our education systems tend to reward us for learning or punish us for not learning, making motivation extrinsic to what is otherwise intrinsically motivating.

Why do we continue to use extrinsic motivation as the primary driver in education, even though we know with some certainty that it is harmful to intrinsic motivation? The answer lies in the nature of the technologies upon which our education systems are based and the rich layers of path dependencies that they embody.

As we have seen, the parts of all technologies, including learning technologies, must be assembled in ways that work, governed by hierarchical constraints in which the bounded are always strongly affected by the limits of their boundaries. Our education systems were developed within a set of clear boundaries, of time, space, purpose, theory, and so on. They started with a limited range of resources and constraints: there were more students than teachers, more readers than books, and so on. These and other phenomena, including many path dependencies, beliefs about human nature, available funding sources, and so on, determined the adjacent possible. This is how the lecture was born: it might not be ideal, but it was the best, most economical solution to scarcity of resources required for learning at a time when no other alternatives were suitable. There had always been alternatives—much softer apprenticeship models, in particular, were and remain powerful educational forms that can be incredibly effective, but being softer they were not as scalable, consistent, reliable, or cheap. The uses to which resources were put also played a large role in determining education systems' forms, especially regarding their later roles in society as filters for employers, babysitters for children, and producers of knowledge of value outside their walls.

To a large extent, much of the purpose of at least the seminal higher education systems of Paris, Oxford, and Bologna, was (at first) to transfer particular doctrines, notably those of specific religions but also philosophical, mathematical, and practical knowledge. They therefore sought hardness in their educational machines, with a clearly defined body of knowledge and clearly defined measures of competence. Given the available phenomena and the intention to replicate doctrine, the orchestration developed—primarily in the form of lectures, seminars, and tutorials—was hard, and it made best use of what could be assembled. It needed scheduled times (timetables) so that students could gather together, lectures so that rare books and wise words could reach the largest number, and classrooms to limit distraction and make the words more audible to more people. This led in turn to a need for a successive procession of counter-technologies (Dubos, 1969) that slowly began to define the process. For example, such classrooms needed rules of behaviour, expectations of conduct, and an innate power structure that favoured the teacher as controller of what went on in the classroom, entailed by the need for lecturers to be heard (lecterns, pulpits, and other paraphernalia of academia reinforced this pattern).

The process needed terms and semesters to cater to intermittent student availability. It needed libraries to house and allocate access to the rare books, and processes for loaning them, so that resources could be fairly allocated. As time went by, universities needed processes to manage both their increasing size and the ever-increasing diversity of lecturers and, in the absence of modern ICTs, hierarchical forms of management were a good solution. Because the intention was to transfer hard doctrines, they needed means to distinguish those who had successfully learned them from those who had not, at first in relatively soft ways (e.g., an oral defence to professors and peers) but, as time wore on, in increasingly hard ways (from written exams starting in the late 18th century to "objective" tests in the late 19th century and early 20th century). Increasingly, they needed specialists, who clustered into disciplines and subject areas and thence into departments, schools, and faculties, which fitted neatly into a hierarchical system of management. The need for comparison with competitors and a "product" to sell led to increasingly standardized curriculums. The list goes on. What this adds up to is a relentless though not inevitable path toward the traditional education system that we still recognize today. However, it is worth remembering that it emerged in the first place as a solution to the one central problem of how to allocate scarce resources (teachers, books, time, etc.) in physical spaces. All the rest built upon that foundation, solving problems that it created. Having solved those problems, most of the rest were counter-technologies designed to limit the side effects and take advantage of the adjacent possibles that the initial technologies opened up.

These solutions to the problem of indoctrination were sensible, in the context of the technologies available in medieval times, and, thanks to the inevitable increase in complexity and refinements introduced over centuries, remain largely compatible with one another and our broader and more open teaching needs to this day, at least in the context of in-person learning. The system has evolved, much like bows and arrows, to be efficient and effective, layering counter-technologies and (not always conscious) exploitation of fortunate happenstances until a system has emerged that educates reasonably well. Many of those serendipitous adjacent possibles have become exaptations that form critical and often overlooked parts of the distributed collective that teaches. Libraries, for instance, provide not only books but also ways of organizing and therefore understanding them, opportunities to bump into different ideas, to learn from librarians, and so on. Corridors do not just connect classrooms but also offer chances to connect with others, to prepare to learn, to make the simple act of getting to a classroom more effortful and therefore more salient. Smokers' areas and dormitory kitchens are incredibly rich environments that connect diverse learners, who can talk about what they are learning and cross-fertilize one another with new ideas. In-person universities, not just the teachers they employ, play a significant teaching role.

The consequences of the designs of education systems are many, but one stands out as more intractable than all the rest: education systems of this kind are systematically antagonistic toward intrinsic motivation (Dron, 2016). As many have shown (e.g., Deci & Ryan, 2008; Reeve et al., 2004; Ryan & Deci, 2000a), intrinsic motivation—through which we do things simply because we love doing them—demands support for learners to experience autonomy (to be in control), gain competence (achieve mastery), and feel relatedness (feel that what they do has value in a social context). Taking support away from any of these fundamental aspects of the process results in diminished or, more often, non-existent intrinsic motivation. The education systems that developed a thousand or more years ago were innately supportive of relatedness, both within and beyond the classroom. However, they inevitably took away autonomy (people had to attend at a place and time and learn what they were told to learn in ways determined by others) and support for competence (the need to cater to the whole class meant that, at best, some would be underchallenged and bored, whereas others would be overchallenged and confused).

The primary and persistent consequence is that, since early teachers (at least) had a strong desire to impart a specific set of knowledge and skills fairly independent of the needs of learners, extrinsic motivation became the primary means to achieve the goal of teaching. We know, and our ancestors knew, that rewards and punishments are highly effective as means of making someone comply with externally regulated requirements (Kohn, 1999), so this made sense in the context of indoctrination. As our education systems evolved, rewards and punishments came to be the technologies of choice, whether in the form of grades, praise, censure for failure to attend, or whatever seemed (in the short term) to work in the context of a classroom. The opportunity for accreditation for learning in the form of degrees, certificates, diplomas, and other proxies for competence was a particularly powerful lure that came to play an increasingly significant role as the centuries rolled by, as education systems began to occupy a more important place in secular society, and as systems of employment began to intertwine with those of education, forming a broader educational ecosystem with needs different from those of learning alone. It was probably also influenced by the regular adoption of such techniques in schools, which faced similar constraints and sought to pass on knowledge and skills at times and places that might not have suited children.

Unfortunately, as decades of research have shown, externally regulated extrinsic motivation can enforce compliance, but it does not add to already high intrinsic motivation. In fact, always and unfailingly, it substantially reduces and, more often than not, totally extinguishes it (Ariely, 2009; Deci, 1972; Deci & Ryan, 2008; Gneezy & Rustichini, 2000; Hidi, 2000; Kohn, 1999; Lin et al., 2003; Ryan & Deci, 2000b). Extrinsic motivation crowds out intrinsic motivation, replacing pleasure or satisfaction in performing the task with the goal of gaining a reward or avoiding a punishment or both. In brief, extrinsic motivation—especially when driven by someone other than the affected individual—is highly antagonistic to intrinsic motivation, mainly because it diverts attention from the task at hand to something external to it, sending a powerful message that the task itself is unenjoyable or insufficient to sustain motivation.

Perhaps the most central design challenge of formal education systems is therefore to overcome or compensate for the loss of intrinsic motivation that its design constraints tend to impose. Although intrinsic motivation is always more desirable than extrinsic motivation, assuming that we are concerned about learners more than doctrines, Ryan and Deci (2017) show that forms of extrinsic motivation which are internally regulated are mostly less harmful, and that higher forms may be positively beneficial. Although doing things because we fear consequences is little better than external regulation, doing things because they help us to achieve goals that matter to us or, better still, because they are part and parcel of our sense of self and identity, may come close to intrinsic motivation in value (Vansteenkiste et al., 2004). Teachers might find it difficult to avoid imposing extrinsic targets altogether, but it is often possible to help learners find those higher forms of extrinsic motivation within themselves through good pedagogical methods and caring support.

Many of our most cherished and deeply embedded pedagogies are in fact designed to motivate, enthuse, challenge, and captivate in order to trigger these higher, self-imposed forms of extrinsic motivation, from scene-setting, attention-drawing introductions to lectures to "hey, wow!" science demonstrations. Good teachers tend to leverage the social aspects of their teaching to emphasize relatedness, with group work, open-ended questions, memorization of students' names and interests, and so on. Many learning designs are based upon ways to increase time on task, for instance through gamified designs or activities intended to enthrall. Others are designed to hold attention or support teacher authority in a classroom. Yet others are intended to sustain enthusiasm or offer meaningful challenges. In fact, the closer one looks at what actually happens in classrooms, the more it becomes apparent that (at least in conventional classrooms) most of the pedagogical methods applied are simply counter-technologies invented to keep people engaged who otherwise would be disengaged. From roll calls to classroom layouts to assessment regimes to chunking of lectures or spacing of learning activities, our education systems are machines made to compensate for the lost intrinsic motivation that is a fundamental consequence of their design.

This is a highly evolved machine, the result of many inventions and inspirations stretching back into prehistory, so despite such problems the system works reasonably well most of the time. It is possible—indeed, I would argue, necessary—for educators to diminish the risks of extrinsic motivation by supporting needs for competence, autonomy, and relatedness. However, as long as the design of education systems systematically diminishes both autonomy and the need for the development of competence for at least some learners, and as long as extrinsic drivers—notably in the form of accreditation—remain the *sine qua non* of education systems, it will always be an uphill struggle. It is perhaps the central problem that in-person pedagogies must solve. Much of educational design and good practice is necessary only because the conditions under which education is "delivered" (a terrible term that reveals much about attitudes toward it) militate against effective learning.

Online learning, without the application of much ingenuity and effort, is the intrinsic motivational inverse of in-person learning. With provisos and exceptions, the relatedness aspect of online learning tends to be weaker in most online teaching, but inherent support for autonomy and competence tends to be greater (illustrated in Figure 3).

Online teachers can never exert the second-by-second control of their in-person counterparts, even in synchronous sessions, because a learner is always inhabiting at least one other significant environment in which teachers have no control: their own environment. What is described as a "virtual learning environment" is actually nothing of the kind: it is just a technology operating in the context of the learner's environment. The

Figure 3. Notional Relative Native Support for Different Factors Affecting Intrinsic Motivation in In-person and Online/Distance Learning

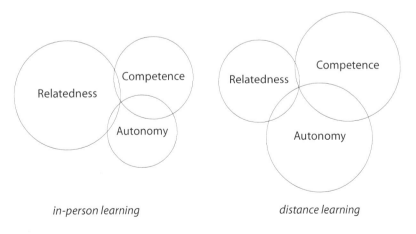

in-person learning　　　　　　distance learning

ability to take detours, or alternative paths, and to make use of alternative resources beyond the constraints of working together in a classroom offers more choice to online and distance learners than to their in-person counterparts. In fact, one of the fundamental (potential and often actual) benefits of online learning is support for autonomy because, no matter how hard teachers try to control it, control rests more firmly in the hands of the learner at all stages of the learning journey. The internet is filled with teachers—labelled as such or not—whom learners can choose to guide as much or as little of their learning trajectories as they wish.

Building upon the work of Morten Paulsen (1993), Terry Anderson and I (Dron & Anderson, 2014a) identified at least 10 types of freedom in online learning that differ from those found in conventional in-person learning, including the common distinctions of time, place, and pace as well as degree of social interaction, choice of media, ability to delegate or assume control, choice of tools, content, and pedagogical method, and so on. I would now subsume some of them under a single category of "choice of technology," but sometimes there is value in subcategorizing different kinds of technology. Our decision to limit the range to only 10 factors was largely pragmatic—to maintain manageable complexity—and based upon informal observation rather than patterns and themes that we had discovered through rigorous empirical research. There might be many other freedoms that emerge from separating learners and teachers in time and space.

Although tempered by the typically greater difficulties in direct communication, competence is generally better supported in online learning than in in-person learning because usually it is much easier for students to take things at their own pace, to explore alternative resources, and to adapt the pedagogies that they use to the need at hand, without having to follow the dictates of the teacher or the rest of the class in lockstep. That said, it can be difficult—at least in typical formal settings—to get timely help when things become complicated, so the benefits are not necessarily so great in practice. Unless there are others in their environments who can help, it can be harder for online students to know what to do next or to get immediate feedback on misconceptions or help with procedural difficulties. The inability to know what to do next to solve a learning problem can be very disempowering. However, at scale and outside a conventional teaching environment, the opposite can be true.

A question posed to a popular forum such as Reddit, Quora, or Stack-Overflow often can be answered within minutes, any hour of the day or night (though the quality of the answers can be difficult to judge). Similar benefits are often found in large-scale MOOCs. For instance, in one of the first MOOCs to exceed 100,000 students, the median response time to questions posed on a discussion forum was 22 minutes (Severance, 2012, p. 9). This advantage also helps to get more of a sense of relatedness, albeit seldom to the extent of the close-knit groups that are the norm for in-person learners.

What is particularly odd (though perfectly understandable from a technological perspective, given the need for interoperability with the rest of the education system, and the nature of technology evolution that builds upon existing pieces) is that distance and online learning systems, though not as constrained by the demands of physics as their in-person counterparts, have substantially replicated the pedagogical methods, notably including those that relate to motivation, designed for the different technological context and problems of the in-person classroom.

Many standard teaching patterns in online and distance learning—especially those that follow an objectivist pattern—are even harder than those usually found within in-person classrooms. Course developers work from an assumption of teacher control, of objectives and lessons set by the teacher, often even more rigidly proscribed than their in-person counterparts. This is especially true of self-paced courses that are designed in their entirety in advance and delivered as a single package because it would be highly disruptive to make more than minor changes to a course while students who have already explored its materials are taking it. Thus, materials tend to be designed with greater care, in more detail, and with more prescriptive tasks and activities than in most in-person or even paced online learning contexts.

Above all, the majority of online teachers use assessments and grades to drive motivation, whether purposefully or not, thereby attempting to claw back much of the teacher control that, inherently, is lost in online learning. In the absence of most of the in-person power structures that allow classroom teachers to control proceedings, grades often play a far more central role in online and distance learning, and there tend to be more of them. Paradoxically, this is even (and perhaps especially) true for self-paced learners who work in different ways from conventional in-person learners and who appear, by default, to have far greater freedom of choice. Self-paced courses, which usually can be taken at any time, without the need for interactions with other students, at a pace to suit the learner, and without a fixed schedule, do not need to be designed like in-person courses. Despite this, they still impose teacher control through grading as well as limits on time and work needed as defined by assumed study time in and content of conventional courses. There is thus a mismatch between the propensities of online learning and the in-person pedagogies that tend to be superimposed on them.

Unsurprisingly, given the consequent effects on motivation, many (though far from all) online courses experience lower completion rates than their in-person counterparts, despite (and perhaps partly because of) their attempts to keep students on track with extrinsic motivation. When grades and credentials are removed from the picture but everything else remains much the same, the results speak for themselves. Most credential-free MOOCs, for instance, are lucky to achieve completion rates of more than about 6%–7% (Jordan, 2016) If some kind of certification is offered then completion rates rise to an average of 15% or more. This still-low figure reflects only partial uptake of the usually paid opportunity to gain transferable credentials. Although not a problem for independent students who attend only part of a course for personal learning reasons, or dabbling, or simply visiting out of interest, this is a damning indictment of the methods and designs that they share in common with credential-bearing courses, when viewed from the teacher's perspective. By way of comparison, my fully online and credential-awarding university (Athabasca University) reckons to achieve average completion rates of about 85%[7] and, in many courses, much higher than that, though it is important to note that, following the almost universal practice by in-person universities

---

7 See https://web.archive.org/web/20130308191411/http://www.athabascau.ca:80/course/documents/course-completion-data.pdf.

of counting only students who turn up for a course in their completion statistics, this excludes 30% or more of registered students who never get as far as submitting their first assignments (our equivalent of identifying attendance in self-paced courses). This, too, is on par with traditional universities.

The differences are stark. Although some of that relatively high persistence rate can be attributable to loss aversion (students who have paid a significant sum of money, been sponsored by their organizations or governments with conditions and expectations attached, or require a course to complete a program that matters to them tend not to drop out as often as those for whom there is no significant commitment) and/or maintaining face with family members, friends, and colleagues who know that they are taking a course, the difference is vast enough to suggest that the traditional course format, without its defining motif of accreditation, is far from sufficiently motivating to learners to be useful or effective. Pedagogically, most MOOCs are at least as well designed as their for-purchase counterparts, and often more so, because they are usually produced by passionate teachers who wish to share their knowledge and expertise with wider audiences rather than as part of their daily duties. Designers and teachers of MOOCs are thus far more likely to be intrinsically motivated and therefore to put greater effort and care into course design and delivery. There is immense structural significance to grades in the overall assembly of online courses, but the consequences for motivation perhaps are even more dire than they are to in-person learners.

There are many ways to reduce such problems, even within a fairly conventional course structure. Getting rid of grades and replacing them with opportunities for discussion and feedback are a good start (Blum & Kohn, 2020; Sharp, 1997), at least until the end. Designing courses that support personal interests, allow students to choose topics, provide negotiable learning outcomes, and so on can be useful. Because much of the extrinsic motivation that drives education results from the need to acquire credentials, one simple solution—relevant to both in-person and online education—would make a large difference: to decouple learning from accreditation. There is also enormous promise in the use of all those myriad teachers found both locally and especially across the internet to support autonomous learning. I will discuss these issues further in the next section.

Revisited: Online Learning Dominates in-Person Learning (except in Formal Education)

Summary: the first ports of call for most internet-connected learners are search engines, help sites, and so on. No one needs to cajole them into learning, yet online learning is notably less popular than in-person learning in formal educational institutions. Are they teaching themselves, or are they being taught?

At least among those with reliable and easily accessed internet connections, the ubiquity and effectiveness of their learning online show conclusively that, freed from its formal and extrinsically motivated fetters, online learning not only works but also dominates the learning landscape in the 21st century. This is easily explained in co-participation terms. There are literally billions of potential teachers just a search term or two away, many of whom attempt to communicate knowledge, be it true or false, or skills, whether effectively or not. This is distributed teaching at its current apogee. Almost any learning orchestration is possible, and, with sufficient care and effective search strategies, almost any can be found. More is different (Anderson, 1972). With scale comes complexity, new interactions, new emergent adjacent possibles, and greater diversity. And the learning occurs precisely when it is needed, without coercion, so learner motivation is high.

Much of the learning accomplished via the internet is orchestrated (at a broader scale) by the learners themselves, pulling together harder (and sometimes softer) pieces such as written tutorials, YouTube videos, Wikipedia articles, MOOCs, email correspondence, and so on to provide unique learning solutions tailored to their needs. It is often possible to gain direct tuition from originators of ideas, research, and theories. This is possible because the internet is an incredibly soft technology, especially thanks to the ease with which its technologies can be assembled with others. For the most part, it uses open standards—the underlying technologies that make it work such as TCP/IP, HTTP, JavaScript, and XML—that allow a diverse range of uses, with a wide range of devices, over highly disparate network substrates, from wired ethernet networks to satellites to undersea cables to cellular networks. Even for the increasing number of commercial and even non-commercial systems that overlay proprietary, locked-in toolsets on top of this open infrastructure (following a design pattern of replacement in order to harden what is essentially soft), interfaces, APIs, gateways, and so on make it relatively simple to connect almost any service, device, or tool to a vast number of others. Increasingly, standards such as xAPI, LTI, Caliper, OpenBadges, and SCORM make it possible to integrate this cornucopia with more formal learning and records of it.

This is an archetypal example, however, of the problem that soft is hard. The internet consists of at least millions of hard technologies enacted in billions of ways every day. The more choices available, the more difficult it is to make them without at least some hardening. Hardening, of course, is exactly what the algorithms and interfaces powering search engines such as Google or those internal to specific sites or toolsets provide. The internet, infamously, is a massive swamp of stuff with a few isolated islands of well-organized, reliable information (Crawford, 1999). It is rich in deliberate falsehoods, distractions, trolls, and echo chambers, albeit perhaps not as disturbingly as is often portrayed in the popular press (Dubois & Blank, 2018). Technologies intended to help harden it to make it easier to find reliable sources for the knowledge that we seek, even when they work well and as advertised, often result in filter bubbles (Pariser, 2011). Unfortunately, without them, the extreme softness can be daunting or overwhelming, even for expert users. Too much choice is as bad as too little choice, especially for learners near the start of their learning journeys.

We need to be able to delegate some choices to others whom we perceive, rightly or wrongly, as sufficiently expert to help us. Unfortunately, the algorithms that filter or provide us with recommendations are seldom designed to support better learning. Although I and some others have designed systems for that purpose (none of which made it far beyond research systems), most are more focused on driving traffic to sites relevant to the subject matter. To make matters much worse, search engine optimization (SEO) strategies are often deliberately designed to subvert this, whether for commercial or propaganda purposes. The chances of finding resources useful to learning, consequently, are diminished.

Some have suggested that at least part of the solution to this problem is better education, especially in digital, network, and social media "literacies" (using the term, as previously discussed, in a fuzzy way). Proponents point to things as diverse as simple operational skills to those of design, legal, ethical, and social behaviours. However, though they definitely can do some good, the problem is only partially susceptible to direct teaching, because the internet, by definition, is a network of networks and, above all, a network of networked communities and cultures, each of which demands at least in part its own distinctive (and sometimes mutually exclusive) literacies.

Many of these networked cultures, not least because of the massive interconnections and scale of interactions supported, are evolving rapidly, so literacies acquired now might soon be out of date. Often, thanks to the structural softness of the most common technologies used (from sites to browsers to protocols), it might not even be clear that we are interacting with a specific culture. For instance, the uniformity of search results or news feeds deliberately masks significant differences in content, design, and other contextual indicators. In such a context, a search for "evolution," say, might well lead to nonsense on intelligent design or radical religious sites, rather than to information about plausible theories, sometimes with little to allow a novice learner to distinguish between reliable and unreliable sources.

It is even more problematic for topics such as the climate crisis, in which deliberately misleading information can be provided by powerful interest groups in forms designed intentionally to deceive or cast doubt. Attempting to solve the problem with greater hardness may introduce new problems of its own, because one size seldom fits all. For instance, efforts by web browser manufacturers to protect their users from scams, privacy intrusions, and malevolent sites often render perfectly legitimate and harmless sites inoperable. Similarly, by taking away agency from those who do understand the problems, the heavy-handed hard filtering sometimes prevents or seriously constrains those who might find alternative, softer solutions from doing anything about it.

The Googlization problem also reveals another set of technological incompatibilities between the pedagogies (and especially the assessments) of traditional in-person learning and the capabilities of this vast, distributed teacher. From teachers who ban cellphones in their classrooms or the use of Wikipedia in assignments and homework to the lament that students just copy their work from internet sources or, worse, use ChatGPT or employ others at the low rates that a vast international network affords to do the work for them, the methods of teaching and assessment typically used in institutional learning have failed to keep pace with the changing ways that we go about learning in an internet-connected age. To a large extent, both problems are direct results of the motivational issues discussed in the previous section.

When we force people to learn things that they might not wish to learn, in ways that might not suit their needs or skills, in a disempowering context, and then we apply extrinsic motivation to make the focus of learning the achievement of grades and credentials, it is little wonder that our students take the quickest, most direct approach to achieving them, and it is hardly surprising that there are plentiful services available to meet this demand. It is unusual for intrinsically motivated learners without extrinsic drivers to take shortcuts or to cheat, because the only people whom they would be cheating would be themselves. Preschool children who learn through play often deeply resent being interrupted in their learning because it is fun. By "fun," I do not mean that every moment makes them laugh for joy. Indeed, watching children at play, it is normal to see much seriousness, and even anger and frustration, as they struggle to overcome challenges of some game or toy, as they practise and struggle until they achieve success. What Csikszentmihalyi et al. (2014) describe as "flow" (a theory highly congruent with self-determination theory) is seldom a state of elation, though it can be highly satisfying and meaningful.

The problem cannot be solved effectively by smarter policing or greater control of the process. In fact, it is likely to make things far worse by further reducing agency in, amplifying the power imbalances, and disrupting the caring, supportive relationships that we strive to nurture between teachers and learners, as well as further emphasizing the importance of the grade, rather than the learning activity itself. Using automated technologies to uncover plagiarism, or tightening restrictions on the use of technologies, is simply to use counter-technologies to harden further a technology already incompatible with the reality of the world around it, making it more difficult to bring about real change. While it remains soft there is at least some potential for flexibility and accommodation of other ways of approaching the learning problems. The more that we harden it, the less compatible with the pedagogies that the distributed internet provides it becomes. The struggle to control the teaching and assessment process has always been an arms race between teachers seeking control and students driven primarily by those teachers' demands to judge and accredit their learning.

When new technologies of cheating (or, more charitably, shortcuts to getting the required grades) evolve and spread ever faster, it can be only a losing battle for educators to continue to teach and assess using the same methods that predate widespread access to the internet or generative AIs. The technologies of cheating are much softer, more agile, and more numerous than the stolid institutional processes that they circumvent. Simply attempting to harden a broken system through counter-technologies can never succeed for more than a moment. Every time that one part is hardened, a mass of soft processes is assembled around it that renders it useless.

The solution to such problems is both simple and difficult because it requires teachers to develop (or accommodate) softer, more flexible, adaptable, and personal (not personalized in the sense of something done to students) ways of teaching and softer, less tightly coupled ways of demonstrating that learning has occurred. It demands changes in how we support learning and in how we judge whether it has occurred.

One of the most harmful consequences of the methods that emerged from formal education's medieval origins is the conflation of formal, judgmental assessment and learning: they must be decoupled, or the entire process must be altered radically, if there is to be any hope of supporting the intrinsic motivation natural to all learners. Although feedback is hugely valuable, summative judgment—especially when linked with credentials—and teaching, for the most part, are largely incompatible technologies. It would make some difference, at least in some cases, were teaching and credentialing to be entirely separate, unaligned activities, performed by different people, with clearly separate purposes. Even when credentials are administered by people other than those teaching, however, it is hard to prevent the almost ubiquitous practice of teaching to the test, as the abysmal effects of SATs in schools clearly show (Baker, 2020; Locker & Cropley, 2004). Notwithstanding the difficulties of implementing such a policy, the general principle of divorcing learning and credentialing as much as possible should be applied whenever, to whatever extent, and however it can be applied. If that is not possible, then we must either use whatever means are at our disposal to reduce the dependencies between learning and credentials or rethink how credentials are given.

One way to get around the fundamental incompatibility of credentialing and effective learning is to make the credential an award (a means of recognizing what we have achieved) rather than a reward (a means of assessing compliance with a specified set of demands). Rather than or at least in addition to imposing "objective" and extrinsically imposed measures of learning, we need to support explicitly flexible, expansive, and open outcomes. We need to recognize the things that have been learned rather than punish learners for the things that they have not learned (yet). Such unplanned outcomes are natural consequences of how we learn, as the example of the lecture in an earthquake reveals. We might make use of portfolios of learning, for example, that are created as part of the learning process and that naturally record such learning and then, as an entirely separate process, provide an award for what has been learned as opposed to achievement of what we intended to teach. In many cases, it might be possible to discover outcomes that match more than one award or to combine the outcomes of different learning activities to match a single award.

To achieve this means a shift in focus from assessment as a reward or punishment to assessment as an award for whatever successes we accomplish, in the spirit of appreciative inquiry (Cooperrider & Whitney, 2011), or outcome harvesting (Wilson-Grau & Britt, 2012), celebrating achievement rather than punishing failure. Appreciative inquiry deliberately seeks the things that work, recognizing that measurement changes what is measured in potentially harmful ways, so (if improvement is sought) it is far better to focus on what worked than on what did not and to explore ways of improving and extending it rather than diagnosing failure. Similarly, outcome harvesting seeks not only to discover whether intended outcomes were achieved but also which other outcomes occurred along the way.

Since there are virtually always learning outcomes in addition to those intended by a teacher, including changes to ways of thinking as well as discoveries and improvements in skill, this offers a far kinder, more precise way to evaluate learning as well as great insights to teachers about the teaching process, not just their own but also across the teaching gestalt. If, at the same time, we also remove the requirement for every course to be some multiple of a predetermined length (as we have seen, an arbitrary quantity determined mainly by the timing of medieval Christian holidays) and instead allow each course to be the length required for the subject matter, then a single course might provide evidence of more than one credential, and multiple courses might be aggregated to provide evidence of a single credential. Rather than being proof of having met the demands of a teacher for a course, credentials can thereby offer evidence of achievement of outcomes, thus becoming more beneficial to employers as well as teachers and students. It would also allow students to assemble learning from beyond the institution, and perhaps from multiple institutions, giving greater personal control over the process.

There is a crucial place for diagnosing problems in teaching and learning. Feedback on success and failure, especially diagnostic feedback, particularly when given promptly or innate to the task, is an extremely important part of most learning journeys, one of the most consistently reliable pedagogical technologies that we have invented, and (along with its counterpart, feedback to the teacher on the teaching process) perhaps the most vital part of any effective educational assembly. However, it should be part of a process of continuous improvement rather than a summative wall that shuts down further learning. If particular learning must be achieved—a necessity in many roles in life, from driving to brain surgery—then multiple attempts should be allowed until success is achieved or until the learner chooses to give up. The only value of negative feedback is as a signal that more learning is needed, not that learning so far has failed.

Timetables and schedules can also be enemies of effective learning. It is a consequence of the constraints of traditional learning that, if it is not perfectly achieved within the time frame that we set for it, on the whole we simply offer a lower grade (including, sometimes, the bizarre and counter-educative notion of a "fail"). Apart from a few special cases, this makes no sense in traditional teaching, assuming that we believe education to be primarily concerned with learning, let alone in the open, flexible, pace-free environment of the internet. When learning without the constraints of timetables and schedules, we should be able to try until we succeed. There is no reason that able students who continue to work at a skill or the acquisition of some knowledge should ever achieve less than total success (however it might be measured) as long as they persist, they are well supported, and there are no learning disabilities or other constraints (e.g., economic or inherent timing sensitivity) to prevent it. Anything less is a failure of teaching, in all its distributed forms, and even when it succeeds teaching can (as the co-participation model implies) always be improved.

It makes a great deal of sense to extend the boundaries of a formal course to encompass the internet, which can be achieved easily through tools of aggregation to syndicate resources from outside, curated lists of resources, student-created social bookmarks, sharing through Twitter hashtags, and a host of other mechanisms. Extending the course boundaries to allow members of the public (or at least a broader university community) to see what students are doing can also be extremely effective, as long as students can choose not to share at least some of their work: control is essential. Such methods are firmly in the complexivist tradition of pedagogies, and they are thus native to an internet-connected world to a far greater extent than in the objectivist and subjectivist methods common in online teaching. They thus tend to be less path dependent.[8]

---

8 For further discussion of such methods and technologies to support them, see Chapter 8 of Dron and Anderson (2014a).

Revisited: There's No Significant Difference in Learning Outcomes No Matter Which Media or Tools You Choose

Summary: extensive research suggests that there is no significant difference between online and in-person learning, that media appear to be largely irrelevant, and that (though some approaches, on average, might be better than others) almost every educational intervention strategy or method works.

The fact that medium or mode of delivery appears to make no difference, on average, is unsurprising given that most such studies provide few controls for method, which might matter much more than medium (Clark, 1983). However, even if methods are as consistent as they can be across media (not really possible thanks to countless dependencies and interactions between technologies used in the assembly), any soft technology can be used well or badly, so it is not remarkable that some online learning is better than some in-person learning, and vice versa, or that the differences tend to balance out. To suggest that all e-learning is comparable to all p-learning (place-based learning) makes no sense given that there are virtually infinite ways to do both and that described methods are only a fraction of what actually goes into any learning experience. Any individual part of the assembly might be better or worse implemented, and the assembly itself might be well or less well orchestrated. This is not to mention the enormous contributions of the pedagogies and working practices of the learners themselves.

It makes no more sense to suggest—without extraordinary evidence— that any one technology, pedagogy, tool, or method is better than another than to suggest that oil paintings are better than watercolours or that blues is better than chamber music. Indeed, typically, there are more differences between two courses using the same modality than between those using two different modalities. There is a world of difference, say, between an online, self-paced, objectivist course and an online, paced, social, subjectivist course or between a small, intimate, in-person tutorial and a large, in-person, impersonal lecture class. There are also many issues related to stakeholders' perceptions of online learning, especially in in-person institutions, where attitudes of faculty, students, and leadership, on average, are negative, especially thanks (mainly in the United States) to their association with for-profit degree mills of dubious quality (Protopsaltis & Baum, 2019).

On a more cautious note, the measurements of effectiveness that we tend to use can conceal a number of important differences. For example, in a well-conducted study, Heller et al. (2019) compare two MOOCs delivered in a paced format (with tutor support) and a self-paced format (with no tutor support) and find no significant difference between the two when measured in terms of course outcomes. Although both versions included discussion forums, discussion on those with tutor mediation, unsurprisingly, was significantly higher, but, perhaps more surprisingly, completion rates for each group differed little. The authors tentatively (and with reservations) suggest that tutors therefore might have done little to improve learning outcome or retention and that other factors such as initial motivation played much larger roles. It is unclear, though, from the study exactly how tutors were expected to contribute and what kind of role they played, nor is there much indication whether there were other benefits such as reduced time on task because tutors clarified questions.

In a longitudinal study of repeat iterations of a similarly constructed MOOC performed at Athabasca University, early attempts to provide moderately intensive tutor support offered little obvious value, much as Heller et al. (2019) found. However, in repeat iterations, when tutors were more carefully coached to encourage students to interact with one another rather than with them, along with a deliberately higher ratio of students to tutors intended to reinforce the message that tutors were there to connect students rather than to answer questions, retention rates improved significantly, though measured outcomes were similar (Mishra et al., 2019). Regardless of the effects on retention, in both cases there were differences in learners' experiences depending on levels of engagement, but in neither case were attempts made to measure the full extent of what the learners actually learned as a result: both studies simply looked at measures such as persistence and achievement of intended outcomes. Everything that we do and experience changes us, so it is virtually impossible for such different experiences to have led to identical learning outcomes. Perhaps students improved techniques for asking questions, or discovered things not assessed but nonetheless useful, or formed relationships that continued to offer learning benefits beyond the course. Perhaps nothing of the sort happened.

The problem is that, because only visible engagement, persistence, and performance to predetermined objectives were measured, we have no way to tell. As Protopsaltis and Baum (2019) argue, there are many aspects of an in-person learning experience that matter, few of which are ever observed let alone measured. This is even more true of online learners, whose presence is measured only by the deliberate traces that they leave in digital spaces but whose learning almost certainly extends into other parts of their lives and interactions with others. If we are to understand education at all, we need better approaches to discovering more about what is learned—and how—than the simple things that we normally choose to record. Again, it would be useful to harvest outcomes (Wilson-Grau & Britt, 2012) rather than measure only those that we expected to occur. It would also help if we were to design learning activities that deliberately made those hidden parts of the process visible, for example by the incorporation of reflective learning diaries that discuss the process in the outputs that we expect of our students.

A similar set of issues underpins Hattie's (2013) findings that just about every method works. In fact, Hattie finds that the average effect size of the improvement reported across all interventions is 0.4 (p. 32). Assuming this as a baseline, he tries to identify an ordered list of effective methods and strategies. Such an ordering is at least partly possible because he restricts his study to a fairly hard and limited set of technologies. The measure of success that he uses is simply the grade achieved in the context of a conventional institutional classroom. Furthermore, Hattie is concerned only with what "works" in a circumscribed, largely in-person, institutional classroom context. He barely considers the myriad other ways of learning that are or could be used were that context to be changed or the many other outcomes, good and bad, that might occur as well.

The studies that Hattie's (2013) work compiles almost all relate to one particular kind of technology (the school or college), with a particular set of purposes (though set in an educational context, far from all educational in nature), by an atypical set of practitioners (those enthusiastic and informed enough to research their practice). Thus, what constitutes success is not generalizable to all human learning, only to the specific subset of common but often inauthentic contexts found in typical educational institutions, mainly in English-speaking countries. To apply this to all education, including everything outside a formal school or college context, would be a little like identifying features such as cylinder size, carburetor efficiency, and number of spark plugs that affect performance in cars, then applying them to electric cars or bicycles.

Hattie (2013) himself is the first to recognize the limitations of his methodology and that no prescriptive list of this kind can ever cater to the specific needs of a given set of learners, so the main message of his book emerges from going beyond simple methods and instead looking for the general patterns that most successful interventions share. Based upon his findings, he observes that passion and artistry in a teacher are usually more important than method. Hattie argues that effective teaching occurs when teachers continuously learn, about what their learners are learning and about how they are teaching, in a responsive process that constantly changes as learners (including teachers) themselves change. He describes this as "visible learning" (discovering what and how students learn) and "visible teaching" (discovering what and how teachers teach). His most significant contribution is less telling us which methods (specifically) we should use to teach than identifying how (in general) to be a teacher. Although stemming from an analysis of empirical data rather than deriving from first principles, these methods are in exact accordance with a co-participation perspective. Having read Hattie's work some years after first developing the ideas in this book, I find it gratifying to know that they stand up to empirical validation.

Revisited: The Best Ways to Teach Are Not the Best Ways to Teach

Summary: to the surprise of many teachers who have been taught otherwise, according to simple measures of achievement of planned learning outcomes, subjectivist approaches to teaching, on average, are far from the most effective.

It is not at all surprising that the evidence to support broadly subjectivist approaches to teaching is patchy and inconsistent or that the average effects on grades are mediocre. Of all pedagogies, those that lie in the subjectivist spectrum are among the softest, so it is inevitable that huge variance will be seen in the results because they will always be instantiated significantly differently—in terms of skill and method—from one context to the next. Indeed, constructivism and other subjectivist models are theories of learning, not of teaching, so inevitably large amounts of detail and process must be filled in if a teaching method based upon the idea is to be put into practice, the details of which can vary enormously. Teachers have to instantiate those pedagogies with creativity and skill. Subjectivist models also implicitly acknowledge that learner pedagogies can and must play a large role in learning, so their skill matters too. Thus, the degree of expertise and the level of engagement with the process must play a dominant role in the effectiveness of the learning technologies.

Far more than in objectivist approaches, the soft technique—the passion, caring, and creativity of teachers (including learners themselves)—leads to success or failure, rarely just the easily described processes, methods, and tools that formally recognized teachers use to bring that about. Unfortunately, simple statistics imply that there are likely to be more average and below-average teachers than those above average, so the chances of this happening are lower, on average, than when using well-proven harder pedagogical methods. The matter is made worse since a casual reading of the literature suggests that minimal guidance is needed for such pedagogies, which is neither normally true nor claimed by most theorists. It is just that the learners themselves are expected to play a more significant role in determining goals, approaches, and methods, with the support of those expected to know more as well as the support of one another. If anything, this demands a more active role from all the teachers involved in the process. This need for skillful technique is not just a problem when considering complex interventions with many possible permutations such as active learning. Arguably, one of the simplest and most uncontroversially valuable pedagogical interventions of all, feedback, on average is a Really Good Thing, but reported results are among the most variable in their influences in educational interventions (Hattie & Gan, 2011, p. 249).

There are many ways of giving feedback that can be great, harmful, or anything in between. Learners can be discouraged by poor feedback as easily as they can be inspired by great feedback. Grades as feedback (perhaps except for some hard, right-answer topics), for example, are almost universally harmful (Kohn, 2011).

Active learning methods demand not only hard skill in applying the method but also soft technique, compassion, and artistry by all teachers involved. Because most reports of successful uses of such methods are made by people with exactly those attributes, it is not surprising that they are reported as being successful or that they fail when enacted by people who are underprepared, have insufficient practice, or are simply not attuned to the methods. In such cases, it might indeed be better to employ a harder pedagogical method (though still sufficiently soft to allow two-way feedback), such as direct instruction or mastery learning, that offers greater assurance of success to teachers who lack the necessary time, energy, or skill to implement softer pedagogies. This speaks to the need for teachers to learn more about how to teach and to engage more actively in reflective practice, to which we turn next.

Knowing more about educational theory and practice can help one to become a better teacher up to a point. Tellingly, pedagogical knowledge gained through education can have some effect on teaching proficiency, but even when it does that effect is not large. Goldhaber (2002) and Goldhaber and Brewer (1999) found that the effect of a teacher on performance is only slightly greater for teachers with full certification than for those with provisional certification following minimal training. Similarly, Hattie (2013, p. 151) observes negligible differences between the effectiveness of teachers with four-year certification and those with alternative forms of training, or even brief emergency certification, though (on average) there are slightly larger improvements among teachers with a few years of experience, and teachers without any training whatsoever tend to fare badly. This seems to imply that some pedagogical/teaching-process knowledge is useful, but there are few gains to be had from being taught a lot about pedagogy. Like a paintbrush, it takes some work to learn the basic strokes, but the real improvement comes about through practice, reflection, and iteration, especially when there are opportunities for feedback and discussion.

For most, there are diminishing returns beyond a certain level of expertise, and it is not uncommon for great teachers to reach a peak relatively early in their careers. This is not unusual in creative occupations as a whole. It would be a brave critic who suggested that Shakespeare's plays from the middle of his career are any worse than those later in his career, for instance, despite presumably being the results of greater knowledge and experience, and for every example of authors, artists, musicians, mathematicians, or scientists producing their greatest work at a venerable age there will be at least as many (I have a hunch more) who did their best work earlier in their careers. Expertise can be developed over time; however, notwithstanding the widespread belief popularized by Gladwell (2008) that expertise follows from 10,000 or more hours of practice, careful studies have revealed that practice in fact might account for as little as a quarter of the skill of an individual (Macnamara & Maitra, 2019), and far from all who excel in their fields put in that many hours, whereas many who do not excel put in more.

The depressing truth is that a lifetime of reflective practice typically leads to a fair level of proficiency and competence, but it will not turn someone with no talent into a genius. Indeed, given that boredom can play a notable role (many teachers, especially in schools, move on to other careers), too much experience within a relatively turgid education system with little scope for growth might be counterproductive, unless teachers constantly and successfully take on new and interesting challenges (Boyd et al., 2011). It is not the pedagogies that need to be better developed but the teachers themselves.

It is important to remember that soft technologies are most suited to orchestrating parts that are fundamentally human and not technological at all—love, passion, interest, excitement, and so on often are of considerably greater importance than the mechanical methods, tools, gadgets, and structures that we use to express them. If you are a teacher and your teaching, of yourself or others, does not inspire your passion, then it might be time to learn new methods, topics, ways of learning, and tools or to get out of the business altogether. In part, this is because passion and compassion are among the key phenomena that can and should be orchestrated in successful teaching, whether of ourselves or others. To a large extent, though, they are what drive us to learn and teach, the energy that makes the educational machine run, without which we might as well be soulless AIs. Passion can be simulated up to a point, but it is usually a bad idea because it is hard to maintain the illusion for more than a little while, and it is difficult to fool everyone all the time. If you find little or no excitement in the subject, in helping learners to learn, and in figuring out how to do that better, then something needs to change. As we have seen, some learners will succeed despite your lack of interest because you are not the only orchestrator of phenomena, but so much more would be possible if you could rekindle your passion.

One approach to doing so is to seek novelty. There is much to be said for learning new technologies of teaching, not because they will improve practice automatically (few if any will do that) but because they encourage reflection, invoke surprise, and maybe even inspire delight in their novelty.

There are also technological means to nurture and engender passion, techniques that can be developed and improved with practice, such as method acting (Stanislavski, 1989). Method acting is used by actors as a means to become entirely immersed in their roles so that they are not so much acting as behaving and feeling like the characters whom they play. It employs a range of soft but formal processes for developing techniques in identifying and replicating sensations, achieving focus (hyper-attention), and removing tension (using relaxation methods common in therapy), and it uses deliberate methods for drawing on relevant memories of past feelings. It can take a long time to learn these techniques well, but some of the basic tricks can be used by anyone: relaxing, focusing, and remembering feelings might be enough to start the process rolling. It is difficult for most teachers to become completely immersed in teaching, inasmuch as few of us love every aspect of our subjects as much as every other, and there is often a need to cater to diversity in both subject and audience, as we flit from one class to the next. However, finding what we do love about what we teach, hopefully, is not a major problem for any teacher.

If deep role immersion is too difficult, imagining ourselves in a slightly different light can make a significant difference to how we think and behave (Brown et al., 2019). Even something as simple as forced smiling can activate parts of the brain associated with pleasure, thus potentially increasing the probability that we will actually feel pleasure (Hennenlotter et al., 2009). Passion is an entirely non-technological phenomenon, but technologies—including music, visual arts, dance, and literature—can stimulate passion and make use of it as part of an orchestration for teaching.

Pedagogical methods can both take advantage of and help to kindle our passions. Telling stories, anecdotes, or snippets of information that reveal our own attitudes and excitement, no matter how small, can make a large difference to how we communicate our passion to others, whether directly or in prepared course materials. One of the innate advantages of in-person teaching is that the effects of such stories can be seen immediately, so feedback loops can drive greater passion among all participants. In an in-person or webinar context, body language can matter. Facial expressions (not faked) certainly do. Responses to questions really matter, and the speed of a response, especially online, matters even more because, especially online, it is a prime indicator of interest in both the subject and the learner (Richardson & Lowenthal, 2017). The infectious nature of passion is yet another reason that social pedagogies are a good idea. In an in-person context, normally, it takes little effort to communicate passion, but online it is important to provide sufficient channels so that learners can be aware of how other learners are experiencing it, not just the teacher.

Discussion forums, backchat channels in webinars, shared blogs, other shared artifacts of learning such as files or bookmarks, and so on can all contribute effectively to an infection model of learning as long as the technologies (including pedagogies) are sufficiently soft to allow free and open expression. Asking a leading question to which answers should be expressed in a largely proscribed format, for example, is rarely an effective way to support infectious passion, still less the sharing of assignment outputs for critical review, though both relatively hard approaches can have a place in the overall assembly. Open questions, questions that encourage learners to connect the current experience to things that they care about, and wicked problems, especially those that incite passionate debate, can be far more effective. Much more could be said on this subject, but the key thing is that development of skill in the soft technologies of teaching is critical to the success of softer approaches to teaching, and without it the results are likely to be disappointing.

The importance of passionate, caring teaching in enacting soft pedagogies suggests that, rather than researching the effectiveness of these particular teaching methods, we should be putting far more energy into researching the effectiveness of particular teachers. If the methods are soft, reliant more on an individual's distinctive technique than on a specific set of processes, then what matters most is developing those techniques in teachers, not honing the methods. The better we can understand what makes a great teacher, the more likely it is that our teaching will be effective (to a point) no matter which methods we use. The emphasis of research on soft methods of teaching should therefore be on raising the bar so that an average teacher of the future is better than a good teacher of today.

Revisited: No One Has Solved the 2 Sigma Problem

Summary: despite a great deal of active research and development, no method of teaching yet devised has consistently matched the average 2 sigma improvements seen in one-to-one or small-group tutoring.

From a co-participation perspective, the most interesting thing about one-to-one tutoring is that it is simply a condition of teaching, not a process, not a method, and certainly not a pedagogy. Because pedagogies are soft technologies, what we describe as a "method" will always leave gaps, to a greater or lesser extent, that need to be filled by technique. One-to-one teaching is nothing but a gap. It allows a teacher and learner complete freedom to apply any method. The reason that the 2 sigma challenge is so hard to meet is that it compares any and every pedagogical method, chosen exactly when needed, in full and open communication with the learner, with specific pedagogical methods. This is an unfair contest. One-to-one tutoring is not a pedagogy: it is a situation in which any and every pedagogy could be used. It allows tutors to ride the wave of the adjacent possible, knowing more about the learner than most (if not all) other forms of teaching and being able to adapt and change almost instantly as both teacher and student learn about themselves and each other. It would still be better even if a particular method met the 2 sigma challenge because tutors simply could adopt it too. Because teaching is a soft technology, such a method cannot be perfect, so there are always ways to improve it, and tutors will still remain ahead.

Revisited: Matching Teaching Style to Learning Style Offers No Significant Benefit

Summary: despite its intuitive appeal, and despite thousands of attempts to prove otherwise, there is no reliable evidence that teaching to students' perceived learning style offers any benefit to learners.

One problem with learning style theories is that it is extremely difficult to find reliable evidence to back their claims because pedagogies are soft. Every enactment of them is unique and deeply determined by context. It is rarely if ever possible to construct directly comparable learning experiences independent of the skill and artistry of their creators. The case is similar to that of the no-significant-difference phenomenon, inasmuch as researchers must attempt to control a single technological variable (whether medium, method, or other factor) without consideration of the usually vast number of other factors that affect and are affected by it. There are, and must ever be, internal consistencies and inconsistencies of the technologies to consider too. For instance, if one wished to create an experience for a learner with a "reading" style, then it would make no sense simply to remove the pictures from an existing text or, vice versa, to remove the text for a "visual" learner.

It becomes significantly more complex when multi-dimensional learning style theories are used, such as the Felder-Silverman model (Felder & Spurlin, 2005), that allow for a wide range of combinations and blends, the absence of any one of which might be harmful (if the theory is valid). There is therefore a wide range of interdependencies among and knock-on effects from all choices made, whether they are about media, structure, attitude, values, or whatever, all of which radically change the technological assembly, making comparison between two instances pointless. If just a word or two or even a verbal emphasis can make a difference to learning (and it can—try shouting an offensive expletive at the top of your voice in the midst of a lesson if you do not believe me), then the massive restructuring involved in choosing a different medium, or in changing the structure of an explanatory text, let alone in altering the underlying pedagogical methods, can never allow us to reliably identify a single aspect of the experience that had the desired effect.

The situation is made worse since, if our preferred model is accurate, then presumably it is also accurate for the person designing the experience, who most likely has more or less skill in designing learning experiences for learners with different learning styles. It would do no good to our research study to assign different learning designers to different learning designs for different learning styles because the skill and artistry of the designer would play an even more prominent role. As a result, all that we can reliably compare is one (highly situated and unrepeatable) assembly with another.

The fact that even enthusiasts agree that all learning style theories appear to work more or less as well as one another (Felder, 1996; Kanadli, 2016) supports this view. Perhaps they just represent facets of a larger whole, but equally any effects that they appear to have might result from something else entirely. Hattie (2013, pp. 246–250) observes that, if learners have a particular learning preference, then it might mean that they enjoy the process more and thus tend to achieve more than they would otherwise; however, if it is enjoyment rather than learning style that matters, then almost certainly there will be better ways to make learning more enjoyable than to match teaching to a learned preference. Ability can make a significant difference across many dimensions, including simple hard literacy concerns such as reading proficiency, typing speed, or skill in operating image manipulation or multimedia editing tools. For instance, Nguyen (2016, p. 33) relates the following quotations from students interviewed about their learning styles:

> I prefer visual, auditory and reflective style and online learning contains those. However, I still haven't got used to this because my computer skill is weak. I can only type slowly.

> When the teacher asks me to upload a video presentation or do an audio reflection, I don't know how to do it. I have to get a lot of help from my friends. Anyway, I will try to improve my computer skill after this course.

If we lack the hard skills needed to cope with whatever a particular theory claims to be our style, then we are more likely to choose another style when offered the option. But hard skills are not innate, and weaknesses do not need to be persistent, for any lack of skill can be corrected through learning. It is also highly context sensitive. If, in our main occupations or activities, we need to exercise different skillsets, then it is highly likely that we will consistently apply appropriate styles in those contexts, regardless of any presumed innate tendencies, and thus we will get better at using them. Larger-scale context can make a big difference too. For example, Carr (2013) notes that there are large cultural differences among learning styles/preferences that exist at least at a national level, making findings that appear to be valid in one culture spurious in another.

Despite all this, were one determined to persist with a certain learning style model, the innate softness of all learning technologies means that there would be little point in doing so. It would still not allow one reliably to predict future improvements/failures to improve because there is always an indefinitely large number of other ways in which one might orchestrate the phenomena differently to achieve a better or worse outcome that we (and everyone else) never thought of and countless ways in which, in the future, we might do it better or worse. Just as in the no-significant-difference phenomenon, so bad methods can be enacted well, and great methods can be enacted badly. It all depends on the assembly, not just on the individual parts of it, and technique (how it is done) often matters more than method (what is done).

Perhaps the most damning indictment of the learning styles concept, though, is one that even dyed-in-the-wool learning style theorists would have to admit: it is extremely likely that, if they exist at all, persistent learning styles are not innate but learned. There is a high probability that individuals were taught or discovered sets of methods and tools that worked for them in the past—most likely in early childhood—and that they have honed their techniques more effectively than other approaches that might be even more effective if they took the time to learn them. Like any technique, practice increases competence. The reasons for initial preferences might be many and varied, from being associated with subjects/skills that we enjoy to liking a teacher. Such effects probably start early in life and certainly are reinforced by schooling. This leads to a self-reinforcing path dependency, a hardness that determines much that follows. The simplest explanation of any learning style—if such a thing exists—is that it is a being-taught habit. It is just a set of pedagogical techniques that we have learned. Because we rarely have a choice in the real world, outside formal education, about how the things that we need to learn are presented to us, it would be foolish to continue to reinforce that habit rather than learn to learn in other ways.

Whether or not learning style theories are valid, they do provide us with stories that help us to make sense of the world in different ways, which can help to catalyze new ideas and imaginative ways of learning and teaching. It is undoubtably a good thing for designers of learning to be aware of a diversity of learning strategies and techniques, and to use them, especially when teaching others. No doubt every learner is different, and all can benefit from approaching a topic or skill in different ways at different times in different contexts. In some ways, learning style models can be seen as coarse, caricatured, but still potentially useful ways of building personas (Pruitt & Grudin, 2003), or parts of them, which have been shown repeatedly to be effective design tools that make it easier for us to imagine the needs, interests, skills, and desires of our target audience. Given that education, fundamentally, is a design/performance discipline, this might be as much as we can hope for in a theory or model.

For example, despite finding the Kolb learning style model extremely problematic, I frequently make use of Kolb's learning cycle—actually, as Kolb and Kolb (2005) acknowledge, the invention of Kurt Lewin—because I know it well, and it serves as a useful reminder of four of the most significant kinds of activity that should be considered in most learning trajectories: abstract conceptualization, reflective observation, active experimentation, and concrete experience. It is not always a cycle, and the order can vary because, being a technology, the best order in any given situation depends on other design choices. These are high-level learning strategies, not styles, and knowing about different strategies can be helpful when faced with a blank screen and a need to develop a learning intervention. Similarly, I often use Pask's (1976b) serialist/holist model of learning strategies to remind myself that there are always different ways to learn the same things and to reduce the likelihood of falling into the trap of teaching the way that I would like to be taught. Such models can be useful intuition pumps whether we believe in them or not. It is almost always possible to distinguish learning or teaching strategies from learning style models, and it can be well worth doing so. Technologies do not have to rely on accurate models of the world in order to be useful. They do not need to be applied science.

Revisited: Experimental Educational Research Appears Not to Work Well

Summary: it seems to be really difficult to perform useful experiments in education, and, despite perhaps millions of attempts, little improvement has been seen in how we teach that can be ascribed to such research.

Reductive research methods, following those of the physical sciences, are mostly intended to seek, confirm, or deny underlying simple causal relationships: if x happens, then y will occur. In most cases, whether the discipline is softer or harder, the main purpose of performing reductive research is thus usually to test some generalizable law or principle, normally by attempting to disprove a hypothesis in a manner that could be replicated. In harder disciplines such as physics or chemistry, studies normally attempt either to replicate both methods and context or to apply different methods to the same context, the assumption being that natural phenomena should behave in the same way no matter where they happen in the universe. In softer disciplines such as education, replications are seldom as direct as those in harder disciplines. Given the situated nature of education and the inevitable softness of the technologies concerned, the context differs every time.

Distributed participation in all learning, with the learner always playing a role in orchestrating the final assembly, means that the same conditions can never hold twice. Although obviously and trivially true when looking at different individuals, the problem is even worse when we attempt to repeat an intervention for a single individual. As Smedslund (2016) argues, once some mental event (e.g., learning) has occurred, it must irreversibly change the person for whom it has happened, so no experiment can ever be repeated on the same person. Even if it could, Smedslund notes, the attempt would be scuppered by a combination of infinite possible contexts (situations that can and do never repeat) and social interactivity (in which there are and always must be many more influences than those controlled by the experimenter). Smedslund argues that, in any intervention that relates to psychological states (especially including learning), it is thus impossible to predict specific outcomes based upon prior observed behaviours and averages.

Following from this, given the complexity and variability of context, in most meaningful educational interventions apart (perhaps) from the hardest and most invariant, it would make little or no sense for researchers to follow identical procedures, because each educational intervention must have unique aspects that need to be controlled for differently and examined differently. As we have seen, virtually all interventions demand soft technique and creativity from their participants, which almost invariably makes all the difference between success and failure. Educational researchers therefore must attempt to follow conceptually similar procedures in necessarily different contexts. Conceptual similarity, however, is a vague concept in itself. These methods are technologies like any other, and there is softness at their heart, and thus small differences in technique that are virtually impossible to identify in their entirety and that are as reliant on skillful use as the phenomena that they seek to examine, can have significant impacts on the results.

When objectivist and reductive methods are applied to human-created technologies, such as pedagogies or tools for teaching, it is unlikely that researchers will find universals that resemble the laws of nature, because technologies are inventions that exist in complex and ever-shifting relationships with one another, continually evolve, rely on technique for their enactment, and seldom occur in similar enough assemblies to reliably infer causal mechanisms. Softer technologies might never occur in the same way twice. In assembly, they might orchestrate dozens, hundreds, or thousands of different phenomena, each of which can affect the whole (and one another) in unpredictable ways. Furthermore, minute differences across many qualitative dimensions (unpredictably) can have large effects, and the vast range of possible combinations can result in emergent phenomena that could not be predicted from simple cause-effect relationships, even if all were known individually.

These phenomena (intentionally or not) can uncover or confirm more atomic phenomena that are parts of the orchestration, such as (in education) ways that people learn or feel about things in general or (in engineering) the load-bearing properties of materials. However, this is not research on the ways and means of teaching and learning. It is simply using the technology in question as part of a different technology, designed to discover natural laws. Unfortunately, as discussed in Chapter 4, in an education system, the laws so discovered might not always be as "natural" as they seem because of the effects of our prior inventions on subjects' behaviour. For instance, it is possible to discover "laws" such as the intermittent punishment effect (Parke et al., 1970) that appear to indicate motivational benefits of rewards and punishments, but this is the case only in a system that, through rewards and punishments, has killed students' intrinsic motivation in the first place (Kohn, 1999).

Unfortunately, though the natural laws that we might uncover can provide (when well researched) a useful set of phenomena to orchestrate, even when we do find consistent causal laws of learning (and almost certainly there are such things), it might not help us much in designing real-life education because it is the assembly, in all its rich and deeply intertwingled complexity, that matters: many causes compete with or enhance one another, and emergent behaviours occur all the way down the line. From a design perspective, it is useful to understand how individual design ingredients tend to work but knowing how people learn (say) does not predict successful teaching any more than knowing how the engines of cars work predicts successful driving or the bristles of a paintbrush predict successful painting. It can help to explain phenomena that occur but not to predict reliably in advance what skillful practitioners can do with those phenomena, in artful assembly with countless others, many of which will never be repeated in the same way again. It could be argued that any knowledge is better than none, but there are complex interactions between these simple parts that make their effects inherently unpredictable. For example, we know that properly spaced learning provides a more effective way to remember than unspaced (or poorly spaced) learning, so it can and often does make sense to use this fact to help remember something, but if what is being remembered is boringly presented, personally irrelevant, or overly traumatic then the results might not be those anticipated. This is a simple example: most real-life situations are far more complex and intertwingled.

All that said, if the technologies that we examine are sufficiently hard and invariant, then we might discover consistent and useful facts about how they behave individually, but on the whole this is mainly valuable in the same way as knowing that steel is harder than paper. It provides us with a better range and understanding of components that we might use to build our technologies, but it does not determine or predict whether those technologies will work how we wish them to work when we put them together.

There are a few useful ways to apply reductive research to technological phenomena, most notably when the assembly itself is very hard—technologies such as SATs, self-paced online courses, and so on—and likely to be repeated with little or no variation many times. Based upon findings, we can make adjustments to those (and only those) hard technologies, adding or changing parts of the assembly, we can observe their effects, and we can explore differences among contexts to gain a fair idea of what works and what does not. Such methods—sometimes described as A/B testing (Dixon et al., 2011)—are common in technology design and often lead to improved inventions.

However, though it can be useful to the creator of that specific hard technology to know whether it works as intended or not, that in itself does not tell us anything that we can generalize reliably for a different tool, method, or process or whether the technology itself makes any sense in the first place. It can tell us little about whether the same technology applied in a different context would work the same way or whether parts of the assembly will behave in similar ways in different configurations. It can help us to understand the pieces, and others might use those pieces in their own assemblies, but it tells us little of value about what happens when they combine in even slightly different ways. This is extremely important if we wish to improve our practices.

Unless we can identify causal relationships, we have no way of knowing what it was about the system we used that did or did not work, and we have no reason to repeat or remove it. But causal relationships in educational contexts are parts of a complex adaptive system that makes it fundamentally impervious to study using methods that reduce complex phenomena to their component parts, as Kauffman (2008, 2009, 2016, 2019) persuasively argues. From those parts, we can never anticipate the boundary conditions of what can emerge in advance, and we can never pre-state what their functions will be by looking at their constituent elements. This means, in a real sense, that the behaviour of the parts does not predict the behaviour of the emergent whole, even though they may cause that behaviour to occur. The problem is not that the smaller-scale phenomena do not mechanistically combine to cause the larger-scale phenomena—of course they do. The problem is that, in a system of any complexity, emergent behaviours are meaningful only in the contexts of the systems to which they belong and cannot be understood by reduction to their component parts. We might know everything worth knowing, say, about cells in a body, but that would not help us to predict or explain the role of a heart in a circulatory system (Kauffman, 2019).

It is tempting to seek reductive empirical knowledge of educational practices because clearly there are causal relationships between what we do and how we learn. We can easily see that some teachers are more consistently successful than others, and it is tempting to ascribe that success to whatever pedagogies and other tools they use: to abstract what they do from how it is done. However, what makes them successful rarely has much to do with any specific method in isolation. Instead, good teachers tend to adapt to the learners and the surrounding contexts as needed. Just as I am at least as reliable a predictor of my local weather as the best meteorologists with the biggest and fastest computers if all I have to do is predict what it will be in five minutes, so too it is possible for a teacher, with sufficient indicators about a learner, to adapt a way of teaching to that individual's needs when it matters. As Hattie (2013, p. 17) puts it, "the art of teaching, and its major successes, relate to 'what happens next'—the manner in which the teacher reacts to how the student interprets, accommodates, rejects, and/or reinvents the content and skills, how the student relates and applies the content to other tasks, and how the student reacts in light of success and failure."

We are good at identifying ways of reacting in the short term, but we are bad at predicting the results of our interventions in the long term, even though we often adopt a convenient illusion—usually based upon average effects—that we do know what has an effect. Unfortunately, averages are not useful when dealing with human beings because, as Rose (2016) observes, almost certainly there is no such thing as an average person. Rose gives the example of aircraft seats designed to fit the average pilot that, because there was literally no average pilot to be found, resulted in many plane crashes. There are reasonable grounds to suppose that education presents a similar case: an intervention intended to suit the average learner, in all likelihood, might suit no learner at all or even be harmful.

Teaching is more like sailing in changeable winds than like driving on well-marked empty roads. Knowing the direction in which we are headed, we must adapt constantly to conditions as they change around us, not keep to an unerring path. There are methods that we can and must learn, techniques that we can and should hone, rules of thumb that we can apply, but each circumstance demands different responses, and there is a high likelihood of encountering novel situations on a regular basis. To do this successfully, we need diverse skills more than mechanical procedures. We must be tinkerers and bricoleurs rather than engineers. Again, this implies that many of the most fruitful research avenues in education lie not in identifying effective teaching methods but in identifying effective teachers and what makes them so. When we find them, we can tell stories, perform design-based research (Anderson & Shattuck, 2012), offer rich case studies, use appreciative inquiry (Cooperrider & Srivastava, 1987; Cooperrider & Whitney, 2011), and so on so that others can gain inspiration, adapt our pedagogies, or imitate our tools in their own orchestrations in their own contexts. In doing so, we can add to and refine the technologies of learning as well as help others to develop their own techniques. This seems to be valuable enough in itself. We do not need to aspire to the kind of predictive certainty found in hard sciences.

The softer the technology, the harder it is to make accurate predictions about it. It would make no sense at all, for instance, to claim that email is good (or bad) for learning, and there is no research method that could be used to prove it unequivocally one way or the other, because there is virtually nothing fixed about the phenomena that it can utilize or the orchestrations of which it can be a part. For very soft technologies, the only research methods that make sense are those that attempt to investigate something about how they are used, not to discover their relative effectiveness in general. However, it is then that the (always unique) orchestration matters rather than the parts of the assembly.

As greater hardening is applied, the number of points of comparison becomes more salient, and it becomes more possible (though seldom particularly wise) to make more general (though always provisional) statements about them. For instance, though LMSs are mostly very soft technologies (for teachers) and can be assembled with other technologies to soften them further, they do impose many pedagogical constraints that lead to greater consistency between instances that, in some cases, can make them more comparable. They create adjacent impossibles as well as possibles. We might be able, for example, to generalize, albeit within a limited domain, about a particular instance of an LMS's discussion tools (e.g., the effects of limiting the size of text boxes on discussion posts) or quiz modules (e.g., the effects of being able to display only a single question at a time) within a specific pedagogical orchestration, though all bets would be off were we to compare different versions of the same tool across different orchestrations. Although they might cause issues in some orchestrations, almost certainly there would be ways of using the constraints to some pedagogical advantage in others, not to mention ways of assembling them with other tools, so we should resist drawing firm general conclusions.

The fact that every meaningful learning transaction is irreducibly unique does not mean that we should despair of seeking patterns or be wary of reifying soft techniques into harder tools and methods. Quite the opposite. This kind of sense making, pattern recognition, and pattern formation is how we make progress, how we learn to teach better, how we learn better in general, both individually and collectively. That said, those of us who seek to understand and research how this happens are left with what appears to be an intractably complex, complicated, and deeply situated view of learning and teaching, which might make one despair of ever being able to come up with any generalizable rules about how it should be done or, indeed, to make any reliable inferences about how learning occurred in any given instance. It is the essence of the art and nature of learning and teaching, a constant and ever-shifting interplay between knowing and discovery, in which what we do affects the structure of how we do it, and that structure in turn affects what we do. It is a constant and never-ending state of becoming, a creative evolutionary process with no beginning and no end. It is what makes us human.

This lack of generalizable predictability should be a cause for celebration, not for despair. If this is the nature of the beast, then we can identify ways to make the most effective use of it and to avoid pitfalls that await us should we get it wrong. What matters most is therefore awareness of how learners are learning and which effects our teaching is having. This has to be combined with a broader understanding of how the technologies of teaching work—all the technologies of teaching, from pedagogies to Google Search—and how they can work together. Teachers—all of us—are orchestrators of technologies that, if used effectively, at the right time, in the right place, with the right people, can lead to learning.

Epilogue

In American legend, John Henry competed with a steam drill to drive spikes into the ground and won, albeit at the cost of his own life, his heart bursting at the moment of victory. His story resonates with those who view technologies as threatening and alien, as competitors to humans. But, as I hope that I have demonstrated, his orchestration of tools was as much a technology as the steam drill, and far from being "other" our technologies must and should include ourselves. The difference between Henry and the steam drill lay ostensibly in the orchestration of phenomena. Were the ends to which they were put the same? Perhaps not. For Henry, there was meaning and value in the accomplishment of the task, not just in the task itself, a meaning so important to him that it cost him his life. We are and should be concerned when the orchestration of phenomena is embedded in machines—instantiated by whatever or whomever— and is no longer the purview of people, because sometimes that orchestration is an important part of what defines our identities, and often the purposes run far deeper than those that dazzle us on the surface. Performing a task with skill, ingenuity, creativity, or simply strength is deeply entangled with our sense of self-worth, part of our identities, and a characteristic delight of being human. This is obviously true of artistic skills, but it is also true of many mechanical tasks in which humans are part of a hard orchestration.

There are countless benefits of simply doing, living, and being. There is value in doing a simple thing well, even when we know that it can be done better, faster, and more efficiently by machines, even when the output is no different from (and likely objectively worse than) what would be achieved by those machines. The ends to which we orchestrate phenomena are not always as straightforward and utilitarian as they might seem to be at first. In all things, no matter how mundane, playing the game usually matters more than getting to the end of it, and the rules of the game might not be those that we see most easily. My grandson's gingerbread house might not be as objectively well built as one assembled by a professional bakery, but I would not swap one for the other. Technologies are often concerned with making our lives and the things that we do with our lives better, but this does not always mean that they should be faster and more efficient, reliable, or cost effective. We should choose what we give up to the machine with inordinate care. This is especially true of education, which is above all about ways of being in human society.

It is equally vital to remove the shackles of prescriptive technologies of which we are unwilling parts. To be an unwilling cog in a machine is a very different state of being than to play the part of a machine out of choice. It is not always obvious when this is happening, and we should constantly be alert to the possibility. When, for example, we trust in an AI tutor to guide us, or accept the verdict of a learning analytics engine that tells us what we should do (or what we are doing wrong), we run the risk of becoming parts of its circuitry rather than it being a part of ours. When the design of an LMS, a timetable, or a classroom encourages us to take the easy path, we are letting ourselves be parts of it rather than orchestrating it as part of us. As soon as we become aware of this, we can take steps to change it: we can assemble it into our own orchestrations as just more stuff in the assembly, or replace it, or (sometimes) modify it. Perhaps we will even accept it as a good or necessary thing.

Many rules that we follow exist for good reasons that benefit not just us but also everyone, and some machines (e.g., the scripts that novice teachers might have to follow or the scales that musicians choose to practise) can help us to learn or do what we want to do more effectively. This is fine as long as we are aware of it, can take ownership of it as part of who we are, and see our place within the technology as part of what it is. The dynamic of the hard influencing the soft more than vice versa is a given that we cannot change, but the hard does not necessarily entail the soft: it enables it. This means that we can adapt our responses in many different ways. But we must never forget that learning is an essentially human process in which technologies mediate, facilitate, and engender but in which the creative, feeling, value-filled human (and the human's society) is and must always be at the centre.

Education is about becoming the best humans that we can be, in a human context, with other humans. We should not blindly learn to be human from a hard machine, even though (and perhaps especially because) that machine might, such as through a generative AI like ChatGPT or Google's LaMDA, embody the thoughts, beliefs, and processes of other humans. A hard machine—even one enacted by people—has no dreams, desires, beliefs, values, or purpose beyond that of its creator or manager, so we need to be wary. Let humans teach humans with, through, about, and to be technologies, of course, but where decisions are at least moderated by a person or people. The parts can and often should be hard, but the assembly and final orchestration must be soft.

Is this book a technology? Of course. It has been many. Some of these technologies are obvious: I am using language, mediated through print (on a paper page, on an e-reader, or perhaps with text-to-speech software) to put a point or two across to achieve some purpose. Some of the technologies are less obvious, such as the book's structure, its approach to building arguments, the models and theories that the book expounds. It is a soft technology, both to me as the writer and to you as the reader, using skill in your interpretation and judgment as well as creativity in how you assemble it with other things that you know. My version of this technology is worlds removed from yours. What it orchestrates for me, and its uses, are utterly different from what it orchestrates for you and the uses to which you will put it. That is exactly as it should be. It is a rich assembly, orchestrated by many people, most of all by you.

If this book has helped you, however slightly, to think about what you know and how you have come to know it a little differently, then it has been a successful learning technology. In fact, even if you hold to all of your previous beliefs and this book has challenged you to defend them, then it has worked just fine too. Even if you disagreed with or misunderstood everything that I said, and even if you disliked the way that I presented it, it might still have been an effective learning technology, even though the learning that I hoped for did not come about. But I am not the one who matters the most here. This is layer upon layer of technology, and in some sense, for some technology, it has done what that technology should do. The book has conveyed words that, even if not understood as I intended them to be, even if not accepted, even if rabidly disagreed with, have done something for your learning. You are a different person now from the person you were when you started reading this book because everything that we do changes us. I do not know how it has changed you, but your mind is not the same as it was before, and ultimately the collectives in which you participate will not be the same either. The technology of print production, a spoken word, a pattern of pixels on a screen, or dots on a braille reader has, I hope, enabled you, at least on occasion, to think, criticize, acknowledge, recognize, synthesize, and react in ways that might have some value in consolidating or extending or even changing what you already know. As a result of bits and bytes flowing over an ether from my fingertips to whatever this page might be to you, knowledge (however obscure or counter to my intentions) has been created in the world, and learning has happened. For all the complexities and issues that emerge from that simple fact, one thing is absolutely certain: this is good.

References

AECT [Association for Education and Communication Technologies]. (1972). The field of educational technology: A statement of definition. *Audiovisual Instruction, 17*, 36–43.

Akerson, V. L., Burgess, A., Gerber, A., Guo, M., Khan, T. A., & Newman, S. (2018). Disentangling the meaning of STEM: Implications for science education and science teacher education. *Journal of Science Teacher Education, 29*(1), 1–8.

Allen, I. E., & Seaman, J. (2013). *Changing course: Ten years of tracking online education in the United States*. http://www.onlinelearningsurvey.com/reports/changingcourse.pdf

Anderson, P. W. (1972). More is different: Broken symmetry and the nature of the hierarchical structure of science. *Science, 177*(4047), 393–396. https://doi.org/10.1126/science.177.4047.393

Anderson, T., & Dron, J. (2011). Three generations of distance education pedagogy. *International Review of Research in Open and Distance Learning, 12*(3). https://doi.org/10.19173/irrodl.v12i3.890

Anderson, T., & Dron, J. (2012). Learning technology through three generations of technology enhanced distance education pedagogy. *European Journal of Open, Disance and E-Learning, 2012*(2). https://old.eurodl.org/?p=archives&year=2012&halfyear=2&article=523

Anderson, T., & Shattuck, J. (2012). Design-based research: A decade of progress in education research? *Educational Researcher, 41*(1), 16–25.

Andrews, T. M., Leonard, M. J., Colgrove, C. A., & Kalinowski, S. T. (2011). Active learning not associated with student learning in a random sample of college biology courses. *CBE—Life Sciences Education, 10*(4), 394–405.

Annand, D. (1999). The problem of computer conferencing for distance-based universities. *Open Learning, 14*(3), 47–52.

Annand, D. (2019). Conceptual failures of the community of inquiry framework. *International Journal of E-Learning & Distance Education, 34*(2). https://www.ijede.ca/index.php/jde/article/view/1133

Ariely, D. (2009). Large stakes and big mistakes. *The Review of Economic Studies, 76*(2), 451–469.

Arthur, W. B. (2009). *The nature of technology: What it is and how it evolves* (Kindle ed.). Free Press. https://doi.org/10.1016/j.futures.2010.08.015

Austin, J. L. (1962). *How to do things with words*. Clarendon Press.

Austin, J. L. (2013). Performative utterances. In M. Ezcurdia & R. J. Stainton (Eds.), *The Semantics-Pragmatics Boundary in Philosophy* (pp. 21–31).

Baker, C. (2020). We need less pressure. *Early Years Educator, 22*(4), 32.

Baldwin, J., & Brand, S. (1978). *Soft-tech*. Penguin.

Bangert-Drowns, R. L. (1993). The word processor as an instructional tool: A meta-analysis of word processing in writing instruction. *Review of Educational Research, 63*(1), 69–93.

Bessant, J., & Francis, D. (2005). Transferring soft technologies: Exploring adaptive theory. *International Journal of Technology Management & Sustainable Development, 4*(2), 93–112.

Bijker, W. E., Hughes, T. P., & Pinch, T. J. (Eds.). (1989). *The social construction of technological systems*. MIT Press.

Bloom, B. S. (1984). The 2 sigma problem: The search for methods of group instruction as effective as one-to-one tutoring. *Educational Researcher, 13*(6), 4–16.

Bloom, H. (2000). *Global brain: The evolution of mass mind*. Wiley.

Blum, S. D., & Kohn, A. (2020). *Ungrading: Why rating students undermines learning (and what to do instead)*. West Virginia University Press.

Boden, M. (1995). Creativity and unpredictability. *Stanford Humanities Review, 4*(2), 123–139.

Bonabeau, E., Dorigo, M., & Theraulaz, G. (1999). *Swarm intelligence: From natural to artificial systems*. Oxford University Press.

Borgmann, A. (1987). *Technology and the character of contemporary life: A philosophical inquiry*. University of Chicago Press.

Boser, U. (2019). *What do teachers know about the science of learning? A survey of educators on how students learn*. https://www.the-learning-agency.com/insights/what-do-teachers-know-about-the-science-of-learning

Bouygues, H. L. (2019). *Does educational technology help students learn?* https://reboot-foundation.org/does-educational-technology-help-students-learn/

Boyd, D., Grossman, P., Ing, M., Lankford, H., Loeb, S., & Wyckoff, J. (2011). The influence of school administrators on teacher retention decisions. *American Educational Research Journal, 48*(2), 303–333.

Boyd, G. M. (1996). Emancipative educational technology. *Canadian Journal of Educational Communication, 25*, 179–186.

Brabazon, T. (2007). *The University of Google: Education in a (post) information age*. Ashgate.

Brand, S. (1997). *How buildings learn*. Phoenix Illustrated.

Brand, S. (2000). *Clock of the long now: Time and responsibility: The ideas behind the world's slowest computer* (Kindle ed.). Basic Books.

Brand, S. (2018). Pace layering: How complex systems learn and keep learning. *Journal of Design and Science*. https://doi.org/10.21428/7f2e5f08

Brown, S., Cockett, P., & Ye, Y. (2019). The neuroscience of Romeo and Juliet: An fMRI study of acting. *Royal Society Open Science, 6*(3). https://doi.org/10.1098/rsos.181908

Brown, T. (2009). *Change by design: How design thinking transforms organizations and inspires innovation*. HarperCollins.

Bruner, J. S. (1966). *Toward a theory of instruction*. Belknap Press of Harvard University Press.

Brusilovsky, P. (2001). Adaptive hypermedia. *User Modeling and User-Adapted Interaction, 11*, 87–110.

Burgess, T. F., & Gules, H. K. (1998). Buyer-supplier relationships in firms adopting advanced manufacturing technology: An empirical analysis of the implementation of hard and soft technologies. *Journal of Engineering and Technology Management, 15*, 127–152.

Bush, V. (1945). As we may think. *Atlantic Monthly, 176*(1), 101–108.

Calvin, W. H. (1997). The six essentials? Minimal requirements for the Darwinian bootstrapping of quality. *Journal of Memetics, 1*, 3–13.

Carr, C. L. (2013). Enhancing EAP students' autonomy by accommodating various learning styles in the second language writing classroom. *INTESOL Journal, 10*(1). 39–52.

Carr, N. (2011). *The shallows: What the internet is doing to our brains*. W.W. Norton & Company.

Cavanaugh, J. K., & Jacquemin, S. J. (2015). A large sample comparison of grade based student learning outcomes in online vs. face-to-face courses. *Online Learning, 19*(2). http://dx.doi.org/10.24059/olj.v19i2.454

Changizi, M. (2013). *Harnessed: How language and music mimicked nature and transformed ape to man*. BenBella Books.

Chang, M.-M., & Hung, H.-T. (2019). Effects of technology-enhanced language learning on second language acquisition: A meta-analysis. *Journal of Educational Technology & Society, 22*(4), 1–17.

Checkland, P. (2000). Soft systems methodology: A thirty year retrospective. *Systems Research and Behavioral Science, 17*, 11–58.

Chen, P.-S. D., Lambert, A. D., & Guidry, K. R. (2010). Engaging online learners: The impact of web-based learning technology on college student engagement. *Computers & Education, 54*(4), 1222–1232.

Chi, M. T. H. (2006). Two approaches to the study of experts' characteristics. In K. A. Ericsson, N. Charness, P. J. Feltovich, & R. R. Hoffman (Eds.), *The Cambridge handbook of expertise and expert performance* (pp. 21–30). Cambridge University Press. https://doi.org/10.1017/CBO9780511816796.002

Chickering, A. W., & Gamson, Z. F. (1987). Seven principles of good practice in undergraduate education. *AAHE Bulletin, March*, 3–6.

Christensen, C. (2008). Disruptive innovation and catalytic change in higher education. *Futures Forum, Harvard Business School*, 43–46.

Christensen, C., Horn, M., & Johnson, C. (2008). *Disrupting class: How disruptive innovation will change the way the world learns.* McGraw Hill.

Churchill, W. (1943). Speech in *House of Commons debates*, October 28, vol.393, c. 403.

Cilliers, P. (2001). Boundaries, hierarchies and networks in complex systems. *International Journal of Innovation Management, 5*(02), 135–147.

Clark, A. (2008). *Supersizing the mind: Embodiment, action, and cognitive extension.* Oxford University Press.

Clark, R. E. (1982). Antagonism between achievement and enjoyment in ATI studies. *Educational Psychologist, 17*(2), 92–101.

Clark, R. E. (1983). Reconsidering research on learning from media. *Review of Educational Research, 53*(4), 445–459.

Coffield, F., Moseley, D., Hall, E., & Ecclestone, K. (2004). *Learning styles and pedagogy in post-16 learning: A systematic and critical review.*

Cohen, J., & Stewart, I. (1997). *Figments of reality: The evolution of the curious mind.* Cambridge University Press.

Cohen, J., & Stewart, I. (2001). Where are the dolphins? *Nature, 409*(6823), 1119.

Collins, A., Brown, J. S., & Holum, A. (1991). Cognitive apprenticeship: Making thinking visible. *American Educator, 15*(3), 6–11.

Cooley, M. (1987). *Architect or bee? The human price of technology.* The Hogarth Press.

Cooperrider, D. L., & Srivastava, S. (1987). Appreciative inquiry in organizational life. *Research in Organizational Change and Development, 1*, 129–169.

Cooperrider, D. L., & Whitney, D. (2000). A positive revolution in change: Appreciative inquiry. In R. T. Golembiewski (Ed.), *Handbook of organizational behavior, revised and expanded* (pp. 633–652). Routledge.

Cormier, D. (2008). Rhizomatic education: Community as curriculum. *Innovate: Journal of Online Education, 4*(5).

Cormier, D. (2014). Community learning—The zombie resurrection. http://davecormier.com/edblog/2014/05/25/community-learning-the-zombie-resurrection/

Crawford, W. (1999). The card catalog and other digital controversies. *American Libraries, 30*(1), 52–58.

Csikszentmihalyi, M., Abuhamdeh, S., & Nakamura, J. (2014). Flow. In M. Csikszentmihalyi & R. Larson (Eds.), *Flow and the foundations of positive psychology: The collected works of Mihaly Csikszentmihalyi* (pp. 227–238). Springer.

Cuban, L. (1986). *Teachers and machines: The classroom of technology since 1920*. Teachers College Press.

Culkin, J. M. (1967). A schoolman's guide to Marshall McLuhan. *The Saturday Review, March*, 51–53, 70.

Curry, L. (1983). An organization of learning styles theory and constructs. Paper prepared for presentation at the American Educational Research Association Annual Meeting, Montréal, QC, April.

Daniel, J., Kanwar, A., & Uvalić-Trumbić, S. (2009). Breaking higher education's iron triangle: Access, cost, and quality. *Change: The Magazine of Higher Learning, 41*(2), 30–35.

Darmody, M., Smyth, E., & Russell, H. (2021). Impacts of the COVID-19 control measures on widening educational inequalities. *YOUNG, 29*(4), 366–380. https://doi.org/10.1177/11033088211027412

Davis, B., & Sumara, D. J. (2006). *Complexity and education: Inquiries into learning, teaching, and research*. Lawrence Erlbaum Associates.

De Bruyckere, P., Kirschner, P. A., & Hulshof, C. D. (2015). *Urban myths about learning and education*. Academic Press.

Deci, E. L. (1972). The effects of contingent and noncontingent rewards and controls on intrinsic motivation. *Organizational Behavior and Human Performance, 8*(2), 217–229.

Deci, E. L., & Moller, A. C. (2005). The concept of competence: A starting place for understanding intrinsic motivation and self-determined extrinsic motivation. In A. J. Elliot & C. S. Dweck (Eds.), *Handbook of competence and motivation* (pp. 579–597). Guilford Press.

Deci, E. L., & Ryan, R. M. (2008). Self-determination theory: A macrotheory of human motivation, development and health. *Canadian Psychology, 49*(3), 182–185.

Dekker, S., Lee, N. C., Howard-Jones, P., & Jolles, J. (2012). Neuromyths in education: Prevalence and predictors of misconceptions among teachers. *Frontiers in Psychology, 3*. https://doi.org/10.3389/fpsyg.2012.00429

Derex, M., Bonnefon, J.-F., Boyd, R., & Mesoudi, A. (2019). Causal understanding is not necessary for the improvement of culturally evolving technology. *Nature Human Behaviour, 3*(5), 446–452.

Derribo, M. H., & Howard, K. (2007). Advice about the use of learning styles: A major myth in education. *Journal of College Reading and Learning, 37*, 2, 101–109.

Deslauriers, L., McCarty, L. S., Miller, K., Callaghan, K., & Kestin, G. (2019). Measuring actual learning versus feeling of learning in response to being actively engaged in the classroom. *Proceedings of the National Academy of Sciences*, 116(39), 19251–19257.

Deutscher, G. (2006). *The unfolding of language: An evolutionary tour of mankind's greatest invention*. Henry Holt and Company.

Dewey, J. (1916). *Democracy and education*. Macmillan.

Dewey, J. (1995). Mind, experience, and behavior. In N. J. Herman & L. T. Reynolds (Eds.), *Symbolic interaction: An introduction to social psychology* (pp. 153–156).

Dixon, E., Enos, E., & Brodmerkle, S. (2011). US Patent No. 7,975,000. US Patent and Trademark Office.

Doctorow, C. (2019). Adversarial interoperability: reviving an elegant weapon from a more civilized age to slay today's monopolies. https://www.eff.org/deeplinks/2019/06/adversarial-interoperability-reviving-elegant-weapon-more-civilized-age-slay

Dosi, G., & Grazzi, M. (2010). On the nature of technologies: Knowledge, procedures, artifacts and production inputs. *Cambridge Journal of Economics, 34*(1), 173–184.

Downes, S. (2008). Places to go: Connectivism & connective knowledge. *Innovate, 5*(1). https://nsuworks.nova.edu/innovate/vol5/iss1/6

Dron, J. (2002). *Achieving self-organisation in network-based learning environments* [Unpublished PhD dissertation]. University of Brighton.

Dron, J. (2004). Termites in the schoolhouse: Stigmergy and transactional distance in an e-learning environment. In L. Cantoni & C. McLoughlin (Eds.), *EdMedia + Innovate Learning 2004* (pp. 263–269). Association for the Advancement of Computing in Education (AACE). https://www.learntechlib.org/p/12942

Dron, J. (2006). Any color you like, as long as it's Blackboard. In T. Reeves & S. Yamashita (Eds.), *E-Learn: World Conference on E-Learning in Corporate, Government, Healthcare, and Higher Education 2006* (pp. 2772–2779). Association for the Advancement of Computing in Education (AACE). https://www.learntechlib.org/p/24125

Dron, J. (2007). *Control and constraint in e-learning: Choosing when to choose*. Idea Group International.

Dron, J. (2016). P-learning's unwelcome legacy. *TD Tecnologie Didattiche, 24*(1), 72–81.

Dron, J. & T. Anderson. (2009). On the design of collective applications. *2009 International Conference on Computational Science and Engineering, 4* (368–374). https://doi.org/10.1109/CSE.2009.469

Dron, J., & Anderson, T. (2014a). *Teaching crowds: Learning & social media*. Athabasca University Press. https://teachingcrowds.ca/discuss-the-chapters/chapter-8-stories-from-the-field

Dron, J., & Anderson, T. (2014b). On the design of social media for learning. *Social Sciences, 3*(3), 378–393. https://doi.org/10.3390/socsci3030378

Dron, J., & Anderson, T. (2022). Pedagogical paradigms in open and distance education. In O. Zawacki-Richter & I. Jung (Eds.), *Handbook of Open, Distance and Digital Education* (pp. 1–17). Springer Singapore. https://doi.org/10.1007/978-981-19-0351-9_9-1

Dubois, E., & Blank, G. (2018). The echo chamber is overstated: The moderating effect of political interest and diverse media. *Information, Communication & Society, 21*(5), 729–745.

Dubos, R. (1969). American Academy of Allergy 25th anniversary series: The spaceship Earth. *Journal of Allergy, 44*(1), 1–9.

Eicher, B., Polepeddi, L., & Goel, A. (2018). Jill Watson doesn't care if you're pregnant: Grounding AI ethics in empirical studies. In *Proceedings of the 2018 AAAI/ACM Conference on AI, Ethics, and Society* (pp. 88–94). https://doi.org/10.1145/3278721.3278760

Ellul, J. (1970). *The technological society* (J. Wilkinson, Trans.). A.A. Knopf.

Engeström, Y. (1999). Activity theory and individual and social transformation. In Y. Engeström, R. Miettinen, & R.-L. Punamäki (Eds.), *Perspectives on activity theory*. (pp. 19–38). Cambridge University Press. https://doi.org/10.1017/CBO9780511812774.003

Fawns, T. (2022). An entangled pedagogy: Looking beyond the pedagogy—technology dichotomy. *Postdigital Science and Education*. https://doi.org/10.1007/s42438-022-00302-7

Feenberg, A. (2006). What is philosophy of technology? In J. R. Dakers (Ed.), *Defining Technological Literacy: Towards an Epistemological Framework* (pp. 5–16). Palgrave Macmillan. https://doi.org/10.1057/9781403983053_2

Feenberg, A., & Callon, M. (2010). *Between reason and experience: Essays in technology and modernity* (Kindle ed.). MIT Press.

Felder, R. M. (1996). Matters of style. *ASEE Prism, 6*(4), 18–23.

Felder, R. M., & Spurlin, J. (2005). Applications, reliability and validity of the index of learning styles. *International Journal of Engineering Education, 21*(1), 103–112.

Ferguson, E. S. (1977). The mind's eye: Nonverbal thought in technology. *Science, 197*(4306), 827–836.

Feyerabend, P. (1987). *Farewell to reason.* Verso.

Feynman, R. (1997). *Surely you're joking, Mr. Feynman!* W.W. Norton & Company.

Frank, A. (2011). *About time: Cosmology and culture at the twilight of the big bang* (Kindle ed.). Free Press.

Franklin, U. M. (1999). *The real world of technology* (Kindle ed.). House of Anansi Press.

Friesen, N. (2007). (Micro-) didactics: A tale of two traditions. In T. Hug (Ed.), *Didactics of microlearning: Concepts, discourses and examples* (pp. 83–97). Waxmann Verlag.

Frisch, M. (1994). *Homo faber.* Houghton Mifflin Harcourt.

Gagne, R. (1985). *The conditions of learning* (4th ed.). Holt, Rhinehart & Winston.

Garland, K. J., & Noyes, J. M. (2004). CRT monitors: Do they interfere with learning? *Behaviour & Information Technology, 23*(1), 43–52.

Garrison, D. R., & Baynton, M. (1987). Beyond independence in distance education: The concept of control. *American Journal of Distance Education, 1*(3), 3–15.

Gibson, J. J. (1977). The theory of affordances. In R. Shaw & J. Bransford (Eds.), *Perceiving, acting, and knowing: Toward an ecological psychology* (pp. 67–82). Lawrence Erlbaum.

Gilster, P., & Glister, P. (1997). *Digital literacy.* Wiley Computer Publishing.

Gladwell, M. (2008). *Outliers: The story of success.* Hachette UK.

Gneezy, U., & Rustichini, A. (2000). A fine is a price. *The Journal of Legal Studies, 29*(1), 1–17. JSTOR. https://doi.org/10.1086/468061

Goel, A. K., & Polepeddi, L. (2018). Jill Watson: A virtual teaching assistant for online education. In C. Dede, J. Richards, & B. Saxberg (Eds.), *Learning engineering for online education* (pp. 120–143). Routledge.

Goertzel, B. (2014). Artificial General Intelligence: Concept, State of the Art, and Future Prospects. In *Journal of Artificial General Intelligence* (Vol. 5, Issue 1, pp. 1–48). https://doi.org/10.2478/jagi-2014-0001

Goldhaber, D. (2002). The mystery of good teaching: The evidence shows that good teachers make a clear difference in student achievement. The problem is that we don't really know what makes a good teacher. *Education Next (Feature), 1,* 50–55.

Goldhaber, D. D., & Brewer, D. J. (1999). Teacher licensing and student achievement. In M. Kanstoroom & C. E. Finn (Eds.), *Better teachers, better schools* (pp. 83–102). Thomas B. Fordham Foundation.

Gould, S. J., & Lewontin, R. C. (1979). The spandrels of San Marco and the panglossian paradigm: A critique of the adaptationist paradigm. *Proceedings of the Royal Society of London, Series B, 205*(1161), 581–598.

Haraway, D. (2013). *Simians, cyborgs, and women: The reinvention of nature.* Routledge.

Hase, S., & Kenyon, C. (2007). Heutagogy: A child of complexity theory. *Complicity: An International Journal of Complexity & Education, 4*(1), 111–117.

Hattie, J. (2013). *Visible learning: A synthesis of over 800 meta-analyses relating to achievement.* Taylor & Francis.

Hattie, J., & Gan, M. (2011). Instruction based on feedback. In R. E. Mayer & P. A. Alexander (Eds.), *Handbook of research on learning and instruction* (1st ed., pp. 249–271). Routledge. https://doi.org/10.4324/9780203839089

Haughey, M., & Muirhead, B. (2005). Evaluating learning objects for schools. *E-Journal of Instructional Science and Technology, 8*(1). https://www.learntechlib.org/p/67809/

Hauser, M. D., Chomsky, N., & Fitch, W. T. (2002). The faculty of language: What is it, who has it, and how did it evolve? *Science, 298*(5598), 1569–1579.

Heller, R. F., Chilolo, E., Elliott, J., Johnson, B., Lipman, D., Ononeze, V., & Richards, J. (2019). Do tutors make a difference in online learning? A comparative study in two open online courses. *Open Praxis, 11*(3), 229–241. http://doi.org/10.5944/openpraxis.11.3.960

Hennenlotter, A., Dresel, C., Castrop, F., Ceballos-Baumann, A. O., Wohlschlager, A. M., & Haslinger, B. (2009). The link between facial feedback and neural activity within central circuitries of emotion—New insights from botulinum toxin-induced denervation of frown muscles. *Cereb Cortex, 19*(3), 537–542.

Henrich, J. (2017). *The secret of our success: How culture is driving human evolution, domesticating our species, and making us smarter.* Princeton University Press.

Heyes, C. (2018). *Cognitive gadgets: The cultural evolution of thinking.* Harvard University Press.

Hidi, S. (2000). An interest researcher's perspective: The effects of extrinsic and intrinsic factors on motivation. In C. Sansone & J. M. Harackiewicz (Eds.), *Intrinsic and extrinsic motivation: The search for optimal motivation and performance* (pp. 309–339). Academic Press.

Higuchi, S., Chaminade, T., Imamizu, H., & Kawato, M. (2009). Shared neural correlates for language and tool use in Broca's area. *Neuroreport, 20*(15), 1376–1381.

Hitchens, C. (2007). *The portable atheist: Essential readings for the nonbeliever* (Kindle ed.). Da Capo Press.

Hlupic, V., Pouloudi, A., & Rzevski, G. (2002). Towards an integrated approach to knowledge management: "Hard," "soft" and "abstract" issues. *Knowledge and Process Management, 9*(2), 90–102.

Hlynka, D., & Jacobsen, M. (2010). What is educational technology, anyway? A commentary on the new AECT definition of the field. *Canadian Journal of Learning and Technology/ La revue canadienne de l'apprentissage et de la technologie, 35*(2). https://doi.org/10.21432/T2N88P

Hofstadter, D. R. (1979). *Gödel, Escher, Bach*. Harvester Press.

Holland, J. H. (2012). *Signals and boundaries: Building blocks for complex adaptive systems*. MIT Press.

Holmberg, B., Bernath, H., & Busch, F. W. (2005). *The evolution, principles and practices of distance education* (Vol. 11). Bis, Bibliotheks-und Informationssystem der Universität Oldenburg.

Husmann, P. R., & O'Loughlin, V. D. (2019). Another nail in the coffin for learning styles? Disparities among undergraduate anatomy students' study strategies, class performance, and reported VARK learning styles. *Anatomical Sciences Education, 12*(1), 6–19.

Illich, I. (1971). *Deschooling society*. Harper & Row.

Jenkins, H. (2006). Confronting the challenges of participatory culture: Media education for the 21st century. An occasional paper on digital media and learning. http://files.eric.ed.gov/fulltext/ED536086.pdf

Johnson, G. M. (2009). Instructionism and constructivism: Reconciling two very good ideas. *International Journal of Special Education, 24*, 90–98.

Johnson, S. (2006). *Everything bad is good for you: How today's popular culture is actually making us smarter*. Riverhead Trade.

Johnson, S. (2010). *Where good ideas come from: The natural history of innovation* (Kindle ed.). Penguin.

Johnson, S. (2012). *Future perfect: The case for progress in a networked age* (Kindle ed.). Riverhead Trade.

Jones, S. (1999). *Almost like a whale*. Doubleday.

Jordan, K. (2016). MOOC completion rates: The data. http://www.katyjordan.com/MOOCproject.html

Jurdi, R., Hage, H. S., & Chow, H. P. H. (2011). Academic dishonesty in the Canadian classroom: Behaviours of a sample of university students. *Canadian Journal of Higher Education, 41*(3), 35. https://doi.org/10.47678/cjhe.v41i3.2488

Juster, N. (1962). *The phantom tollbooth*. Collins.

Kanadli, S. (2016). A meta-analysis on the effect of instructional designs based on the learning styles models on academic achievement, attitude and retention. *Educational Sciences: Theory and Practice, 16*(6), 2057–2086.

Katz, E. (1992). The big lie: Human restoration of nature. *Research in Philosophy and Technology, 12*, 93–107.

Kauffman, S. (1995). *At home in the universe: The search for laws of complexity*. Oxford University Press.

Kauffman, S. (2000). *Investigations* (Kindle ed.). Oxford University Press.

Kauffman, S. (2008). *Reinventing the sacred: A new view of science, reason and religion*. Basic Books.

Kauffman, S. (2009). *Towards a post reductionist science: The open universe*. arXiv. https://doi.org/10.48550/ARXIV.0907.2492

Kauffman, S. A. (2016). *Humanity in a creative universe*. Oxford University Press.

Kauffman, S. A. (2019). *A world beyond physics: The emergence and evolution of life*. Oxford University Press.

Kay, A. (1996). Revealing the elephant: The use and misuse of computers in education. *The Educom Review, 31*(4), 22–28.

Keen, A. (2007). *The cult of the amateur*. Nicholas Brealey Publishing.

Kelly, K. (2010). *What technology wants* (Kindle ed.). Viking.

Kerker, M. (1961). Science and the steam engine. *Technology and Culture, 2*(4), 381–390.

Klahr, D., & Nigam, M. (2004). The equivalence of learning paths in early science instruction: Effects of direct instruction and discovery learning. *Psychological Science, 15*(10), 661–667.

Knowles, M. S. (1975). *Self-directed learning: A guide for learners and teachers*. Association Press.

Kohn, A. (1999). *Punished by rewards: The trouble with gold stars, incentive plans, A's, praise, and other bribes* (Kindle ed.). Mariner Books.

Kohn, A. (2011). The case against grades. *Educational Leadership, 69*(3), 28–33.

Kolb, A. Y., & Kolb, D. A. (2005). Learning styles and learning spaces: Enhancing experiential learning in higher education. *Academy of Management Learning & Education, 4*(2), 193–212.

Koltay, T. (2011). The media and the literacies: Media literacy, information literacy, digital literacy. *Media, Culture & Society, 33*(2), 211–221.

Lakhana, A. (2014). What is educational technology? An inquiry into the meaning, use, and reciprocity of technology. *Canadian Journal of Learning and Technology, 40*(3). https://cjlt.ca/index.php/cjlt/article/view/26280

Lakoff, G., & Johnson, M. (1980). *Metaphors we live by* (Kindle ed.). University of Chicago Press.

Lane, L. M. (2009). Insidious pedagogy: How course management systems affect teaching. *First Monday, 14*(10). https://doi.org/10.5210/fm.v14i10.2530

Lankshear, C., & Knobel, M. (2006). Digital literacy and digital literacies: Policy, pedagogy and research considerations for education. *Nordic Journal of Digital Literacy, 1*, 12–24.

Laszlo, A. (2003). The evolutionary challenge for technology. *World Futures: Journal of General Evolution, 59*(8), 639–645.

Latour, B. (1987). *Science in action: How to follow scientists and engineers through society*. Harvard University Press.

Latour, B. (2005). *Reassembling the social: An introduction to actor-network theory* (Kindle ed.). Oxford University Press.

Law, J. (1992). Notes on the theory of the actor network: Ordering, strategy and heterogeneity. *Systems Practice, 5*, 379–393.

Lin, Y. G., McKeachie, W. J., & Kim, Y. C. (2003). College student intrinsic and/or extrinsic motivation and learning. *Learning and Individual Differences, 13*(3), 251–258.

Locker, J., & Cropley, M. (2004). Anxiety, depression and self-esteem in secondary school children: An investigation into the impact of standard assessment tests (SATs) and other important school examinations. *School Psychology International, 25*(3), 333–345.

Longo, G., Montévil, M., & Kauffman, S. (2012). No entailing laws, but enablement in the evolution of the biosphere. Paper presented at the 14th Annual Conference on Genetic and Evolutionary Computation, Philadelphia.

Ma, Y., McCabe, D., & Liu, R. (2013). Students' academic cheating in Chinese universities: Prevalence, influencing factors, and proposed action. *Journal of Academic Ethics, 11*(3), 169–184.

Macnamara, B. N., & Maitra, M. (2019). The role of deliberate practice in expert performance: Revisiting Ericsson, Krampe & Tesch-Römer (1993). *Royal Society Open Science, 6*(8), https://doi.org/10.1098/rsos.190327

Maguire, E. A., Gadian, D. G., Johnsrude, I. S., Good, C. D., Ashburner, J., Frackowiak, R. S. J., & Frith, C. D. (2000). Navigation-related structural change in the hippocampi of taxi drivers. *Proceedings of the National Academy of Sciences, 97*(8), 4398–4403. https://doi.org/10.1073/pnas.070039597

Makel, M. C., & Plucker, J. A. (2014). Facts are more important than novelty: Replication in the education sciences. *Educational Researcher, 43*(6), 304–316.

Mayer, R. (2004). Should there be a three-strikes rule against pure discovery learning? The case for guided methods of instruction. *American Psychologist, 59*(1), 14–19.

McCabe, D. L., & Trevino, L. K. (1996). What we know about cheating in college: Longitudinal trends and recent developments. *Change, 28*(1), 28–33.

McDonough, E. F., & Kahn, K. B. (1996). Using "hard" and "soft" technologies for global new product development. *R&D Management, 26*(3), 241–253.

McLuhan, M. (1994). *Understanding media: The extensions of man*. MIT Press.

McLuhan, M., & McLuhan, E. (1992). *Laws of media: The new science*. University of Toronto Press.

Means, B., Toyama, Y., Murphy, R., Bakia, M., & Jones, K. (2009). *Evaluation of evidence-based practices in online learning: A meta-analysis and review of online learning studies*. US Department of Education.

Melville, H. (1984). Hawthorne and his mosses. In H. Hayford, A. A. MacDougal, & G. T. Tanselle (Eds.), *The piazza tales and other prose pieces, 1839–1860* (Vol. 9). Northwestern University Press, 1154–1171.

Mishra, S., Cleveland-Innes, M., & Ostashewski, N. (2019). A Case Study of the Technology-Enabled Learning (TEL) Massive Open Online Courses. In K. Zhang, C. J. Bonk, T. Reeves, & T. Reynolds (Eds.), *MOOCs and open education in the global south: Challenges, successes, and opportunities*. Routledge. https://doi.org/10.4324/9780429398919

Mitcham, C. (2009). Philosophy of information technology. In C. Hanks (Ed.), *Technology and values: Essential readings* (pp. 481–490). Wiley.

Mitra, S. (2012). *Beyond the Hole in the Wall: Discover the power of self-organized learning* (Kindle ed.). TED Books.

Mumford, L. (1934). *Technics and civilization*. Harcourt, Brace and Company.

Nelson, Ted (1974). *Computer Lib/Dream Machines*. http://archive.org/details/computer-lib-dream-machines

Nguyen, N. V. (2016). An investigation of Vietnamese students' learning styles in online language learning. *Tạp chí Khoa học, 1*(79), 25–34.

Noë, A. (2016). *Strange tools: Art and human nature*. Farrar, Straus and Giroux.

Norman, D. A. (1993). *Things that make us smart: Defending human attributes in the age of the machine*. Perseus Publishing.

Norton, A. (1909). *Readings in the history of education: Medieval universities*. Harvard University Press.

Nuthall, G. (2005). The cultural myths and realities of classroom teaching and learning: A personal journey. *Teachers College Record, 107*(5), 895–934.

Nye, D. E. (2006). *Technology matters: Questions to live with*. MIT Press.

OECD. (2015). *Students, computers and learning: Making the connection*. OECD Publishing. https://doi.org/10.1787/9789264239555-en

Oliver, S., & Young, T. (1939). *T'aint what you do (it's the way that you do it)*. Vocalion.

Olson, J. K. (2013). The purposes of schooling and the nature of technology: The end of education. In M. P. Clough, J. K. Olson, & D. S. Niederhauser (Eds.), *The nature of technology* (pp. 217–248). Brill Sense.

Oppenheimer, T. (2003). *The flickering mind: The false promise of technology in the classroom, and how learning can be saved*. Random House.

Orlikowski, W. J. (1992). The duality of technology: Rethinking the concept of technology in organizations. *Organization Science, 3*(3), 398–427.

Page, S. E. (2011). *Diversity and complexity*. Princeton University Press.

Papert, S. (1987). A critique of technocentrism in thinking about the school of the future. *Children in an Information Age: Opportunities for Creativity, Innovation and New Activities*, Sofia, Bulgaria.

Papert, S., & Harel, I. (1991). Situating constructionism. In S. Papert & I. Harel (Eds.), *Constructionism* (pp. 1–11). Ablex Publishing Corporation.

Pariser, E. (2011). *The filter bubble: What the internet is hiding from you* (Kindle ed.). Penguin.

Parke, R. D., Deur, J. L., & Sawin, D. B. (1970). The intermittent punishment effect in humans: Conditioning or adaptation? *Psychonomic Science, 18*(4), 193–194.

Pashler, H., McDaniel, M., Rohrer, D., & Bjork, R. (2008). Learning styles concepts and evidence. *Psychological Science in the Public Interest, 9*(3), 105–119.

Pask, G. (1976a). *Conversation theory—Applications in education and epistemology*. Elsevier.

Pask, G. (1976b). Styles and strategies of learning. *British Journal of Educational Psychology, 46*, 128–148.

Patel, N. (2003). Deferred system's design: Countering the primacy of reflective IS development with action-based information systems. In N. Patel (Ed.), *Adaptive evolutionary information systems* (pp. 1–29). Idea Group Publishing.

Paulsen, M. (1993). The hexagon of cooperative freedom: A distance education theory attuned to computer conferencing. *DEOSNEWS, 3*(2), https://web.archive.org/web/20030814011330/http://www.ed.psu.edu/acsde/deos/deosnews/deosnews3_2.asp.

Pausch, R. (2008). *The last lecture*. Hachette.

Pea, R. (1993). Practices of distributed intelligence and designs for education. In G. Saloman (Ed.), *Distributed cognitions: Psychological and educational considerations* (pp. 47–87). Cambridge University Press.

Pei, L., & Wu, H. (2019). Does online learning work better than offline learning in undergraduate medical education? A systematic review and meta-analysis. *Medical Education Online, 24*(1), 1666538. https://doi.org/10.1080/10872981.2019.1666538

Pelecanos, G. (2003). *Soul circus*. Little, Brown.

Pestalozzi, J. H. (1894). *How Gertrude teaches her children* (L. T. Hooland & F. C. Turner, Trans.). Swan Sonnenshchein & Co.

Piaget, J. (1952). *The origins of intelligence in children*. Basic Books.

Pinker, S. (1994). *The language instinct: How the mind creates language*. HarperCollins.

Pinker, S. (2010, June 11). Mind over mass media. *New York Times*, 31.

Plato. (360 BCE). *The Phaedrus* (B. Jowett, Trans.). Project Gutenberg.

Plutarch. (1927). De auditu. In Frank Cole Babbitt (Trans.), *Moralia* (Vol. 1, pp. 201–259). Harvard University Press.

Popper, K. R. (1972). *Objective knowledge: An evolutionary approach*. Clarendon Press.

Postman, N. (2000). *Building a bridge to the eighteenth century: How the past can improve our future*. Vintage Books.

Postman, N. (2011). *The end of education: Redefining the value of school*. Knopf Doubleday Publishing Group.

Potter, W. J. (2013). *Media literacy*. SAGE Publications.

Powers, R. (2006). Richard Powers: Each try launches another. Interview with Melody Joy Kramer, November 20. https://www.npr.org/templates/story/story.php?storyId=6515434

Prieto, L. P., Dimitriadis, Y., & Looi, C.-K. (2015). Orchestration in learning technology research: Evaluation of a conceptual framework. *Research in Learning Technology*, 23. https://doi.org/10.3402/rlt.v23.28019

Protopsaltis, S., & Baum, S. (2019). Does online education live up to its promise? A look at the evidence and implications for federal policy. Arnold Ventures.

Pruitt, J., & Grudin, J. (2003). Personas: Practice and theory. Microsoft Research.

Purkey, W. W. (1991, February 22). *What is invitational education and how does it work?* Annual California State Conference on Self-Esteem, Santa Clara, CA. http://files.eric.ed.gov/fulltext/ED334488.pdf

Read, L. E. (2019). I, pencil. In C. Newmark (Ed.), *Readings in applied microeconomics: The power of the market* (pp. 32–36). Routledge.

Reeve, J., Deci, E. L., & Ryan, R. M. (2004). Self-determination theory: A dialectical framework for understanding sociocultural influences on student motivation. In D. M. McInerney & S. Van Etten (Eds.), *Big theories revisited* (Vol. 4 of *Research on sociocultural influences on motivation and learning*, pp. 31–60). Information Age Publishing.

Reuell, P. (2019, August 22). Clever crows. *The Harvard Gazette*. https://news.harvard.edu/gazette/story/2019/08/like-humans-crows-are-more-optimistic-after-making-tools-to-solve-a-problem/

Rheingold, H. (2012). *Mind amplifier: Can our digital tools make us smarter?* (Kindle ed.). TED Books.

Richardson, E. (2006). *Hiphop literacies*. Routledge.

Richardson, J. C., & Lowenthal, P. (2017). Instructor social presence: Learners' needs and a neglected component of the community of inquiry framework. In A. Whiteside, G. Dikkers, & K. Swan (Eds.), *Social presence in online learning: Multiple perspectives on practice and research* (pp. 86–98). Stylus Publishing.

Ridley, M. (2010). *The rational optimist: How prosperity evolves*. HarperCollins e-books.

Ridley, M. (2015). *The evolution of everything: How ideas emerge*. HarperCollins.

Riener, C., & Willingham, D. (2010). The myth of learning styles. *Change: The Magazine of Higher Learning, 42*(5), 32–35.

Rivoltella, P. (Ed.). (2008). *Digital literacy: Tools and methodologies for information society*. IGI Global.

Robbins, T. (1990). *Another roadside attraction*. Random House Publishing Group.

Rose, F. (2012). *The art of immersion: How the digital generation is remaking Hollywood, Madison Avenue, and the way we tell stories* (Kindle ed.). W.W. Norton.

Rose, T. (2016). *The end of average: How we succeed in a world that values sameness*. HarperCollins Canada.

Rosen, W. (2010). *The most powerful idea in the world: A story of steam, industry, and invention* (Kindle ed.). Random House.

Russell, T. L. (1999). *The no significant difference phenomenon: As reported in 355 research reports, summaries and papers*. North Carolina State University.

Ryan, R. M., & Deci, E. L. (2000a). Self-determination theory and the facilitation of intrinsic motivation, social development, and well-being. *American Psychologist, 55*(1), 68–78.

Ryan, R. M., & Deci, E. L. (2000b). Intrinsic and extrinsic motivations: Classic definitions and new directions. *Contemporary Educational Psychology, 25*(1), 54–67.

Ryan, R. M., & Deci, E. L. (2017). *Self-determination theory: Basic psychological needs in motivation, development, and wellness*. Guilford Press.

Saloman, G. (1993). *Distributed cognitions: Psychological and educational considerations*. Cambridge University Press.

Salomon, G., & Perkins, D. N. (1998). Individual and social aspects of learning. *Review of Research in Education, 23*, 1–24.

Schatzburg, E. (2018). *Technology: Critical history of a concept*. University of Chicago Press.

Schwartz, B. (1997). Psychology, idea technology, and ideology. *Psychological Science, 8*(1), 21–27.

Schwartz, B. (2004). *The paradox of choice: Why less is more*. HarperCollins.

Schwartz, B. (2015). *Why we work*. Simon & Schuster; TED Books.
Scott, J., & Marshall, G. (n.d.). Pedagogy. In *A Dictionary of Sociology*. http://www.oxfordreference.com/view/10.1093/acref/9780199533008.001.0001/acref-9780199533008-e-1697
Seely Brown, J., & Duguid, P. (2000). *The social life of information*. Harvard Business School Press.
Segaran, T. (2007). *Programming collective intelligence* (Kindle ed.). O'Reilly.
Severance, C. (2012). Teaching the world: Daphne Koller and Coursera. *Computer*, 45(8), 8–9.
Sharkey, J., & Brandt, D. S. (2008). Integrating technology literacy and information literacy. In P. Rivoltella (Ed.), *Digital literacy: Tools and methodologies for information society* (pp. 85–97). IGI Global.
Sharp, J. E. (1997). *Ungrading: Adding learning intensive writing assignments without increasing grading load*. https://peer.asee.org/ungrading-adding-learning-intensive-writing-assignments-without-increasing-grading-load.pdf
Shirky, C. (2007). The (Bayesian) advantage of youth. http://many.corante.com/archives/2007/05/19/the_bayesian_advantage_of_youth.php
Shulman, L. S., & Wilson, S. M. (2004). *The wisdom of practice: Essays on teaching, learning, and learning to teach*. Jossey-Bass.
Siemens, G. (2005). Connectivism: A learning theory for the digital age. *International Journal of Instructional Technology and Distance Learning*, 2(1), https://www.itdl.org/Journal/Jan_05/article01.htm
Skinner, B. F. (1960). Teaching machines. *The Review of Economics and Statistics*, 42(3), 189–191. https://doi.org/10.2307/1926170
Skulmowski, A., & Rey, G. D. (2017). Bodily effort enhances learning and metacognition: Investigating the relation between physical effort and cognition using dual-process models of embodiment. *Adv Cogn Psychol*, 13(1), 3–10. https://doi.org/10.5709/acp-0202-9
Smedslund, J. (2016). Why psychology cannot be an empirical science. *Integrative Psychological and Behavioural Science*, 50(2), 185–195. https://doi.org/10.1007/s12124-015-9339-x
Stanislavski, C. (1989). *An actor prepares*. Routledge.
Steinbeck, J., Benson, J. J., & Shillinglaw, S. (2003). *America and Americans and selected nonfiction*. Penguin Classics.
Stiegler, B. (1998). *Technics and time, 1: The fault of Epimetheus (1)*. Stanford University Press.
Stockard, J., Wood, T. W., Coughlin, C., & Rasplica Khoury, C. (2018). The effectiveness of direct instruction curricula: A meta-analysis of a half century of research. *Review of Educational Research*, 88(4), 479–507.

Stout, D., & Chaminade, T. (2012). Stone tools, language and the brain in human evolution. *Philosophical Transactions of the Royal Society B: Biological Sciences, 367*(1585), 75–87.

Taft, S. H., Kesten, K., & El-Banna, M. M. (2019). One size does not fit all: Toward an evidence-based framework for determining online course enrollment sizes in higher education. *Online Learning, 23* (3). https://olj.onlinelearningconsortium.org/index.php/olj/article/view/1534

Tamim, R. M., Bernard, R. M., Borokhovski, E., Abrami, P. C., & Schmid, R. F. (2011). What forty years of research says about the impact of technology on learning. *Review of Educational Research, 81*(1), 4–28.

Taylor, A. H., Hunt, G. R., Medina, F. S., & Gray, R. D. (2008). Do New Caledonian crows solve physical problems through causal reasoning? *Proceedings of the Royal Society B: Biological Sciences, 276*(1655), 247–254.

Taylor, T. (2010). *The artificial ape: How technology changed the course of human evolution* (Kindle ed.). Palgrave Macmillan.

Turing, A. (2004). Intelligent machinery (1948). *The Essential Turing*, 395.

Turkle, S., & Papert, S. (1992). Epistemological pluralism and the revaluation of the concrete. *Journal of Mathematical Behavior, 11*(1), 3–33.

UNESCO. (2006). *Literacy for life: Education for all global monitoring report.* http://unesdoc.unesco.org/images/0014/001416/141639e.pdf

Uomini, N. T., & Meyer, G. F. (2013). Shared brain lateralization patterns in language and Acheulean stone tool production: A functional transcranial Doppler ultrasound study. *PLoS ONE, 8*(8), e72693.

Bob Uttl, Amy Siegenthaler, & Anne Tseu. (2018). The end of Flynn effect: A meta-analysis of the WAIS-R vocabulary scores (Issue 8110393). *International Institute of Social and Economic Sciences.* https://ideas.repec.org/p/sek/iacpro/8110393.html

Vaidhyanathan, S. (2012). *The Googlization of everything (and why we should worry).* University of California Press.

Vandenberg, D. (2002). The transcendental phases of learning. *Educational Philosophy and Theory, 34*(3), 321–344.

Vansteenkiste, M., Simons, J., Lens, W., Sheldon, K. M., & Deci, E. L. (2004). Motivating learning, performance, and persistence: The synergistic effects of intrinsic goal contents and autonomy-supportive contexts. *Journal of Personality and Social Psychology, 87*(2), 246–260.

Vygotsky, L. S. (1978). *Mind and society: The development of higher psychological processes.* Harvard University Press.

Walters, C. (Director). (1962). *Billy Rose's Jumbo.*

Watson, R. A., & Szathmáry, E. (2016). How can evolution learn? *Trends in Ecology & Evolution, 31*(2), 147–157. https://doi.org/10.1016/j.tree.2015.11.009

Watts, D. (2003). *Six degrees: The science of a connected age*. Norton.

Wenger, E. (1998). *Communities of practice: Learning, meaning and identity*. Cambridge University Press.

Wenger, E., Trayner, B., & de Laat, M. (2011). *Promoting and assessing value creation in communities and networks: A conceptual framework* (No. 18; Rapport). Ruud de Moor Centrum.

Williams, W. C. (1969). The wedge. In *Selected essays of William Carlos Williams* (p. 256). New Directions.

Wilson-Grau, R., & Britt, H. (2012). Outcome harvesting. Ford Foundation. https://web.archive.org/web/20160307142445/http://managingforimpact.org/sites/default/files/resource/outome_harvesting_brief_final_2012-05-2-1.pdf

Wilson, E. O. (2012). *The social conquest of Earth* (Kindle ed.). Liveright Publishing Corporation.

Wittgenstein, L. (2001). *Philosophical investigations: The German text, with a revised English translation* (Trans. G. E. M Anscombe). John Wiley & Sons.

Zegarac, V. (1998). What is "phatic communication?" *Pragmatics and Beyond, New Series*, 327–362.

Zhouying, J. (2004). Technological progress in history: A survey of evolution and shift of research emphasis from "hard-tech" to "soft-tech" development. *International Journal of Technology Management & Sustainable Development*, 3(2), 133–148.